LEIBNIZ

LEIBNIZ

by

HERBERT WILDON CARR

DOVER PUBLICATIONS, INC.
NEW YORK   NEW YORK

Published in the United Kingdom by
Constable and Company Limited,
10 Orange Street, London, W.C. 2.

This new Dover edition, first published in
1960, is an unabridged and unaltered republica-
tion of the first edition published in 1929.

This edition is dedicated
to the memory of

HERBERT WILDON CARR

the last years of whose life
were spent in the United States of America
as Fellow of the School of Philosophy
in the University of Southern California

*"In interpreting the great thinkers of the past
we form the philosopohy of the future."*

H.W.C.

Manufactured in the United States of America

Dover Publications, Inc.
180 Varick Street
New York 14, N.Y.

CONTENTS

PART I

LIFE AND TIMES

PART II

DOCTRINE

v

CONTENTS

PART III

INFLUENCE

PART I
LIFE AND TIMES

I

THE HISTORICAL BACKGROUND

To understand the extraordinary intellectual force of the philosopher Leibniz and the influence of his ideas in determining the course of the historical development of philosophy, it is not enough to be acquainted with his particular theories : we must know something of the man himself, view him in his true historical setting and realize the nature and extent of his multitudinous activities. Voltaire, writing in the succeeding age, with his genius for pithy, incisive characterization, thus describes him : " In intellectual achievements he was perhaps the most erudite man in Europe : a historian unwearying in documentary research and a profound jurisconsult, illuminating by philosophy alone the study of law, to the practice of which he was apparently a total stranger ; a metaphysician so unbiassed as to think it possible to reconcile theology with metaphysics ; even a Latin poet, and a mathematician so accomplished that he could dispute with the great Newton the invention of the infinitesimal calculus and leave their rival claims a long time doubtful."

Leibniz lives to-day in his philosophy alone, yet he was not a professorial philosopher. He held no university appointment and he wrote no formal treatise. The collected editions of his philosophical writings consist entirely of occasional criticisms and essays. Only one considerable work of philosophy was prepared by him for publication and published in his lifetime, the *Théodicée*, and this also was occasional. It was called forth by the challenge of Bayle, the writer of the famous *Dictionary*, to reconcile by reason the divine attributes of omniscience, omnipotence and benevolence. The fullest exposition of his metaphysical principles is contained in his *Nouveaux Essais*. This was not published in his lifetime. It is a detailed criticism of Locke's *Essay on the Understanding*, in the form of a dialogue. It is complete and was written for publication, but since his letters to Locke failed to elicit a reply, and because Locke died before the publication could be arranged, it was laid aside. Not till 1765, nearly fifty years after Leibniz's death, was this momentous work discovered among the manuscripts in the Hanover Library and published. For a complete account of the logical principles and metaphysical doctrine of this profoundly original thinker, we are, in fact, entirely dependent on his correspondence and the occasional articles he contributed to the academical journals of his time.

The active life of Leibniz coincides with the age of Louis XIV. He lived through the brilliant opening of that reign and to its disastrous close. In English political history he is contemporaneous with the Stuart restoration, with the successful Revolution of 1688, with the rise of the House of Hanover, and he witnessed the growing predominance of the Protestant power following the Catholic reaction. In all the stirring political changes of that age he was the consultant and the consulted, the adviser of princes, the active diplomatist, the trusted counsellor. It is to this political activity that we owe the preservation of his papers. When he died, his death passed unnoticed by the world, in which for half a century he had played so notable a part, but it aroused no small anxiety among scheming political factions, who believed him possessed of important Court secrets. Accordingly, his papers and manuscripts were at once put under seal, the rights of the heirs to their possession having been purchased for a trifling sum, and they remain to this day in the custody of the Library at Hanover. Leibniz seems to have preserved methodically all his correspondence, together with memoranda of his replies to letters received, and copies of all his important writings, whether they were answers to letters or occasional articles. From time to time selections have been made by students, and what seemed of sufficient importance published. The Prussian Academy of Sciences has now taken in hand the publication of a complete edition of all the papers. The scope of this work can be judged by the prospectus. It contemplates the publication altogether of forty quarto volumes. They are to be issued in seven different sets. (1) General, Political and Historical correspondence, eleven volumes. (2) Philosophical correspondence, six volumes. (3) Mathematical, Scientific and Technical correspondence, five volumes. (4) Political writings, four volumes. (5) Historical writings, four volumes. (6) Philosophical writings, six volumes. (7) Mathematical, Scientific and Technical writings, four volumes. The coming generation of Leibniz students will therefore have at its disposal an unexampled mass of documentary material.

In order to understand the important position which Leibniz occupied in the intellectual, political and diplomatic life of his age we must first cast a glance at the general state of Europe in the second half of the seventeenth century.

It is often a source of wonder to the student of history that the character of an age should seem to establish itself without reference to the hard school of experience through which the chief actors in it have had to pass. The wonder leads to curious moral reflections. It seems strange, for example, almost to the point of incredibility, that a king like our Charles II, who, as a prince, had lived through the tragedy of his father's disastrous reign, and himself

6 LEIBNIZ

known the misery of proscription and exile, should at his restoration become at once the " merry monarch " and abandon himself to the luxuries of a dissolute Court. It is usual to explain the England of the Restoration as a simple though extreme reaction from the austerities of the Puritan Commonwealth. Such a facile explanation, however, will only pass at the cost of some derogation from our ideal of the dignity of human nature. To understand the character of an age we must endeavour to discern its true alignment. The change from the austere religious ideals of the first half of the seventeenth century to the brilliant social and intellectual expansion and illumination of the second half was not special to any one country, but general throughout Europe, and the centre and chief source of the enlightenment and its principal manifestation was the policy of Louis XIV. For fifty years following the assumption by Louis of personal rule on the death of the Cardinal Mazarin in 1661, the politics of Europe was determined by the ambitions and schemes and undertakings of the French Court. The restored Stuart family was to all intents and purposes a dependent of France. The royal family of England was, in fact, so closely related to the royal family of France as to be practically at home there. Versailles was its spiritual home. Charles's young sister, the Princess Henrietta, born when the royalist cause in England was *in extremis*, the daughter whom her father never saw, the infant her mother had to leave behind in her perilous escape to France, was at the Restoration the first lady of France, always referred to as " Madame," the wife of the Duke of Orleans, Louis's only brother. Young, beautiful and popular in both Courts, she had as maids of honour both the king's mistress, Mademoiselle de Vallière, and Charles's mistress, Louise de Kerouaille, afterwards Duchess of Portsmouth. When, in 1670, Louis wished to make sure of the English navy in his designs against the independence of the Dutch republic, the delicate negotiation was entrusted solely to his sister-in-law, and carried through by her without any diplomatic aid. During the whole reign of Charles II, and during the reign of his successor James II, up to the time of the English Revolution of 1688, the Court policy of England was to conceal as well as it could from the people of England that they were being used to aid and abet the schemes of Louis XIV. During this period France was extending her frontiers, her armies seemed invincible, her leadership unchallengeable. At home the capital, Paris, and the royal demesne, Versailles, were being adorned with magnificent buildings and artistic embellishments to the wonder of the world. It was part of Louis's design to draw to his capital and attach to his Court, painters, poets, musicians, architects and distinguished men of all kinds, whatever their nationality. He bestowed pensions lavishly. Had this magnanimity been accompanied with toleration in religion, his ideal might have been attained and the history of Europe would have been different.

The English Revolution of 1688, which expelled James II and placed the Prince of Orange on the throne as William III, not only marks the successful establishment in England of the principle of constitutional monarchy, it sets the definite limit to the ascendancy of France in Europe. From it we may trace the dramatic reversal of the fortunes of Louis. From this time forward he finds himself confronted with an alliance of the northern Protestant powers, growing continually stronger, their armies receiving constant accessions from the vast numbers of his own subjects, whom he was driving into exile by his religious persecution. The interest now centres in the growing power of the loosely-federated German states and free cities. The Elector of Brandenburg becomes ruler of the new-founded Kingdom of Prussia. The House of Brunswick becomes established and independent in the

Electorate of Hanover and its princes are named in the English Act of Settlement and will succeed to the English throne.

Leibniz lived, therefore, throughout the great formative period of modern Europe, when stirring and momentous changes followed rapidly one another. The outstanding historical events are : the invasion by Louis of the Austrian Netherlands and the spectacular success of his campaign ; the building of the great fortresses under the direction of the military genius, Vauban ; the simultaneous conquest of Franche Comté on the Eastern frontier, and the extension of the frontiers on the Spanish border into Catalonia and on the Italian border into Savoy ; then follow the attack on Holland, with the narrow escape of that republic from extinction, and the laying waste of the Palatinate, both of which expeditions by their ruthlessness had the effect of alarming other threatened powers and bringing into alliance mutually jealous nationalities. These events mark the expansion of France. Then follow the revocation of the Edict of Nantes, which has the fatal consequence of driving a chief part of the industrial population of France into exile ; the expulsion of James II from England and his refuge in the French Court ; the campaigns of William III, which though marked by defeats on the battle-field succeeded in wearing out the strength of the French King and securing the treaty of Ryswick ; lastly, the wars of Marlborough and Prince Eugene, which deprived Louis of all his earlier conquests and made it difficult for him to find security within his old frontiers.

Gottfried Wilhelm Leibniz was born at Leipzig, in Saxony, on 23rd June 1646. His father, who was Registrar of the University and Professor of Moral Philosophy, died in his seventy-first year, when his son was six years old. His mother was his father's third wife, the daughter

of a professor and doctor of law. The family belonged to
the class of the nobility. The name in the older histories
of philosophy is usually given as Leibnitz ; both forms of
spelling are used in the first collected edition of his writings
by Dutens, 1768. The termination " tz " is apparently
due to the latinization of the name. The family must
have been well-to-do and independent, for when the
father died there was no change in the home and the
mother had entire charge of the young child's education.
He was brought up without the necessity of specializing
for any particular profession, and though in later life he
was always in receipt of Court pensions for his services,
he seems to have been able to live where and as he pleased.
His father had collected a large library of choice books,
and at an early age the boy entered into possession of
these and had rare enjoyment in the opportunity it gave
him to become acquainted with the treasures of literature.
His life seems to have been passed in affluence and unen-
cumbered with domestic ties of any kind. He travelled
widely, and wherever he made his home he enjoyed complete comfort. He never married, and we know nothing
of his family relations. Fontenelle, in his *Eulogy*, tells
us that when about fifty years of age he made a proposal
of marriage, but that the lady took time to consider and
afforded him the leisure to repent and withdraw. When
he died the only heir to his considerable fortune was a
nephew, his sister's son, curé of a parish near Leipzig,
and the story goes that the wife of the nephew was so
overcome by the sudden news of the wealth which had
fallen to her that she died of shock. These trivialities are
not unimportant ; they help us to understand how Leibniz
was able to play the part he did in the great events of his
age. We never find him like the typical philosopher
retiring from the world, seeking seclusion and retreat
in order to reflect on the deeper problems; on the contrary
he is always immersed in practical schemes, interested in

all that is going on in politics, in religion, in the natural sciences, in mathematics and in philosophy.

The introduction and first essential to education in the seventeenth century was the mastery of Latin. Until one could read and write it the world of science and philosophy was a closed door. The young Leibniz began to learn Latin at the age of eight, and at twelve was proficient. Till then he could only read the German books in his father's library, now the higher literature was open to him. He acquired remarkable facility in writing Latin verse. His earlier writings and correspondence are in Latin, very seldom in German, later he wrote French. At fifteen he entered the University of Leipzig as a student of law, and at the age of seventeen, in 1663, he defended his bachelor's dissertation, entitled *Disputatio Metaphysica de principio individui*. It is significant that the subject should thus anticipate the doctrine on which his fame as a philosopher rests. After graduation he devoted three years to the study of law, and in 1666 applied for a doctorate. This was refused on account of his youth. Thereupon he left his native town and applied to the University of Altdorf, belonging to the free city of Nuremberg. The doctorate was conferred on him and his dissertation on the half philosophical, half juridical thesis *De Casibus Perplexis in Jure* was considered so brilliant that he was offered a professor's chair in the university. This he declined. It was on this occasion that he came to know Johann Christian Boyneburg, a distinguished statesman, who had been First Minister to the Elector of Mainz, one of the episcopal electorates of the Empire, and through him Leibniz was introduced to the Elector, and soon after entered his service. In this way he made his entry into the political world.

One of the first things on which he was employed was the election of the King of Poland, and the memorial he wrote on this occasion is one of the curiosities of literature. In 1668 Casimir, King of Poland, abdicated,

and among the candidates for the vacant throne was
the Count Palatine, Philip William of Neuburg. The
Elector of Mainz espoused his cause, and in support of
his claim Leibniz composed a Latin tractate. It bore a
pseudonym and professed to have been written ten years
earlier with prophetic insight into the future. Its full
title is : *Specimen demonstrationum politicarum pro rege
Polonorum eligendo, Novo scribendi genere ad claram
certitudinem exactum. Auctore : Georgio Ulicovio
Lithuano. Juxta exemplar editum Vilnae* 1659. This
extraordinary treatise, which we might be inclined to
regard as a mere political squib, is of great biographical
interest. Leibniz was only twenty-two years old, and
he wrote it, not as a political joke, but in perfect serious-
ness. In a preface he refers to Galileo, Descartes, Hobbes
and Bacon as having introduced precision and exactitude
in their methods and made the ideal of mathematical
proof the aim of their science. He then sets forth in sixty
propositions, following one another in geometrical order
with corollaries and lemmas, the demonstration leading
to four absolute conclusions, the first three containing
the rejection of each of the other three candidates and
the fourth the election of the Count Palatine King of
Poland. Notwithstanding the rigour of the argument, it
did not, in fact, correspond with the issue of the election.
The candidate was rejected. What makes it of particular
interest to philosophy is the fact that at this very time
Spinoza was writing his *Ethica* in this form, *ordine geo-
metrico demonstrata,* and Leibniz's treatise shows that he
was only exercising himself in what was then a recognized
modern method of writing. The treatise, though it did
not effect its purpose, had a notable success.

Another political writing which he produced at this
time attracted considerable notice, being first printed in
Holland and later in four successive editions in Germany.
It bore the pseudonym Cesarinus Fustenerius, and

describes the ceremonial rights and privileges of the free princes of the Empire who were not Electors. It bears evidence of the extraordinary diligence of Leibniz in searching out neglected and obscure historical records, also it shows his love of exact definitions and unambiguous terms. Several other important and quite remarkable writings—essays on subjects of arithmetical, logical and juridical interest—belong to this early period.

The five years which followed, 1668 to 1673, were a period of excessive anxiety in the free cities and states of the Empire, with continual alarm as to the intentions of Louis XIV, in consequence of his policy of aggression. Besides conquest, Louis's scheme included the conversion of the Protestants and the restoration of the Catholic religion. The threatened countries, Holland and the German Electorates, had more to fear than a change of rulers or new imperial alignment. It was during this period that Leibniz played the important part which brought him on the stage of world events and made him a player in the political drama.

The only great power in Europe at this time which stood in rivalry to the ambitious plans of Louis was Austria, and it was only the difficulties of the Emperor Joseph I, defending his Eastern frontiers against the revived Turkish power, which gave Louis freedom to pursue his schemes against Holland and Germany. At one time, however, the Turkish government threatened Louis also, and there was likelihood of a breach. Leibniz saw in this an opportunity, and conceived the possibility of averting the threatened attack on Holland and Germany by directing Louis to an enterprise which offered substantial advantages and greater aggrandisement. He wrote in German a pamphlet entitled, " Thoughts on Public Safety," in which he urged the Christian powers of Europe instead of fighting one another to combine against the infidel, and suggested that in such a united war against the Turks, Egypt, one of the best situated lands in the world, would fall to France. At the same time he wrote a memorial, directed to Louis himself, pointing out that the surest way of attacking a mercantile power like Holland was through Egypt, as the trade route to the East, and that nothing would more effectually establish the predominance of France in Europe than the conquest of Egypt. Leibniz consulted with his friend Boyneburg, and the memorial was sent to Louis. Leibniz received an invitation from the Secretary of State to visit Paris. The political project does not seem to have received further attention, and Leibniz never had the personal interview with Louis he expected, but he visited Paris. Before he arrived the French relations with Turkey had undergone a change, and the threatened quarrel was averted, so that the project was no longer practical. The sequel is curious, however, inasmuch as the same idea commended itself more than a century later to Napoleon. Leibniz's memorial, together with the reason of his visit to Paris, were in the Library of Hanover, and discovered there by Napoleon when he took possession of Hanover in 1803. The important thing to Leibniz himself was the visit to Paris, for it brought him to the centre of literature and science, and introduced him personally to the intellectual leaders.

Thus at the age of twenty-six Leibniz came to Paris, nominally in the service of the Elector of Mainz, but to all intents and purposes free to carry on his own researches and studies. From Paris he visited London, and received introductions into learned circles there. In 1673, when settled in Paris, he left the service of the Elector of Mainz and entered that of the Duke of Brunswick-Lüneburg, one of the Electoral families rapidly rising to the front in the political changes of Europe, and for the rest of his life he was attached to that family. In his correspondence he always refers to its head as " my prince." The Duke

John Frederick died in 1679, and Leibniz composed in his memory a Latin poem which was greatly admired. He continued in the service of his successor, and in fact served under three successive princes. In 1676 the Duke invited him to leave Paris and come to Hanover, and thenceforward his headquarters were in that city, where he had charge of the Ducal Library. The special service for which he was retained was to defend the dynastic claims and write the history of the House of Brunswick. The service was thoroughly congenial, for it gave him the opportunity of travel and access to historical records. In later life he was the councillor of the Electress Sophia throughout the delicate negotiations connected with the English Act of Settlement, and he lived to see her son, the Elector of Hanover, ascend the throne of England.

Honours were heaped upon Leibniz in his last years. In 1700 he had founded the Akademie der Wissenschaften of Berlin, having been invited there by the Electress Sophie-Charlotte, wife of the Elector of Brandenburg, known as the Great Elector, and her mother, the Electress Sophia. He was appointed life president. At the same time he was made a privy councillor to the Elector of Brandenburg and also to the Elector of Hanover, and in 1712 he received the much-coveted honour of an imperial privy councillorship and was made a baron of the Empire.

When George I went to England for his coronation Leibniz was at Vienna, and greatly wished to attend the Court in London, but he received peremptory orders to return to Hanover and continue his work in the library. He died at Hanover 14th November 1716, strangely neglected. His death attracted no notice either in London or in Berlin, and at his funeral the sole mourner was his secretary, Eckhard. At Paris he received adequate recognition of his great genius and extraordinary erudition. In the French Academy a worthy eulogy was pronounced on the anniversary of his death by Fontenelle, and inscribed in its archives.

II

THE INTELLECTUAL WORLD OF THE
SEVENTEENTH CENTURY

LEIBNIZ's four years' residence in Paris, 1673–1676, was the important period of his life in so far as the determination and direction of his philosophical activities is concerned. It was then he received his introduction to the mathematicians, philosophers and leaders in church and state, and was brought into the intellectual movement of the age. Up to this time his articles and correspondence had been in Latin, henceforward he usually writes in French.

The intellectual world of the latter half of the seventeenth century is a different world in its ideals and in its character from the intellectual world of the beginning of the century. There is a wider outlook and a more tolerant spirit in theology, in philosophy, in literature and in science. The ideal of toleration in religion is still, indeed, far off, and rival principles in practice and doctrine are as irreconcilable as ever, yet there is a distinct advance towards a more rational, a humaner and broader policy. The struggle to enforce uniformity no longer bears cruelly on the individual in pursuance of the desperate notion that heresy can be extinguished at its source by the ruthless destruction of the heretic. Louis was, indeed, engaged throughout his reign in the definite and well-considered policy of enforcing uniformity, and he did, in fact, pursue a relentless plan which had the effect of expatriating vast numbers of his subjects to the lasting injury of the state, but the predominant motive was statesmanship:

craven superstition and religious bigotry played a quite subordinate part. The motive which in a previous age had inspired the massacre of the Eve of St. Bartholomew was dead. The revocation of the Edict of Nantes was not a despotic act prompted by crafty prelates, it was the carrying out of a consistent state policy. The Huguenots, under the edict, were acquiring a privileged position in the towns, a kind of *imperium in imperio*, an exterritoriality which in a measure enabled them to defy the common law, and to many political thinkers this seemed to be nurturing a disruptive element within the commonwealth. It was not, however, his Huguenot subjects alone who had imposed on Louis the necessity of a religious repressive policy; there was internal dissension in the Catholic Church by reason of the powerful philosophical reform in doctrine and practice which had been attempted by the Jansenist faction. At the time when Leibniz resided in Paris there was a pause in this spiritual warfare. A pacific Pope, Clement IX, had accepted the ambiguous formulary which the Jansenists at last after much persuasion had consented to sign, and their leaders were now free to come out of their hiding places. In particular the great party leader, Antoine Arnauld, was able to return and live openly in Paris. Leibniz came to know him, he had already corresponded with him, but not at this time in relation to theology. Arnauld was a distinguished philosopher and mathematician, part author of the Port-Royal Logic, *L'art de Penser*, and it was on logical and mathematical questions that Leibniz communicated with him. There is an interesting note on one of Leibniz's mathematical papers, dated February 1676, which shows that he had consulted Arnauld on the subject of his great mathematical discovery, the calculus. " M. Arnauld had given me the rule or theorem, and I have now worked out for him the proof by my calculus. The specimen may serve for an example of the art of finding proofs by the calculus ; it shows in what way the expression or the characters must be changed to be successful."

Leibniz had come to Paris in response to an invitation of the Secretary of State, but, as we have seen, the particular political situation to which the invitation had reference had undergone an entire change. Leibniz, however, was still impressed with the idea that the disunion of Christendom was disastrous in its political consequences, and that it might and should be ended. It was not, however, till some years later that a practical proposal was submitted to him which at least might secure the entry of the Lutheran Church into reunion with Catholicism. Through Leibniz's energy, supported by his extraordinary historical erudition, the scheme was seriously discussed 1691–1701. The story is interesting and affords an insight into the character of Leibniz, his conspicuous clearness in presenting the end to be attained together with his untiring perseverance in removing the difficulties. To understand the story it is important to bear in mind that at this time, notwithstanding the intolerance of theologians and the oppression of statesmen, there is, in fact, a very close approximation of the rival religious creeds, as is evidenced by the frequent cases of conversion which are clearly the result of conviction and not of expediency. The divisions in Christian Europe at this period are political and practical, and no dissentient Church could claim a monopoly of the spiritual life. Not only princes and rulers, like Queen Christina of Sweden and James II of England, who had everything to lose and nothing to gain, were then announcing their conversion to Catholicism, but also many notable leaders in the intellectual world.

The leading prelate in France at this time, and the director and executant of Louis's ecclesiastical policy, was Jacques Bénigne Bossuet (1627–1704), famous for his funeral orations, his sermons and his theological writings. It was between Bossuet at Paris and Leibniz, then at the library of the Duke of Brunswick at Wolfenbüttel, that the practicability of reunion between the Catholics and Protestants was discussed. The proposal itself was originated by the Duchess of Hanover, a daughter of the Princess Elizabeth of England, wife of the Prince Palatine. A sister of the Duchess, Princess Louise-Hollandine, had gone to Paris to make open profession of the Roman Catholic religion, and had entered the Abbey of Maubuisson, of which she was now the Abbess. Another very talented lady of the French Court, Madame de Brinon, who had been lady superior of St. Cyr, the religious establishment founded by Madame de Maintenon, was now secretary to the Abbess. It was through these two ladies, the Abbess of Maubuisson and her secretary, Madame de Brinon, that the project was committed to Bossuet and Leibniz for their decision. The letters had to pass through reliable and confidential channels, and the two ladies undertook the charge.

The Duchess of Hanover wrote to her sister the Abbess, who had manifested the zeal of a new convert by seeking to draw her sister along the same path, a letter in which she tells her that she had sent their correspondence to Leibniz, and then recounts how she had read that a papal nuncio journeying to Mount Lebanon had admitted members of the Greek Church to the Catholic communion. " Yet their differences," she writes, " are greater than those of our Lutheran Church. Why, then, should Lutherans not be received and at the same time allowed, as the Greeks are, to retain their rites, if it can be shown that the doctrinal differences which divide them concern unessentials ? Such a project has been actually formulated by the Bishop of Neustadt and brought by him to the notice of the Emperor on behalf of the Protestant states."

This letter was sent to Bossuet because it was thought useless to put forward any proposal which would meet with his opposition, and Bossuet's reply was sent to Leibniz. Thereafter the letters are directed by each to the other and forwarded by the Abbess.

Bossuet takes up the position : That Rome can never relax any point of doctrine defined by the church in a council, or make any capitulation thereon ; that the doctrine defined by the Council of Trent is received by Roman Catholics not only in France, but everywhere ; and that acceptance of the decisions of that council is a necessary condition of re-entry into the Catholic Church. Undiscouraged by this apparent *non possumus*, Leibniz puts the question in this form : Recognizing that agreement is impossible on such a subject as transubstantiation, is it possible, nevertheless, waiving for the time such disagreement, to re-establish ecclesiastical communion between all parties by the three following means ? First, granting the Protestants what they ask on certain points of discipline, such as the communion in two kinds, the marriage of the clergy, the use of the vulgar tongue, etc. Second, giving them explanations on controversial points which concern the faith (such as Bossuet has himself published), showing that when taken in the proper sense many learned and moderately-minded Protestants have acknowledged that, even if not entirely acceptable as true, these variations of practice no longer appear as damnable. Third, allowing a truce to certain controversies in regard to which the Church itself is not agreed, as, for example, the controversy concerning freewill and sufficient grace. A reunion on these conditions would then, he suggests, be on the understanding that a new general council would be called in the future in which all the reconciled Protestant nations would have representatives, animated by goodwill, whose decisions would be acknowledged.

Bossuet's reply is courteous, guarded and incisive.
Anyone, he declares, who accepts the doctrine of the infallibility of the œcumenical council must acknowledge
the authority of the Council of Trent. Could anyone,
for example, after the Councils of Nicæa and Chalcedon,
with good conscience have doubted the doctrines settled
therein ? Whatever disposition, therefore, one has for
the peace of the Church, he can never be really pacific
and in a state of surety until he is actually himself re-
united with the Church—a pointed hint to Leibniz to
announce his own adhesion.

Leibniz in reply argues at great length on the subject
of the infallibility of the councils, particularly questioning
whether the Church itself had uniformly accepted the
finality of the decisions of the Council of Trent. This
letter as soon as it was acknowledged was followed by
another. Leibniz's passion for historical research was
aroused, and he was now able to enclose a case in point.
The Council of Bâle, in 1436, had actually itself, on
receiving a remonstrance from the Protestant party in
Bohemia, the Calixtins, suspended in its favour a notorious
decree of a former council, the Council of Constance,
which had decided the question whether the communion
in two kinds is incumbent on all the faithful. The Calixtins
had refused to recognize the authority of the Council of
Constance. The Pope Eugenius and the Council of Bâle
overruled the decree, relieved the protesters from even
temporary submission, and referred the matter for a
new decision to a future council. This order, Leibniz
points out, had the effect of preventing a schism, and it
actually reconciled dissentient factions. It was in all
respects and to the minutest details a complete precedent
for the project he was putting forward, namely, the
suspension of some of the decisions of the Council of
Trent and their reference to a future council.

The case appears to have disconcerted Bossuet, and he

took council with another of Louis's ecclesiastical administrators, Paul Pélisson (1624–1693), one of the remarkable men of his age. Pélisson, a Huguenot, had been converted from Calvinism to Catholicism, and was at this time engaged in dispensing a fund which the king had put at his disposal, and was carrying out the conversion of Huguenots on a wholesale scale by financial bargaining.

If Leibniz expected that his dialectical triumph would secure the adoption of his project he was soon disappointed. There was no way of discrediting his precedent, but there were plenty of ways of raising other issues. It is evident from the correspondence that there was no real intention on the Catholic side of agreeing, but only the hope of effecting a notable conversion; and it is equally clear that Leibniz had no intention of stultifying himself by a preliminary submission.

Bossuet stands out in history as the unbending champion of orthodoxy in the age of Louis XIV. Theology in itself had really little interest for him, all he cared for was that it should carry the hall-mark. Leibniz, on the contrary, had a purely philosophical interest in theology, but it was profound and earnest. His ideal was the realization of a rational theology.

The predominantly theological interest of Leibniz's philosophy had found marked expression some five years before the discussion of the project with Bossuet, in a lengthy correspondence he had had with the Catholic prince, Ernest of Hesse-Rheinfels. The outcome of it was the *Discours de Métaphysique*, 1686, and the correspondence with Arnauld in regard to it. This correspondence was published by Foucher de Careil in 1857, and was seen at once to throw an interesting light on the genesis of what in his later writings Leibniz calls his new system.

The form of publication makes it appear as though

Leibniz had composed the "Discourse on Metaphysics" with a view to its submission to Arnauld, and that the princely correspondent was only employed as the friendly intermediary. Leibniz, however, had no need of an introduction to Arnauld, with whom he had been corresponding for fifteen years. Moreover, at this time Arnauld was an old man in his seventy-fifth year, living in seclusion and practically excommunicated. Leibniz therefore could have had nothing to gain by his approval or disapproval of the *Discours*. The *Discours* was really composed for the prince, and in fact only a summary of it was submitted to Arnauld. It was part of a long correspondence which dealt with all the theological disputes of the time, and particularly with the points at issue between the Catholic and Protestant doctrines. The *Discours* is consequently of especial interest from the fact that it is the philosophical counterpart of Leibniz's idea of a possible reconciliation. In all these efforts towards mutual understanding, the primary aim on the Catholic side seems to have been to win over Leibniz to a declaration of adhesion to the Catholic Church, and it was with this idea that the prince asked permission to submit the *Discours* to Arnauld. Notwithstanding his continual trouble with the ecclesiastical authorities, Arnauld was a staunch Catholic. There is for the historical and philosophical student, therefore, the curious revelation of a double motive in the controversy, for Arnauld is not only a Jansenist in theology, but also a Cartesian in philosophy. While he devotes his logical skill to bringing Leibniz to the Catholic view, Leibniz devotes his metaphysical clearness to demonstrating to Arnauld the weakness of the Cartesian position.

The contemporary philosopher of most fame in Paris when Leibniz was resident there was Nicolas Malebranche (1638-1715). He was a Catholic priest. He belonged to the French Oratory, a privileged institution which had been founded originally as a training college, and had since become a nursery of clerical scholars, and therefore a refuge for the philosophical recluse. Malebranche was attracted to philosophy by the writings of Descartes, and more especially by the scientific treatises, and he came to be regarded as his direct successor and representative, developing the Cartesian system on its spiritual or idealistic side. His great work, *La Recherche de la Vérité*, made him universally famous, and distinguished visitors to Paris regarded an interview with Malebranche as one of the privileges of the city. Leibniz paid him a visit during his residence in Paris and engaged him in a warm discussion on Descartes's principles, particularly arguing against the doctrine which Leibniz found unacceptable, the indestructibility of movement. On returning home he seems to have sat down and written a long letter on the subject, repeating his arguments in form. Malebranche replied in a short and courteous letter, declaring himself convinced by Descartes's arguments and saying that he found it easier to clear up misunderstandings in conversation. Leibniz answered this with a longer and more argumentative letter, and Malebranche, evidently irritated at his persistence, politely declined to continue. In 1677 Malebranche published his *Entretiens Chrétiens*. Leibniz read this with his usual care and penetration and annotated it fully, sending his notes to Malebranche and inviting him to further correspondence. What the correspondence shows, however, is how little intellectual sympathy there is between the two philosophers. Leibniz at this time found himself diverging more and more completely from the whole Cartesian conception. " Nothing useful," he remarks in one of his letters to Malebranche, " has come from Descartes to compare with the experiments of Galileo."

Of greater interest to the philosophical student is
Leibniz's relation to the contemporary philosopher
Spinoza (1632–1677). Leibniz visited him at the Hague
on his journey from Paris to Hanover in 1676, the year
before Spinoza died. He had written to him five years
before, but not on philosophy. Spinoza was a grinder of
lenses of considerable repute, and Leibniz had written
about optics and theories of transparency with remarks on
current treatises. Spinoza had replied, enclosing a
schedule. When Leibniz proposed to visit him, Spinoza,
who had forgotten the old correspondence and only knew
him by repute as a learned diplomatic courtier, was
naturally suspicious, for at that time the Dutch were in
continual alarm as to the hostile intentions of the French
king and Spinoza feared Leibniz's visit might be prompted
by other than philosophical interest. They met and discussed philosophy. Leibniz was shown the manuscript
of the *Ethica*, and was lent a copy from which, according
to his practice, he took extensive notes before he returned
it. This interesting and quite ordinary friendliness of two
philosophers was later the occasion of an absurd calumny
on Leibniz's good faith, which has to be noticed, for it
finds currency in some quarters even to-day. It was
suggested that Leibniz plagiarized the *Ethica* and con-
cealed his theft by affected indignation at the consequences of a doctrine in all essentials identical with his
own. The best answer to the calumny is to quote some
of Leibniz's letters to his friends. These show that his
attitude to Spinoza's doctrines is never the least ambiguous.
He is aware that Spinoza's opinions are shocking from the
standpoint of popular religious teaching, but he recognizes
their philosophical ground, and he is always confident of
his power to disprove them by reason.

There is a note of a letter addressed by him to a friend
(ex epistola mea ad Placcium), dated 14th February 1678,
the year following Spinoza's death and the publication

of the *Ethica*. The note, which is in Latin, runs : " Although Spinoza has occasionally beautiful thoughts, and not at all abhorrent, as I have shown, yet, nevertheless, his main doctrines are not capable of the least proof, and, in fact, are not proved by him despite his claim to have given the demonstration. For him there is one only substance, and this is God. Creatures he regards as modes or affections of God. God is without understanding and will, does not act according to final causes, but by a necessity of his nature, just as the properties of the circle follow from its essence. He believes, indeed, that our mind will survive death, but it will no longer perceive the present, will the future or remember the past. All happiness, stripped of its specious wrappings, comes to this, that recognizing the inevitable necessity of things we should be content to accept them as they come. Is not the Christian view better and truer ? He says, indeed, many noble things of the affections. He grants us providence and the future life, yet it is in word only, the reality is gone. I cannot think how with such a theory one could expect to persuade men to undertake the duties of life. Yet I do not deny that there are those who, like the Stoics, have cultivated virtue without incentives, and who have even held that the good and pure life is only for those who are not incited to it by the hope of reward and the fear of punishment. For all this I fear your judgment of the work will be adverse."

There is also one of the letters addressed to Prince Ernest of Hesse-Rheinfels of special interest for its reference to the visit in 1676. The letter is in French, and dated 14th August 1683 : " With regard to Spinoza, whom M. Arnauld calls the most impious and dangerous man of this age, it is true that he is an atheist in the meaning that he did not admit the existence of a providence dispensing rewards and penalties according to justice, and he believed he had demonstrated its non-existence. The

God who fills his background is not like ours. He has neither understanding nor will. Spinoza also had a strange opinion regarding the immortality of the soul, which he conceived on the analogy of the Platonic Idea. He thinks our soul is immortal in the same sense in which the idea of the circle or of the triangle is eternal, and that we ought to strive to perfect ourselves in every kind of virtue in order to leave after us when we die an eternal essence or Platonic Idea as perfect as is possible ; as though such idea were not already existing in nature, whether I strive to resemble it or not, and as though it could be any use to me after my death to resemble this perfect idea if I am no longer anything. Such strange thoughts as these are dealt with in his posthumous work, *De Deo*, in such a way as makes it seem that he is saying something different. He makes great boast of his demonstrations, but it would have been better if he had had fuller knowledge of the art of demonstrating, his knowledge of analysis and geometry being only mediocre and best employed in making microscope lenses. I spent several hours in discussion with him when I was passing through the Hague, and the rest I have learnt from some of his followers whom I know quite intimately."

When we come to consider Leibniz's philosophy we shall see that while it rests on the same metaphysical basis as Spinoza's it is completely opposite in its arguments and conclusions.

The leading philosopher in England during the early part of Leibniz's active life was Thomas Hobbes (1588–1679). Hobbes's philosophy belongs, however, to the earlier part of the century, and his real contemporaries were Descartes and Gassendi, and even in his younger days Francis Bacon. Hobbes is generally coupled with Spinoza in the reproach of atheism, not on account of any positive teaching, but because his frank materialism, like Spinoza's pantheism, was thought to imply it. Like Spinoza also, Hobbes had earned the obloquy of Catholic and Protestant alike by his free criticism and rationalization of Scripture. Leibniz corresponded with him. There is a letter from Germany dated 1670, and another a few years later from Paris. At the time of the first of these letters Hobbes was over eighty and Leibniz only twenty-five. What is interesting, however, is the evidence of Leibniz's great admiration and sympathy with a philosopher whose philosophy appears to us to have little in common with his own. The reason undoubtedly is that Leibniz even at this early time was in revolt against the Cartesianism which was then daily growing in popularity and fast establishing itself as philosophical orthodoxy. Hobbes in England and Gassendi in France were the contemporaries of Descartes, who by their intellectual eminence and originality could challenge his philosophical leadership. Gassendi (1592–1655) was particularly attractive to Leibniz from the fact that he revived and modernized the ancient atomic theory ; and Hobbes's empiricism offered a complete alternative to Descartes's theory of the deceptiveness of the senses which to Leibniz was peculiarly unacceptable. With all his admiration for Hobbes, however, Leibniz was fully sensible of the defectiveness of his philosophy and of its cause. " He combines," he says in a note, " a marvellously penetrating mind with a strange obtuseness. It is because he had not profited by mathematics sufficiently to save himself from paralogisms." This note has peculiar significance in the case of Hobbes, who had managed to subject himself to humiliation at the hands of the English mathematician, Wallis, by the confidence with which he had claimed to have solved the problem of squaring the circle. He had acquired his knowledge of mathematics in middle life, and after his reputation in political philosophy was established, and he found himself accordingly attempting mathematical research without mathematical discipline. Leibniz, on the other hand, gained his main force in dialectics from his mathematical discipline. Mathematics seems, indeed, to have come naturally to him, for we find him engaged in the study of pure mathematical problems, apparently for their intellectual interest alone and with no practical incentive. It was by its mathematical conceptions and its geometrical method that the new philosophy of the seventeenth century marked its departure from scholasticism. This is not surprising when we remember that the new science had its origin in an astronomical hypothesis.

The first part of the seventeenth century was the golden age of mathematics, and it was then that the foundations of the new physics were being laid down. The liberation of physical science from the mediæval astrology and alchemy was the work of the mathematicians. Besides the well-known names of Galileo, Kepler, Torricelli, Descartes and Pascal, there were Cavalieri, Huygens, Roberval, Fermat, and in England Isaac Barrow, and later his more distinguished pupil Newton. Mathematical problems would seem to have been a hobby of Leibniz rather than a serious occupation; they were evidently his diversion in his spare hours. A curious example of this is his arithmetical machine, the design of which he thought out as a young man, inspired no doubt by the instrument which Pascal had invented and which was deposited in the *Bibliothèque Nationale* at Paris. This machine of Pascal's had excited the marvel of the preceding generation. It enabled calculations to be made mechanically in the three denotations of the currency—livres, schillings and deniers. Leibniz set to work to make an improvement and invent a machine which would do complicated arithmetical calculations, such as extracting square roots. He seems to have kept working at it, and only brought it to a satisfactory working perfection near the end of his life.

Leibniz was evidently a self-taught mathematician, and this is entirely in keeping with his character. He was ambitious to be in the front rank in every form of erudition, and in that age to be of no account in mathematics was to be negligible. We get a most illuminating insight into the kind of interest which drew him to mathematics in one of his papers published by Foucher de Careil, entitled *Animadversiones ad Weigelium*. Erhard Weigel (1625–1699), the subject of these critical remarks, was a somewhat eccentric contemporary German mathematician and astronomer. He was professor of mathematics at Jena and author of numerous treatises. He conceived the odd idea of substituting for the mythological constellations heraldic signs to represent the reigning dynasties of Europe (*Der Europäische Wappen-Himmel*, 1688). He also constructed an ingenious celestial globe as a copper sphere with the earth poised within it. The work, however, which seems to be referred to in the first part of the *Animadversiones* is *Arithmetische Beschreibung der Moral-Weisheit*, 1674. It would appear to have propounded an ingenious scheme for inculcating morals in children by the teaching of mathematics. It won the admiration of Leibniz : " I entirely approve the excellent designs of our Weigel for inculcating useful ideas into children's minds while yet they are pliant in such a way that the practice of virtue will always be linked to them. . . . There is nothing more delightful than the analogies he draws from mathematical things and applies in various ways to moral things ; nothing better fitted to fix in the mind these two orders of truths and make them shine forth in act on occasion." He then proceeds to apply this to his own work, and in particular to the reflection which had led him to the discovery of the calculus. " Each of these things (theory and practice, or mathematics and morals) should be the goal of our endeavours, seeing that God has given us the power to accomplish them. I, too,

strive to contribute my mite, following my feeble powers,
and especially I seek to extend beyond its present limitations the art of inventing which mathematicians term
analysis. For the science of quantity in general or estima-
tion (scientia de quantitate in universum vel de æsti-
matione), as our celebrated Weigel names it, appears to
me to be treated only partially. We are familiar enough
with that part which deals with finite quantities ; but
besides this there is that part of general mathematics
which is the highest matter, to wit, the science of the
infinite, a science often necessary even for research concerning finite quantities, and which I have perhaps been
the first to enrich with analytical precepts. Indeed, I
have proposed a new kind of calculus to which the ablest
men of different countries have generally had recourse.
Huygens, an excellent judge in such matters, even declares
that by means of it he has obtained solutions of problems
which without it would have been inaccessible." This
leads him on to a further consideration, very important in
its bearing on what to him was his main interest, metaphysic. "The art of proving metaphysical propositions,
in any view, demands extreme precautions and a greater
precision even than those required in mathematics. The
reason is that when we are dealing with numbers and the
figures and ideas which depend on them, our mind is in
possession of an Ariadne's thread to guide it, namely,
imagination and the example ; this, moreover, gives it
the means of control which arithmeticians call proofs, and
which quickly lead us to expose paralogisms. In ordinary
metaphysics, on the other hand, we have no such aids,
and we have to make rigorous reasoning supply their
place. And although many well-intentioned philosophers
have held out to us the promise of metaphysical demonstration, they turn out for the most part to be self-decep-
tion. In fact, we possess very few and very rare metaphysical demonstrations worthy of the name." He then

proceeds further to illustrate this remark by submitting to criticism some of the demonstrations from another of Weigel's books, *Speculum Virtutum*. He singles out for special examination the proof of the Cartesian doctrine that the creation of the world by God implies as a consequence the world's conservation—that is, its continual creation from moment to moment, a fundamental proposition of Descartes which Leibniz disputes. Leibniz held that the creation is self-sustaining and justified this by the attribute of omniscience in the Creator.

One of Leibniz's great contemporaries was Christiaan Huygens (1629–1695), referred to in the remarks on Weigel. Leibniz was in continual personal relations with him. He was a Dutch mathematician distinguished among other things for the great improvements he introduced into the construction of telescopes, and for the invention of the pendulum clock. His most important work, most momentous in the development of scientific theory, was his formulation of the wave theory of light, made possible by his discovery of the mathematics of the advancing wave front. He was one of the distinguished foreigners whom Louis XIV had attracted by the offer of a liberal pension to reside at his Court. He was living in Paris during the years of Leibniz's residence there. Later he returned to Holland, determined to this by his resentment of Louis's ecclesiastical policy which bore heavily on his co-religionists. Leibniz would seem to have made his personal acquaintance on his arrival in Paris in 1673, after his first visit to London and before he had met Newton. Huygens led him to read Descartes's *Géometrie*, and appears to have been his chief director in the choice of his mathematical studies. It may, indeed, have been Huygens's early mathematical writings, in particular his *De Circuli Magnitudine Inventa*, in which he deals with the problem of finding the ratio of the circumference to the diameter of the circle (the familiar problem of squaring the circle), which put Leibniz on the line of mathematical discovery with which his name is associated, that of the calculus.

From the time Leibniz left Paris in 1677 to take up his official duties in Hanover, his profession and main occupation was history. He was appointed to write the history of the House of Brunswick, and this necessitated the undertaking of genealogical researches in Germany and Italy. From 1687 to 1690 he journeyed through these two countries examining records and searching registers. It was an immense work, and it occupied him throughout his life. The amazing thing is that the continual minute detailed investigation it involved in no way prevented him pursuing steadily his mathematical and metaphysical critical studies or impaired in any way the high level of his attainment in those fields of research.

The philosophical work is that by which he lives, and this belongs to the last twenty years of his life. It was elaborated in notes and criticisms of the work of rival philosophers, and of three in particular, Pierre Bayle, John Locke and Isaac Newton. Though no philosopher has left behind him more definite doctrine, more clearly enunciated theory and bolder speculation than Leibniz, yet with the exception of the semi-theological *Théodicée* the whole of his collected philosophical works consists of occasional papers, notes, letters, commentaries selected from the mass of unedited manuscripts he left behind.

III

BAYLE, LOCKE AND NEWTON

THE philosophical writings to which we go for a consistent account of Leibniz's metaphysical system—the *Théodicée*, the *Nouveaux Essais* and the correspondence with Clarke— are without exception controversial. The *Monadologie* is only a summary of his " new system," one of many summaries, such as he seems to have been always ready to furnish to his friends. It differs from others only in being more complete. While, therefore, no philosopher of the modern period had so definite a metaphysical system as Leibniz, he only found expression for it in the clash of dialectical rivalry.

The three contemporaries who stand out as the opposition in this dialectical contest are widely different from one another in their position, their particular interests and their individual problems. Two of them, Newton and Locke, are the most famous Englishmen of their age, and this had its unfortunate consequence for Leibniz. The English race has always been open to the charge of insularity, a characteristic which makes it ever ready to adopt a can-any-good-thing-come-out-of-Nazareth attitude towards a new gospel. This showed itself almost to the discredit of our nationality in the case of Newton, whose followers organized themselves into a defensive guard against what they chose to represent as the insolent claims of the foreigner. Apart from this, however, if we would understand the position which Leibniz occupies in the historical development of philosophical theory we must know something of the work of his three famous contemporary rivals and the nature of his opposition.

Pierre Bayle (1647–1706) was one of those philosophers whose reputation in their life-time is out of all proportion to the value which posterity has assigned to their work. He was a person of wide and varied knowledge, the result of omnivorous reading, and he had a swift and ready pen. He was a formidable critic in an age of bitter theological disputes on which political action depended. He was the son of a French Protestant minister. His love of books was remarked from his boyhood, and he seems to have had a tendency to overstudy, for his education was frequently interrupted by illness. His favourite authors were Plutarch and Montaigne. He lived at home till the age of twenty-one, when he went to study logic at the Jesuit College of Toulouse. Within a month of his residence he abjured his Protestantism and became a Catholic, manifesting hot enthusiasm for his new religion, and seeking in his zeal to bring over his brother, who had entered the Protestant ministry. His ardour, however, cooled as quickly as it had become enflamed, and after a few months turned to rather bitter regret and finally led at the end of sixteen months to his return to Protestantism. The relapse of a convert in that age was dealt with very stringently, and to avoid the penalty he had to leave France and take refuge in Geneva. For the next few years he supported himself by becoming private preceptor in various families, some of these in France, where he disguised his identity by adopting a French spelling and naming himself Béle. His whole training at Toulouse had been in mediæval scholastic Aristotelianism, but at Geneva he was initiated into the philosophy of the reform, particularly the Calvinist philosophy, and also, what was of greater consequence, into the principles of Cartesianism. It was his staunch adherence to the philosophy of Descartes which later was to bring him into controversy with Leibniz. In 1675 a thesis on *Time*, defended with great brilliancy before the Protestant Academy of Sedan, led to his selection from among several applicants for the chair of Philosophy at that Academy. The principality to which Sedan belonged was at that time attached to the kingdom of France, but it enjoyed special privileges. Bayle first came prominently into public notice by the part he played in his vigorous opposition to the craven superstitions which were widely prevalent in spite of the great progress toward rationalism. The Duke of Luxembourg had been charged with having made a pact with Satan and solemnly was put on his trial before his peers. He was acquitted. Bayle composed his defence and published it as the speech the Duke had delivered. A short time afterwards the whole nation was terrified by the horrible portent of a comet, which appeared in 1680. Bayle published *Pensées sur la Comète écrites à un Docteur de la Sorbonne*, which on account of its scepticism and rationalism attracted the unwelcome attention of the ecclesiastical authorities. In 1682 Louis XIV, disregarding the privileges of the principality, suppressed the Academy of Sedan and Bayle was again forced into exile. He had established his reputation, however, and was almost immediately offered the chair of Philosophy and History at Rotterdam. The same year there appeared the *Histoire du Calvinisme*, by Père Maimbourg, an eloquent but unscrupulous cleric, and his book offended deeply the Protestant communities. Bayle responded immediately, and in fifteen days had prepared his *Critique Générale*, a complete vindication against the calumnies. His book was condemned and ordered to be burnt in the Place du Grève, Paris. In effect this secured its success. Three editions followed rapidly, and Bayle became famous. In 1684 he started a successful journal, *Nouvelles de la République des Lettres*, the pioneer of literary journals. Even the abdicated queen Christina of Sweden, the former pupil of Descartes, wrote to him from her place of retreat in Rome asking him to send her his journal and keep her furnished with all the important books which appeared in Latin, French, Italian or Spanish, not excepting romances. Another work of this period was his *Commentaire Philosophique sur ces Paroles de l'Evangile : Contrains les d'Entrer* (Philosophical Commentary on the Gospel Text " Compel them to come in "). At this time the Catholic clergy were doing their utmost to justify to the mind and conscience of the people the severe measures which Louis XIV was putting in force against his Protestant subjects. With extraordinary insight they had seized on the Gospel parable of the king's wedding feast, at which the invited guests had not appeared, but with one consent had made excuse. The king in his anger had sent his servants into the highways and hedges to collect guests with the instruction, " Compel them to come in " (Luke xiv. 23). The parable, if we include the sequel of the punishment of the guest who entered without a wedding garment, was so strikingly appropriate to the situation as almost to suggest that the parable had had in view precisely the case in point of Louis and his obstinate subjects. It was a favourite text, and the great Bossuet himself had set the example of preaching from it. Bayle therefore in arguing against this application of it was representing the dissenting bodies everywhere.

While at Rotterdam he had had from the beginning of his professorship the misfortune to arouse the hostility of one of his colleagues, a writer of distinction, Jurieu. The quarrel developed into personalities and petty jealousies, which at last, in 1693, led to the dismissal of Bayle from his post and the refusal to him by the city authorities of the right to teach. Thereafter he settled to private life and devoted himself to the work by which he is known to posterity, the *Dictionnaire Historique et*

Critique. It occupied him for many years, and was first published in 1699 in two folio volumes. The dictionary was proscribed both in France and in Holland, but it was translated into all the European languages and reprinted many times after the author's death. This remarkable book is only a dictionary in form. It seems to have taken Bayle's fancy as a convenient, however fantastic, way of expressing his own opinion on current controversies, to append his commentaries to biographies, for the most part slight and sketchy, of more or less striking personalities. Thus under the heading " Rorarius " he gives a brief account of a little-known sixteenth-century writer who had quaint notions regarding the nature of the souls or minds of the lower animals. This furnishes him with a peg whereon to hang lengthy dissertations on the views of leading Cartesians and other philosophers of his time and the particular opportunity to criticize the philosophical principles of Leibniz.

Bayle became the leading representative of a philosophical position which combines scepticism and dogmatism. In philosophy he maintains the rational principles of Descartes, in theology he defends the rational basis of the reformed religion, that is, the conception of God on which the Christian belief in historical revelation rests. Instead, however, of following Descartes and assigning to separate compartments the things of reason and the things which concern the faith, he makes it his definite aim to discover in reason a reconciliation. This was also the aim of Leibniz, but there is a striking difference in their methods. Leibniz finds such a reconciliation absolutely inconsistent with the acceptance of Descartes's conception of material substance, and accordingly for him the first thing necessary, the essential thing, is a reform of the conception of substance. This reform is not called for in the interest of religion or of theology, it is necessary in the interest of philosophy. This, then, is the occasion of Leibniz's *Théodicée*. Bayle had applied the Cartesian method of doubt to the theological conception of the attributes of God. He had found, in the true Cartesian spirit, in the search through doubt for a sure foundation, that it is impossible to deny the attributes of goodness and power to God, defined as the infinitely perfect being whose essence involves existence. Equally he had found that it is impossible to reconcile these attributes by appealing to the evidence of them in the creation. Are they then irreconcilable ? Yes, if the appeal is to reason. No, if the appeal is to faith. In this antithesis of faith and reason there is nothing irrational ; it is no more than the recognition that the infinity of God is incomprehensible by the finite creature. Faith supplements without opposing reason ; but there is no way by following reason to effect the reconciliation.

To this position of the philosophical Christian there was an alternative. It seemed a cruelly logical alternative, and it was ever-present to the reflection of the seventeenth century. All turned away from it with abhorrence. It was the conception of God to which Spinoza, developing the Cartesian definition, had given expression, the conception of the one substance, without intelligence or will, from the necessity of whose nature had proceeded the moral and physical world. It was anathematized as atheism.

Leibniz turned away from both these alternatives. For him there must be and there is an absolute conformity between faith and reason. To demonstrate this is the aim of his *Essais de Théodicée sur la Bonté de Dieu, la Liberté de l'Homme et l'Origine du Mal*. The grandeur and boldness of Leibniz's argument is that he disdains the Calvinist doctrine of the sovereignty of God, the conception of a kind of *fiat* in the nature of God ; and equally he is unappalled and undeterred by the Pauline challenge : Who art thou, O man, who repliest against God ? He takes far higher ground. If there is contradiction in our idea of God it is clear evidence that we have failed to conceive God truly. On the other hand, there is no escape by denying the reality of evil or by relieving the creature of responsibility. There must be no transmutation of values. Evil is the contradictory of good. There is no higher court of appeal than human reason and reason is adequate to the task. Let us look, then, at the argument ; it is stated with logical precision.

Descartes had conceived God as *ens realissimum*. God is the idea of perfect being, infinite existence. Spinoza had shown that following out the definition to its consequences God must be conceived as the one substance, and no reality can fall outside the divine nature. Leibniz demonstrates that this definition of God suffers by defect, for there is more in God than infinite actuality, there is infinite possibility. At first sight this may seem to be a mere logomachy; for possibility has no meaning apart from actuality. Leibniz shows it to be a real distinction. Take, for example, a living being or a rational soul. Its substance is more than actuality. Its substance is its potentiality, and this potentiality must be included in its definition. God, then, is more than infinite actuality, He is infinite potentiality. Descartes had taken extension and movement as the actuality of material substance, but the reality of a living being is force or potentiality, which is more than its actuality at any and every moment. The creation of the world was the creation of possibilities, and these to be actualized must be compossible. Creation, therefore, implies a choice among possibilities and a pre-established harmony. Evil, therefore, may be necessary, and yet the world may be the best of all possible worlds.

The *Théodicée*, in which this new system is expounded, is the most sustained and the most discursive of Leibniz's philosophical writings. It has lost interest, however, for the modern reader, and it is peculiarly difficult to read, both on account of its matter and of its form. To us of the modern period the attempt to deduce the nature of the physical and moral world a priori, by consideration of the divine attributes, and to pass judgments of value on the universe regarded as the handiwork of a transcendent God with infinite perfections, seems not only extravagant but otiose. It has entirely lost its attraction. But the form even more than the matter of the book detracts from its present value. It is filled with lengthy quotations from Bayle, exhaustive consideration of all his objections, and detailed verbal criticisms of his expressions. It is only when we are able to read the book in the spirit of the age that its magnificence and the profundity of its metaphysical insight impresses us.

Like the *Republic* of Plato (also a dialogue concerning Justice) the *Theodicy* of Leibniz concludes with a legend. This is the vision of Theodore, priest of Jupiter, father of the gods, in the temple of Pallas Athene, goddess of wisdom. Sextus Tarquinius Superbus, the last of the Roman kings, had, so runs the legend, before his journey to Rome, sought the advice of the oracle of Apollo at Delphi. The god's response was :

> Exul inopsque cades irata pulsus ab urbe
> (Driven out of the enraged city poor and in exile wilt thou fall slain).

He would avoid his cruel fate, but Apollo has no power. The god foreknows his fate, but cannot avert it. His fate is determined by Jupiter. It is Jupiter who has made the ravenous wolf, the timid hare, the foolish ass, the roaring lion. " Jupiter has given thee a soul, wicked and incorrigible ; thou wilt act according to thy nature and he will reward thee according to thy works—such is the oath he has sworn to fate." In dismay Sextus leaves Delphi and goes to the oracle of Jupiter at Dodona, where he consults the god. " Why hast thou condemned me to be wicked and unhappy ? Either change my lot or recognize that thou, not I, art responsible for the wrong thou dost." " Yes, Sextus, renounce thy journey to Rome and then the fates will spin thee other destinies ; thou wilt be wise and happy." " Why must I renounce the hope of a crown ? Can I not be a good king ? " " No, Sextus, go to Rome and thou art lost." The sacrifice is too great, and Sextus leaves the temple to follow his fate.

The faithful priest of Jupiter, Theodore, has witnessed the supplication and humbly addresses the god. " Thou hast convinced this man of his wrong ; he must now impute his misfortune to his bad will ; he cannot complain. Yet we, thy faithful worshippers, are amazed. We would adore thy goodness as well as thy power. Did it not, then, depend on thee to give this man a good will ? " Jupiter bids his servant go to his daughter, the goddess of wisdom, for enlightenment. Theodore accordingly repairs to the temple at Athens. There he sees in a vision all the possible worlds, each in its individuality spreading out around him and all forming a pyramid. He is conducted by the goddess, and there he sees Sextus leaving the temple of Dodona, Sextus repentant, the Sextus who will obey the god and renounce Rome. He sees him settle at Corinth, buy a plot of land, and while cultivating his estate discover a treasure. He becomes a rich man, respected and beloved, and dies in old age, mourned by the city. He is shown then, as it were, in a panorama, the whole possible world of which this Sextus is a part. He is conducted to another tier of the pyramid. He sees another possible world, in which another Sextus, also resolved to obey Jupiter, goes to Thrace, weds a king's daughter, succeeds to a kingdom and proves a good king. There are infinite other possibilities for there are infinite possible worlds. He is conducted to the apex of the pyramid and is shown the world which actually is. Here he sees Sextus such as he is and as he actually will be. He is leaving the temple in wrath, disdaining the counsel of the god. Pallas then interprets the vision to Theodore. " Had my father Jupiter not chosen this world, which surpasses in perfection all the others, he would have renounced his wisdom, he would have banished me, his child. It is not, then, my father who has made Sextus wicked ; he was wicked from all eternity and always of his own freewill. All that the god has done is to give existence to the world which contains him as a part, an existence he could not refuse. This world the god has made to pass from the region of the possibles that it may become actual. Sextus's crime serves great purposes ; from it will be born a great empire which will set forth noble examples. Yet is this partial good as nothing to the value of the whole, the beauty of which will be thy admiration, when having passed from this mortal state to another and better state the gods shall have rendered thee capable of knowing it."

Theodore awakens from his vision, gives thanks to the goddess, acknowledges the divine justice, and returns to the duties of his priesthood with enlightenment in his mind and all the joy in his heart of which a mortal is capable. Leibniz closes with this word of interpretation : If Apollo truly represents the divine wisdom in its direct vision, that is, the knowledge which concerns *existences*, Pallas may well stand for that pure intellectual knowledge which regards all the *possibilities*, for it is to these we must go if we would seek the ultimate source of things.

The work of Leibniz which has been by far the most influential in modern philosophy is the *Nouveaux Essais sur l'Entendement Humain*. It is a complete work, prepared by Leibniz for publication, but not published in his lifetime. The book is not, as we might expect, a collection of essays, but a connected work, unique in form and direct in purpose. It is a dialogue between two persons, one of whom expounds, chapter by chapter and point by point, the theories of Locke in the *Essay on the Human Understanding*, and the other, representing Leibniz himself, gives his reasons for agreeing or disagreeing, and generally opposes to the principles of Locke the principles of the " new system."

Philosophy at the close of the seventeenth century definitely turned its back on theodicies and directed its attention to the more immediate problems of sense perception and logical reasoning. It was a descent from heaven to dwell among men. Mankind losing interest in theology, found a new problem in the study of the nature of the human mind and the limitations of human knowledge. The leader in this new departure was John Locke. He introduced and adopted the principle of empiricism, the direct interrogation of experience, the subordination of all questions of genesis to the preliminary analysis of the actual immediate data of consciousness. Leibniz was in no sense opposed to this principle, but he was acutely critical of it. He had, indeed, from the very first indicated his pronounced divergence from the Cartesian doctrine of sense perception, with its disparagement of sense knowledge and condemnation of it as deception, yet he was by no means prepared to subordinate the truths of reason to the a posteriori judgments of experience, or to postpone the metaphysical problem until the epistemological problem was solved. A theory of sense perception is, indeed, an integral part of Leibniz's " new system." The *New Essays*, therefore, when at last it came into the possession of the philosophic world, exercised an immediate and determining influence on the modern development. This was not, however, in Locke's lifetime. Locke had, indeed, the opportunity to consider Leibniz's criticisms, but they did not interest him. Locke's successors, Berkeley and Hume, developed the logical implications of the empirical principle long before Leibniz's book was published. In fact, the new movement which Locke's

Essay inaugurated had run its course before the contemporaneous criticism of it by Leibniz was known.

Though Locke and Leibniz were contemporaries, both
in the duration of their lives and in the period of their
philosophical activity, and though they were well enough
known to each other by repute, they never came into
personal relations. Like so many of the great intellectual
leaders of the seventeenth century, Locke had spent many
years of his life in exile, and had consequently consorted
with the political refugees in France and Holland. He
was in Paris when Leibniz was residing there, but they
do not seem to have met. Leibniz did, indeed, send his
notes and criticisms of the Essay to Locke, but he received no acknowledgment. They had, in fact, little in
common, and there was no real intellectual sympathy
between them possible. Leibniz was a mathematical
genius, Locke had neither knowledge of mathematics nor
interest in purely mathematical problems. He returned
from exile at the English Revolution with William and
Mary, and in the political peace which followed he wrote
the *Essay on the Human Understanding*, the fruit of many
years of philosophical reflection and research and which
thenceforward became the focus of philosophical interest.

It is easy to understand why Locke had no relish for
a discussion of his theories with Leibniz. He was one of
those minds which think out their problems in retirement
and work methodically. Leibniz, on the other hand, was
one of those who, like Socrates, are incited to activity by
the dialectics of the forum. For them the only test of the
truth of a principle is its survival in the clash of open
discussion. Leibniz was disappointed at Locke's refusal
to be drawn into controversial correspondence, yet he was
too interested in the new principle to set the book aside.
He completed his work, bestowing on it more than usual
care and not grudging the time, and when in 1704 it was
ready for publication, he heard of Locke's death. He

thereupon gave up his intention of publishing the book and set it entirely aside. Ten years later he refers in a letter to his reasons for having done so. This letter is from Vienna, dated 14th March 1714. Referring to one of his friends, a Mr. Hugoni, he writes : " He also saw my very extensive reflections on the work of Mr. Locke which treats of the human understanding. But I dislike publishing refutations of authors after their death, though it is right enough that they should appear in their lifetime and be communicated to them." It is hardly probable that this was the only or the real reason for withholding publication. The death of Bayle did not prevent him publishing the *Théodicée*. At the time of Locke's death Leibniz was occupied with unpleasant controversies in England and was concerned to answer the charge against him of having made use of a paper by Newton in publishing a discovery he claimed to be original. The report of a committee of the Royal Society, while nominally exonerating him, had cast what he considered most unjust aspersions on his good faith. It was clearly not the time to embroil himself in disputes with the followers of another leading English philosopher. Whatever the reason, the manuscript remained among his papers for fifty years following his death. It was first published by Erich Raspe in 1765.

When the *New Essays* did appear there is clear evidence that it exercised an immediate and powerful determining influence on the mind of Kant. It seems almost certain that it is from this book he received the suggestion of the line along which it was possible to meet the scepticism of Hume, and it may have given him the basis of the transcendental principle. Locke's empiricism may be summed up in the maxim that there is nothing in the understanding which has not entered through the senses (nihil est in intellectu quod non prius fuerit in sensu). Leibniz assents, but with a reservation which in effect turns the whole position—"except the understanding itself" (nisi intellectus ipse). The whole Kantian reconciliation between dogmatism and empiricism may be said to hinge on this reservation. In Kant's doctrine the understanding, while dependent for all the content of knowledge on the data of sense, provides inwardly from its own nature the forms or frames or moulds into which the sense material is received. This distinction of form and content is not explicit or implicit in Leibniz, yet without his criticism on Locke's theory the idea of it might never have occurred to Kant. Thus this masterpiece of reflective thought, the *New Essays on the Human Understanding*, has a strange history and a prime importance in the development of modern theory.

The *New Essays* would be sufficient of itself to place Leibniz in the front rank of those leaders of thought who have made the modern period. It concentrates attention on the nature of the activity which we experience as mind. According to Locke this experience could be exhaustively described as a sensitiveness to external influences possessed as an endowment or quality by certain material structures, such, for example, as the animal brain. All knowledge could be analyzed into ideas which are the objects formed by immediate sense-impressions and ideas which are formed by reflection, a reflection made possible by the power of receiving sense-impressions. Locke's first principle, therefore, is that there are no ready-formed ideas in the mind anticipating experience, no innate ideas such as Descartes had declared the idea of God to be. The mind before experience is purely expectant and dependent on what experience will bring forth. For Leibniz, quite as much as for Locke, knowledge must wait upon experience, but he conceives perception in an entirely different way. Perception is the universal form of activity, the expression of *vis viva*, the living force itself, and it does not imply consciousness.

Perception admits of degree. Consciousness marks a
degree in the clearness and distinctness of perception and
depends on a power of self-reflection in the mind's activity.
Ideas, therefore, are not imposed on the mind from
without by any kind of impression or external influence ;
they are in their very nature and definition formed within.
Ideas are not impressions, but expressions. There is no
classical work of the modern period which so clearly brings
out the antithesis between the two methods of approaching
the problem of knowledge and reality which divide the
philosophical world to-day into two camps, the realists
and the idealists.

When Leibniz died in 1716 he was engaged in a controversy with Samuel Clarke (1675–1729), the most
distinguished disciple of Newton, on the subject of the
conceptions which form the metaphysical background of
Newton's system of physics. In the light of the development of modern physical theory this correspondence is in
some respects the most important of all Leibniz's philosophical writings. The correspondence arose out of a
letter of Leibniz to the Princess of Wales, Caroline of
Anspach, who became Queen of England when her husband
succeeded as George II. The Princess had formerly
resided at the Court of the Prussian Queen Charlotte,
daughter of the Electress Sophia, and Leibniz's correspondence with her had extended over several years. He
had been her adviser in the delicate negotiations which
concerned the Hanoverian succession in England. She
was deeply interested in philosophy, had read the *Théodicée*
and had questioned Leibniz on points in his philosophy
which seemed to conflict with the views of Newton, who
at that time was a frequent visitor at the English Court.
The letter she received in reply was shown to Dr. Samuel
Clarke, and he was asked to answer it. The correspondence
which followed between the two philosophers passed

through the Princess's hands. The letter which occasioned
the correspondence was dated December 1715 ; four letters
were written in succession to the four replies of Leibniz ;
a fifth letter by Clarke in reply to Leibniz's fourth remained
unanswered, for Leibniz died on November 14, 1716. His
death was sudden, the result of a fit, though he suffered
from gout and had been in poor health for some time. Up
to within an hour of the fit which proved fatal he was in
full possession of his powers and discoursing with his
friends. The letters represent therefore the work of
Leibniz in the fullness of his intellectual vigour. There is
little doubt he would himself have published them in
some form. They have all the conciseness of a dialogue,
each person dealing in order point by point with the
subject in dispute. We are entitled to rank this correspondence, therefore, as equal in importance to the other
two philosophical writings we have just considered.

It is impossible, however, in considering the value of this
correspondence, to pass over the reason why Clarke should
have been asked to reply, and not Newton himself.
Leibniz had met Newton many years before. When Leibniz
visited London the first time in 1672 he brought an introduction to Henry Oldenburg (1615–1677), the first secretary
of the Royal Society, the friend of Spinoza, and through
him he came to know the intellectual leaders of the time.
He did not meet Newton at this time, though he was made
a foreign corresponding member of the Royal Society and
dedicated a communication to it. He was then chiefly
interested in mathematics, and was working at the problem
of an infinitesimal calculus, and so also, quite independently,
was Newton. In the following year Leibniz had solved
his problem and discovered the method of the differential
calculus which he named " transmutation." Newton had
made the same discovery by a method which he named
" fluxions." Leibniz sent an account of his method to
Huygens, and a little later to Oldenburg, with inquiries

as to Newton's discoveries. The dates of the following
letters are important in regard to the subsequent dispute
which arose. In July 1676 Leibniz received an answer to
his inquiry in a letter from Newton to Oldenburg, and he
replied to Newton's letter in August. In October Newton
wrote a long letter to Oldenburg giving him the results of
his discovery, but concealing the formula in an anagram
in which the letters were transposed. Though this letter
was written in October 1676, it was not dispatched till May
1677. After seeing it Leibniz, in June 1677, gave Newton
a complete account of his own differential calculus. He
received no reply. There was no question of rivalry at the
time, for neither philosopher had yet become famous.
The dispute concerning priority arose twenty-two years
later, in 1699. It arose from an insinuation that Leibniz
had seen Newton's letter to Oldenburg in 1676, and stolen
his idea from it. Leibniz at once appealed to Newton very
earnestly to exonerate him from the charge, recalling all
the circumstances, but Newton did not reply. The matter
was taken up by Newton's friends in a jealous and hostile
spirit. The Royal Society appointed a committee of
investigation of a notoriously partisan constitution, whose
report, while clearing Leibniz of the charge, left an aspersion on his character. It is difficult to-day to read the
account of this calumny without a feeling of shame, and
it is impossible to acquit Newton of pettiness and
ungenerosity in the matter. The only thing we can put
forward in explanation is that Newton himself on several
occasions, as in the case of the anagram, showed himself
naturally secretive and suspicious. In 1704 he published
his *Optics* and included two treatises dealing with the
calculus. In the Preface to this book he gave the following
reason for their inclusion : " In a letter written to Mr.
Leibnitz in the year 1676, and published by Dr. Wallis,
I mentioned a Method by which I had found some general
theorems about squaring curvilinear figures or comparing

them with the conic sections, or other the simplest figures with which they may be compared. And some years ago I lent out a manuscript containing such theorems, and having since met with some things copied out of it, I have on this occasion made it public, prefixing to it an Introduction and subjoining a Scholium concerning that method. And I have joined with it another small Tract concerning the curvilinear figures of the second kind, which was also written many years ago, and made known to some friends who solicited the making it public." This fanned the dispute into a new flame, and the prejudice in the English mind against any criticism of Newton was excessive. We can easily understand, therefore, that the Princess would not like to engage Newton himself in the controversy. There was also another reason for selecting Clarke to reply. It is that Leibniz's aspersion in the letter was not particularly against Newton's conceptions, but against the materialism of English philosophy in its two representatives, Locke and Newton. Clarke was a doctor of divinity as well as a mathematician, and it was most fitting that he should be selected. Leibniz's letters were written in French, Clarke's in English, but Clarke himself had had his letters translated into French, and the whole correspondence was published in French by Des Maizeaux a few years after Leibniz's death.

The extraordinary interest of this correspondence is that by its criticism of the Newtonian concepts of the framework of the physical universe, it foreshadows the very defects which, when brought home to it three centuries later by scientific observations and experiments, have led to its rejection and the formulation of the general principle of relativity.

IV

THE MONADOLOGY

THERE is another side to Leibniz's philosophical activity besides that which found expression in his criticisms of Bayle, Locke and Newton. He is himself the propounder of a constructive metaphysical theory which as the work of an individual thinker is original and unique, and which marks an entirely new stage in the historical development of speculative thought. The distinctive work of Leibniz is the *Monadology*. It contains, in the form of a series of syllogistic propositions, a complete metaphysical system, based upon a pluralistic conception of substance. It is a theory of monads or individual substances. It is completely non-controversial, written expressly for the purpose of expounding a metaphysical system from its own standpoint and no other.

There is a letter of Leibniz addressed from Vienna, August 26, 1714, to M. Remond, the same correspondent to whom he had written the letter already quoted about the *Nouveaux Essais*, in which he says : " I am also sending you a brief discourse on my philosophy which I wrote for Prince Eugene of Savoy." The work which we name the *Monadology* is believed to be the brief discourse referred to in the letter. It was found among the manuscripts in the Hanover Library in French without any title or superscription. It was first published in 1720 in a German translation entitled *Lehrsätze über die Monadologie*. A Latin translation appeared in 1721 in a Leipzig journal, *Acta Eruditorum Lipsiensium*, and this translation was included in Dutens's collected edition, 1768, and entitled *Principia Philosophiæ, seu Theses in gratiam principis Eugenii conscriptæ.* The original French manuscript was first published in 1840 by Erdmann in his collected edition, and by him was given the title by which it has since been known, the *Monadologie.*

The story brings out the curious fact that the philosophy of Leibniz, which has challenged every leader of thought since his time, has its focus of interest in a casual exposition drawn up for a personal correspondent without any idea of wider publication. It appears to have been a characteristic of Leibniz to give these expositions of his theory to correspondents whenever they requested them, and the requests were frequent. Usually he could get enough into the limits of an ordinary letter, but occasionally when a prince or princess took a specially intelligent interest in his philosophy, as the Hanoverian princesses certainly did, he was at the pains to write a separate discourse and enclose it in the letter. There are among the works published three such brief discourses. One is the *Discours de Métaphysique,* written for Prince Ernest of Hesse-Rheinfels, which occasioned the correspondence with Arnauld ; a second is *Les Principes de la Nature et de la Grace fondés en Raison,* which belongs to the same period as the *Monadology* and may have been the brief discourse sent to Prince Eugene ; and the third is the *Monadology,* the most finished and complete.

It is interesting to compare the *Monadology* with the *Discours de Métaphysique.* They are separated by about thirty years, the one being written at the beginning, the other at the end of Leibniz's philosophical activity, yet the change is not from immaturity to maturity, but rather from a predominantly theological to a paramount metaphysical interest. The comparison also brings out a very important fact in regard to the sequence of the ideas which enter into the " new system." Most of the critics of Leibniz, finding an impasse in his concept of non-interacting substances, imagine that Leibniz himself to meet this difficulty introduced the idea of the pre-established harmony as a way of escape. His system, it is generally said, can only be made workable by introducing the *Deus ex machina*, the *Deus* being the god of the pre-established harmony. The direct contrary would seem to be true. The pre-established harmony is the original idea and the theory of monads follows naturally from it. It is true that such a discovery only increases the difficulty of the modern interpreter, for it is the concept of the pre-established harmony which is most antithetical to the spirit of modern science.

Another curious fact is that the *Monadology* is the first presentation of the philosophy as a theory of monads. Up to this time Leibniz had hardly ever used the word monad, and never as a distinctive term of his theory, nor did he describe his philosophy as monadology. On the few occasions of his introduction of the word " monad " it is put forward tentatively and as an alternative. Thus, for example, in the *Nouveaux Essais*, in the chapter on " Our knowledge of God's existence " (Bk. IV, Chap. X, Sect. 10), referring to Locke's remark that matter cannot be taken to be a thing single in number, he adds : " Or (as I have been wont to state it) as a true and perfect *monad* or *unity*." It is not, however, until the *Monadology* that the term is used as distinctive of his metaphysical theory. Before this, whenever he makes reference to his own philosophy it is as " my system of the pre-established harmony." It is interesting, therefore, to look into the origin of the word and its use in the modern period.

The word monad originally was used to denote the unit of arithmetic, the monad, the dyad, the triad, etc. Yet even in the ancient philosophy it was sometimes used to mean simply the individual, something which like the atom of Democritus was by definition indivisible. Leibniz means by it a living being, using it to denote the individual which is really indivisible, as distinguished from a mathematical unit individual or atom, which is only indivisible by definition and cannot be indicated in any real existent. In modern philosophy the word had been used by Giordano Bruno in the identical meaning which Leibniz afterwards gave it, and Bruno had developed from it a doctrine in all essentials resembling Leibniz's conception. So striking is the resemblance that it seems as though Leibniz must have derived his doctrine from him. This cannot be the case, however, for Leibniz had worked out his system long before he adopted the name, and he had thought it out independently of any previously existing doctrine and of the name he afterwards gave it. The name monad is, in fact, employed for a new definition of substance, a definition intended to express the distinctive meaning of a new concept.

It is curiously characteristic of Leibniz that the *Monadology*, his most important contribution to philosophy, the most challenging and influential metaphysical theory of the modern period, was not designed to attract attention or to startle by its novelty. It was a personal statement written for a friend and patron at the friend's request, and not even preserved by that friend, merely left by the author as a memorandum of what he had written among his personal papers, and by this fortunate accident preserved. Leibniz, in fact, was not by profession a philosopher. The metaphysical problem forced itself upon him by the very depth of his intellectual interest and the range of his humanistic studies. By profession he was an historian, and undertook as the serious and continuous work of his life the searching of records for the writing of the history of the House of Brunswick, for the glorification of its head and the furtherance of its political schemes. His home was the Royal Library. The enormous mass of papers he left disclose no romantic friendships and no intimate confidences. No loved and loving kindred cherished him in old age, and no one was perturbed by his death, so that John Ker of Kersland, the famous spy employed by the government at the time of the Jacobite plots, could record in his journals : " He was buried more like a robber than what he really was, the ornament of his country."

His unpopularity during his life, notwithstanding the universal recognition of his erudition and admiration of his genius, is not difficult to understand. On the Continent he was engaged in trying to reconcile the two warring religious factions and thereby earning the enmity and hatred of both. In England the philosophers resented his criticisms and suspected his good faith. Posterity has made amends. He has come to represent in the modern world what Plato stands for in the ancient.

PART II
DOCTRINE

I

THE WORLD-VIEW

THE title-page of Leibniz's unpublished criticism of Locke's Essay is : *Nouveaux Essais sur l'Entendement Humain*, par l'Auteur du Système de l'Harmonie Préétablie. This new system of the pre-established harmony was always put forward by Leibniz as his original and special contribution to philosophy. Leibniz's philosophy, however, is not a system in the same meaning in which Descartes's mechanistic conception of the whole scheme of the natural world can be so described. Nor is it a system in the same meaning as is Hegel's conception of the genesis of the actual world by the pure agency of a universal logical thinking. Leibniz's " system " is really a principle by which he could explain how a world of free agents could have originated in an act of creation. Had Leibniz's philosophy been this and nothing more he would have no place among philosophy's leaders, though he might perhaps have secured a niche in the philosophic hall of fame by reason of an ingenious hypothesis. He was not one of the world's great system makers, and it is not his system we study to-day. His intellectual leadership is due to his insight into the nature of existence and to the sure way in which he indicated the true line of the scientific advance. Yet though Leibniz had no system of philosophy he had a very complete and a very distinctive world-view and every particular problem he dealt with took shape and derived its meaning from his conception of the whole. In studying Leibniz the first essential is to understand this world-view.

Leibniz, as we have seen, was an indefatigable correspondent, and always ready to pour forth, as it were, his whole philosophy of human life in a letter to a sympathetic inquirer. We cannot do better, therefore, than begin by selecting one of his letters and quoting it in full. This letter is to the Electress Sophia of Hanover, one of a series extending over many years. The correspondence dealt with dynastic and political and diplomatic questions, but the letter selected is exclusively devoted to philosophy, and evidently a reply to the question or questions the Electress had addressed to Leibniz. In this reply he gives a clear account of his new system and of his principles generally in a way which enables us to see his scheme as a whole. The original is in French, dated Hanover, 6th February 1706. It belongs, therefore, to the time of Leibniz's full philosophical activity. The *New Essays* had been set aside and the *Théodicée* was as yet unpublished, and it is eight years before he wrote the *Monadology*. Five years earlier the Electress had been placed by the English parliament in the direct line of succession to the English throne, but at this time Queen Anne's infant son, the Prince of Denmark, was still living. I will now give the letter, preserving the short paragraphs of the original.

" Your Electoral Highness asks me what a simple substance is. I reply that its nature is to have perception, and consequently to represent composite things.

" I shall be asked how the composite can be represented in the simple, or the multitude in the unity. I reply that it is in much the same way as an infinite number of rays meet and form angles in the centre of a sphere, simple and indivisible as the centre is.

" And these rays do not consist only in the lines, but also in the tendencies or efforts along the lines, which are cut without being confused together, as the movement of fluids helps us to understand.

" For it is thus that, throwing several stones into a pond at the same time, we see on the surface of the water each stone make circles which are clear-cut and not confused, the circle made by each stone spreading as though it were all alone. We see also that rays of light interpenetrate without being intermingled. We know, in fact, that one and the same body can receive at the same time an infinite number of impressions, each of which has its effect ; and in a mass of tendencies or efforts under pressure the minutest part resists the efforts of all the rest, and this could not happen unless each received the impression of all. This is what makes us conclude that the *Unities* themselves, from which all the rest results, must be modified in relation to everything which surrounds them, and, in fact, it constitutes the representation which is attributed to them.

" God is to Himself a simple substance, but as He is the original and universal centre which includes and produces all, He is outside the series (*hors de rang*). The other simple substances are what we call *souls*, and of these all nature is full.

" Each *soul* is a world in miniature, representing things without, according to its point of view, and confusedly or distinctly according to the organs which accompany it, whereas God includes all distinctly and eminently.

" Thus by souls, as by so many mirrors, the Divine Author of things has found the means of multiplying the universe itself, as it were, that is to say, the means of varying the views of it, as one and the same city appears differently according to the different standpoints from which it is beheld.

" And each soul being a mirror of the universe after its manner, it is easy to conclude that the soul is as imperishable and incorruptible as the universe itself.

" This follows, moreover, from the fact that the soul is a simple substance or unity. Having no parts it cannot have been formed by the composition of parts nor be destroyed by their dispersion. Souls are unities, bodies are multitudes.

" The universe being in a kind of way fluid, all of one piece and like a boundless ocean, all movements are conserved in it and propagate themselves to infinity, howbeit insensibly, just as the circles I spoke about, which are produced by a stone thrown into a pond. The waves are propagated visibly for some distance, and though they fade away at last into invisibility the impression does not cease ; it continues and extends to infinity, as the laws of movement make known to us.

" This communication of movements brings it about that everything is bound up with everything else, and each is affected by all. Though generally things distant do not act on us sensibly.

" Yet light, sound, the loadstone and other examples prove that there are some notable actions at a distance.

" Since our bodies are affected by neighbouring bodies, and these again by other bodies in their neighbourhood, it follows that we are affected immediately by all the others, and since our soul represents bodies, according to its sense organs, it too is affected by all that is happening.

" We may infer also that a soul is never completely deprived of an organic body. For order requires that every substance should always be bound up with the rest of things, it may even be said to be the proof that there is this universal interconnexion.

" From this it follows that not only the soul, but even the animal subsists always. Nature, indeed, never makes leaps and does not pass from one kind to another.

" To-day, as a result of direct observation, we know that the apparent generation of a new plant or of a new animal is not a new birth, but only a growth and a transformation of a plant or an animal, which already subsisted in the seeds.

"It is not, however, only the direct experiments of Swammerdam, Leeuwenhoek and M. Dodard, but reason itself which leads us to this conclusion. For there is no mechanical principle by which a body endowed with an infinite number of organs, such as an animal's, can be derived from a formless mass. Apart from miracle, we may say there must of necessity be a preformation, that is a formation in advance of actualization. What surprises me is that, having recognized that the animal can only have its origin with the origin of the world, and that generation only effects change and development, we have not also recognized that the animal must endure while the world endures, and that death is only a diminution and envelopment, not extinction.

"It would appear also by all this that each soul, being a mirror of the universe, must follow its course, like the universe itself which it represents, without this regulated course being ever completely interrupted by death. For death is only a slumber, that is to say, a state in which the perceptions are more confused, and it lasts only till the perceptions are re-developed.

"And just as there is ground for concluding that even the universe itself is progressively developing, and that all is tending to some end, since all derives from an Author whose wisdom is perfect, we have equal grounds for believing that the souls, which endure as long as the universe, also go from better to better, at least physically (*au moins physiquement*, i.e. in the natural as distinct from the moral world), and that their perfections go on increasing, although it may be only insensibly and sometimes after long periods of retrogression.

"It is often necessary to recoil in order to leap. There would be no death and no suffering in the universe were they not necessary for the great upward changes, just as a grain appears to perish in the earth before it pushes forth the blade.

"And as there are two kinds of perceptions, one simple and the other accompanied by the reflections which are the origin of the sciences and of reasoning, so there are two kinds of souls, to wit, common souls whose perception is without reflection and also reasonable souls who think about what they are doing. The first are mirrors of the universe, the second are also imitations of the divinity.

" Common souls are ruled like empirics, purely by sense examples ; but rational souls examine by reason (wherever possible) how far past examples are applicable to their present case. The brute souls, therefore, cannot apprehend necessary and general truths, just as an empiric can never be sure that what has often succeeded with him, without his knowing why, will again succeed with him in the future.

" It is probable there are rational souls more perfect than we are, we think of them as Genii and hope to be one day of their number. The order of the universe seems to require it.

" The rational soul has self-knowledge by reflection ; that is to say, in actual thinking it knows itself and comes to know itself as an enduring self ; for when waking from sleep or passing from some distraction which may have interrupted its attention, it knows itself as the same self. This self, which subsists throughout all states, is not only the same soul physically, but also the same person morally. This renders it susceptible to punishments and rewards under the most perfect government, that of God.

" Thus the highest conclusion we can draw from the true science of principles is the importance of the practice of virtue.

" It is true that well-born souls, or those early habituated, practise good without thinking, finding their pleasure therein. Yet since every one does not enjoy this advantage, and since custom and passions often draw the soul aside from the path of virtue, it is important that good principles should be established, that so even those who have inherited or acquired contrary inclinations should be able gradually to adopt good principles intrinsically, and make them natural by their efforts, regulating and choosing their conduct. For it is possible to change even one's character.

" Besides, by joining good inclination to reason we make our action nobler and more constant. For there is satisfaction and happiness in knowing that we are acting in conformity with reason. Nothing raises us higher above the brute and nothing brings us so near the divinity. Those divine rays of wisdom and goodness which shine so brightly in some eminent persons with whom I have had the honour and privilege to be associated and whom I will not dare to name to you, Madame, lest I should be thought a flatterer, may serve as examples to the human race.

" I am, with devotion, etc.

" P.S.—I have forgotten to add that matter by itself alone is one, in the sense that it, in fact, receives all impressions and compounds them, but without the soul the order of the impressions which matter has received could not be disengaged and the impressions would be only confused. Each assignable point of matter has its own movement, different from the movement of every other point, and this movement is compounded of all the precedent impressions ; but this compounded impression is as simple as those which compose it, and we do not recognize composition in it. The movement which is the whole effect, however, since it must always be the expression of the cause, must be something other than matter. And wherever precedent impressions are distinguished and preserved there is a soul. Thus there is soul everywhere. It is true and most remarkable, that at the point where the soul is joined to the surrounding matter there exists the means of unravelling the past. For all the impressions can be gathered up, so to say, into the infinite varieties of figures and movements which exist at that point and preserve something of all the precedent effects. And this also is why every soul is accompanied by an organic body which responds to it."

In this characteristic letter Leibniz presents a complete epitome of his metaphysical theory, and also reveals the central interest of his philosophizing. The letter refers at every point and in every one of its expressions to the metaphysical problem as it existed in the seventeenth century, and yet it is quite modern and touches the very core of the problem as it exists for us in the twentieth century. The universe which presents to us the aspect of a material or unthinking reality which we call Nature, and a spiritual reality which we call Mind, consists of simple substances which are souls and their perceptions. The unity and wholeness which we attribute to Nature is a block or mass effect of the perceptions of the soul. All our perceptions are at first confused, and only with the developing activity of the soul do they grow distinct and clear, a differentiation which is a process to infinity. Souls differ from one another by the degree of clearness and distinctness in their perceptions, from the perfect and eminent degree of distinctness in God to the total con- fusedness of the perception of the dormant soul.

Souls are simple substances. Each is individual and exists with its perceptions absolutely. The soul is not composite or compounded, and its unity is not the unity of confused perceptions, as that of matter is. A soul, therefore, is indestructible. It can only be said to come into existence and go out of existence in the same sense in which we may say the world has come into existence and may go out of existence by the creative or annihilative act of God.

The soul undergoes change, but this change is only in the degree of its activity. Every soul is accompanied by a body, for pure disembodied souls would not have perception, and would not supply us with any principle by which past, present and future would be continuous. Such a principle is secured in organization, and organization is provided by the body to which every soul is attached. The body is not a substance, for it is not, like the soul, simple but composite. The body is the means or instrument by which order is imposed on the multitudinous impressions which converge on the soul from every centre of activity in the universe. This order of nature is the important point which Leibniz explains to the Electress in his postscript. The impressions and influences in their aggregation constitute Nature. They are a whole, and in that sense a unity, but without the soul they would be merely a collection without any order in themselves. The order of the world is the active work of the soul, brought about by the principle of organization. To take an example, were there no sense organs by which the impressions of light, sound, touch, etc., could pass to the soul, nature would lack the characteristic order the impressions possess for the soul. This natural order, which is the direct consequence of the embodiment of the soul and the principle of organization, is in its turn the condition of a higher order, a moral order to which rational or reflective souls can attain. There is no reason to suppose that we who are able to philosophize have attained the highest sphere of our activity. It is reasonable to believe that there are higher degrees of intelligence, and that we may ourselves rise in the hierarchy. What we do know is that, while the body is never at two moments materially identical, it is in fact just as enduring as the soul, and it is the means by which we are subject to chastisements and rewards under the government of the absolutely perfect ruler, God.

These principles are based on reason. They are logical deductions which can be tested at every step by the inner light of intellect reflecting on experience, guided by the law of contradiction and the principle of sufficient reason. But they are also confirmed by observation and experiment. Leibniz pointed to this as the peculiar triumph of scientific research. Swammerdam and Leeuwenhoek and others, by the new invention, the microscope, are able to show us worlds within worlds, and there is every reason to infer that with better microscopes this would hold to infinity.

This is the world-view which Leibniz unfolds to the Electress. Let us now look a little closely at the form of expression. It depends on two leading principles, one of which we may call the principle of individuality, the other, the principle of organization. Let us see how each of these principles is expressed in the letter. We will take them in order, and first the principle of individuality.

Leibniz begins by directly answering the questions the Electress has put to him. We have not her letter, but the reply makes it easy to see what her difficulty was. The universe, according to Leibniz, consists of simple substances. This at once gives rise to a dilemma. The universe is one, therefore if it consists of simple substances these must be parts of it. But simple substances cannot be parts of anything, and therefore the universe is not one with many parts, but many universes. It is the old problem, How are the many one? but it assumes a new form in Leibniz's doctrine of substance. It seems as though we ought to deny that there is a universe and affirm that there is a multitude of universes. A very little reflection will convince us that the idea of the universe as not one, but many, is fundamentally unsound and essentially irrational. It cannot, in fact, be even propounded in intelligible terms. Leibniz has, therefore, to show that his theory that there are simple substances does

not imply that there are simple universes. The universe
is not simple, but composite, not many, but one. To
meet the Electress's difficulty he has therefore to explain
the nature of a simple substance. The nature of a simple
substance is to have perception. Perception is not an
external relation, but an internal activity. To perceive
is to *represent* composites. To represent the simple would
be meaningless. We do not, in fact, perceive the simple
substances which compose the universe, we perceive the
universe which is composed of them. Our perception is
not the universe, it is the representation of the universe.
In modern phrase we should say that knowledge, of which
perception is a mode, is ideal or pictorial ; it gives us not
the real itself, but a representation of the real. To Leibniz
this is the very meaning of individuality, because every
representation of the universe must be individual. Representation is always from a point of view, and he gives the
illustration that the various views of a city are views of
the one city, though as views they have nothing in common. Even more clearly does the principle of individuality
come out in his other illustration. The handful of stones
thrown into the pond gives a composite ruffled surface, and
this composite is represented in perception. The reality
is not composite. Each stone has given rise to its own
circle, visibly widening and insensibly fading away, though
really preserving its individuality to infinity. The activity
which is the substance of reality is individual, and each
individual in its perception represents the universe. It
should be noted that perception with Leibniz does not
imply consciousness. There is only consciousness when
perception produces the reflection which leads to self-
knowledge. Such reflection characterizes rational souls.
Leibniz is not, therefore, in this letter propounding what
we should now call subjective idealism. Souls are simple
substances ; simple substances compose the universe ;
and in the perceptions of souls the universe is represented.

Let us now turn to the other principle which is equally important in Leibniz's world-view, the principle of organization. The argument that the soul is simple is the rational proof that it is immortal. It is not one of the things that comes to be by composition or ceases to be by disruption or decomposition. But this substantial reality of the soul does not of itself give us the order of the universe. This arises from the perceptions of the soul which represent the universe. This is the subject of the postscript. Nature, he says, might be the aggregate of all the impressions and influences radiating from every active centre and converging in every assignable point, and this would, indeed, account for the unity of the universe. But were there no souls with their perceptions there would be no order, or as we should now say, there would be no laws of nature. The idea of order cannot arise from the mechanistic principle (for example from the propagation of motion in a plenum or the composition of the waves in the illustration of the stones thrown into the pond) ; it arises in organization, and organization requires that the soul should be attached to a body. The soul must receive its impressions and influences through the body, and the body gives order to the perceptions which represent the universe. The body is not simple, but composite. Therefore, Leibniz adds, he finds it necessary to infer that the animal, that is the soul in its attachment to the body, is as enduring as the pure soul. Accordingly, he regards birth not as generation, but as development, and death not as decease, but as envelopment. This imperishability of the body does not mean that the composite body is naturally indestructible like the soul, for the soul is indestructible because it is simple and without parts. What is meant is that every soul has an individual nature, according to which a particular order enters into its perceptions, and the condition of such a nature is embodiment. Therefore to give meaning to the immortality of the soul we must infer the indestructibility of its embodiment which, however much it undergoes change, endures.

The reason of Leibniz's insistence on this idea of the endurance of the embodiment of the soul appears when we come to his moral theory of which it is the basis. This is the main interest of his letter. He wants to show how the ethical theory rests on the metaphysical foundation. There is a hierarchy of souls culminating in the idea of a perfect God, the moral ruler of the universe. Rational souls attaining to the knowledge of general and necessary truths are in effect morally responsible agents. In the monadology he will speak of them as emanations or fulgurations of the divinity.

II

SPIRITUAL PLURALISM

THERE are certain aspects of the world-view presented by Leibniz in his letter to the Electress which require to be elucidated before we proceed to examine in detail the metaphysical basis of the philosophy.

This world-view might seem to the modern historical and scientific student to be one of the artificial, more or less fantastic, divine-legation schemes and dispensations, the offspring of the fertile imagination of the Christian apologists. Also it might seem to be marked by a glaring defect, inasmuch as it leaves out of view the vast range of inanimate nature. Neither of these charges would be well-founded. A fuller understanding will show that the anthropocentric character of the world-scheme is not based on myth or preconceived opinion, but is a direct consequence of its logical and metaphysical basis. So far from ignoring the scientific problem of the physical reality of the universe, Leibniz's philosophy is, in effect, ultra-scientific. It is true, however, that it had its origin in theological and juristic concepts, and it bears throughout the marks of its origin.

One thing which is particularly noticeable in all the writings of Leibniz, and which is emphasized in every line of the *Théodicée*, is that the problem of the relation of God to man, as creator, providence and moral ruler, is never conceived within the narrow limits of the Christian theology or from an ecclesiastical standpoint, Catholic or Protestant. God is the God of the whole world. The optimism which is so distinctive of the philosophy is not based upon, or in any way bound up with, the Christian scheme of salvation and the idea of the election to grace. The Christian revelation can find a place in the scheme, but it is not the scheme, nor in any way essential to it. In this Leibniz stands in marked contrast to Pascal and even to Malebranche. As an instance we may take the myth of Theodore with which the *Théodicée* closes (page 40). The good for which Tarquin's crime is the necessary evil is that noble and moral characters will be developed in the Roman Republic which that crime of Tarquin will bring into existence. The problem of God and man, creator and creature, is for Leibniz a metaphysical problem. How is a creation of free agents possible ? If such a creation is fact, what is implied therein ? Leibniz answers that the creation implies the actualization of beings able to express their nature in their actions. Granted the creation of such free beings, what will be the nature of their freedom ? Their freedom will depend on the range of their activity, and it will differ in degree and consequently in character proportionately to the extent of such range of activity. In itself each such nature will consist in a living force, ready to find expression when the occasion arises. A universe of such beings will be a universe of free forces mutually limiting one another, and also mutually providing for one another the scope for actions.

In this conception of the universe Leibniz has left behind, as of no account, the idea of material substance, or of extension, either as a substance or as the essential attribute of a substance. Matter drops out of Leibniz's world as completely as it disappeared for Berkeley when he discovered that *esse* is *percipi*. For Leibniz, however, material substance had not to be rejected ; it has no place when substance is defined as activity. Material substance becomes a contradiction in terms, for matter is inertia, and if it changes it is because movement is imparted to it or imposed on it. In Leibniz's world-view, therefore, matter is not needed, and matter conceived as a self-subsistent existence can find no place. The idea of a God who, as a condition of creating a world, must first create a plastic material and then mould it into form, and finally endow the forms he has moulded with qualities, was not merely repugnant to the idea of omniscience and omnipotence, but in the light of those attributes self-contradictory. This does not mean that the distinctions of form and matter, soul and body, thought and extension, creator and creature, have no reality ; what it means is that matter and materiality are always taken *ad hoc* and can never claim self-subsistence. While therefore the doctrine of the creation of Adam, the fall and its consequences, the incarnation of the Son of God, and the atoning sacrifice on Calvary all have their place in Leibniz's world-view, and their interpretation in his philosophy, yet his philosophy is not pivoted on historical facts and does not revolve round any central beliefs, authoritative or rational.

The world-view is expressed in the letter in the crisp statement, " simple substances are what we call *souls*, and of these all nature is full." This is not an animistic conception. It has nothing in common with those modern theories which affirm an animating principle active throughout the natural world. It has no relation whatever to the mind-stuff or mind-dust hypotheses. These suppose that every isolable bit of matter has its equally isolable bit of soul. When Leibniz says there are souls everywhere he means that there is nothing else anywhere. To the scientific materialism of the nineteenth century such a theory was simply unintelligible, to the relativist principle of science in the twentieth century it appears as an anticipation. Even in his own century it was not put forward by Leibniz as contradicting science, but as supported by science and interpretative of it.

To understand the full significance of the disappearance

of material substance from Leibniz's world-view, we cannot do better than compare the two completely different principles which led Berkeley and Leibniz to an identical conclusion. The two philosophers were contemporaneous in their writings, though Berkeley (1685–1753) was young and Leibniz was old. Berkeley's *Treatise concerning the Principles of Human Knowledge* was published in the same year (1710) as Leibniz's *Théodicée*, his *New Theory of Vision* was a year earlier, and his *Dialogues of Hylas and Philonous* three years later. Berkeley's argument for the rejection of the idea of material substance, his denial that matter exists, was based on the full acceptance of Locke's empirical principle and its application to Locke's own account of the origin of the idea. With material substance eliminated, Berkeley's world-view became, like Leibniz's, the conception of a spiritual pluralism. Leibniz's spiritual pluralism was reached, however, in an entirely different way and with no reference whatever to Locke or to the empirical principle. It had arisen in the course of his reaction to much older doctrines, and it was based on intelligible and logical principles solely. His new system is an alternative to the theories of Descartes, Spinoza and Malebranche, all of which seemed to him open to direct logical refutation. Descartes had come to the conclusion that there are two substances, thought and extension ; mind, a substance whose essential character is thinking in its various modes ; matter, a substance whose essential quality is extension. The science of the one is psychology, of the other geometry. Thinking substance, the soul, is known to us innately in the activity of thinking itself ; matter, or extended substance, is the innate, clear and distinct idea of an existence external to us ; and the truth of this idea depends on our conception of God, who is the cause of the idea, and on the impossibility that God is deceiving us. Malebranche had sought to rationalize this principle by the theory of vision in God. The existences which correspond to our ideas are in God, who occasions in us the ideas. God sees all things in Himself in their true nature and being, and in God are the ideas of all things. In God therefore we see the ideas. Spinoza, however, had given the full logical development to the doctrine of substance and had made it consistent by identifying substance with God. The union of soul and body, thought and extension, was not the relation of two realities substantially distinct, but the necessary double aspect of one substance known under two essential attributes. Such was the state of the philosophical problem when Leibniz made it the subject of meditation. His first idea was to escape from the difficulty by reverting to the old doctrine of atoms and the void. It is a very attractive doctrine. It affords the most obvious reconciliation of the conflicting principles of individuality and continuity, and it appeals to common sense by the powerful aid it brings to the imagination in presenting the foundation for the construction of physics. But Leibniz's mathematical reflections at once exposed the inconsistency of the concept and the unsoundness of the theory. The concept of the atom will not supply the type of a real unity or offer the basis of a real compound.

Leibniz has told us himself the way in which in his mind the conception of material substance came to be discarded. In an article in the *Journal des Savants*, in 1695, he gives us this piece of mental autobiography :

"Although I am one of those who have worked intensively at mathematics, yet I have never ceased from my youth to meditate on philosophy ; for it has always seemed possible to me to reach solid results by clear demonstrations. I had already penetrated deeply into the world of the scholastics when mathematics and our modern authors drew me away from it while still young. The excellent manner in which the moderns explain nature mechanically charmed me, and I soon and rightly came to despise the method of those who refer us to forms and faculties from which there is nothing to be learnt. But when I had striven to fathom the principles of mechanics, in order to find the ground of the laws of nature which we know from experience, I came to see that the notion of *extended mass* taken alone is insufficient, we must also employ the notion of force, a very intelligible notion, though its source may be metaphysical. It also appeared to me that the opinion of those who transform or degrade the brutes into pure machines may, indeed, be a possible one, but it is most unlikely, and even contrary to the nature of things.

" In the beginning,when I had freed myself from the yoke of Aristotle, I turned to the idea of the void and the atoms, for that doctrine more than any other fills the imagination ; but when I came to review it I saw after much meditation how impossible it is to find the *principles* of a real unity in matter alone, or in what is purely passive; for in matter the whole is only a collection or massing of parts to infinity. Now since multitude can only have for its reality *real unities*, and as real unities are a quite different thing from mathematical points, for it is agreed that the continuous cannot be composed of points, so in order to find these *real unities*, since a material being cannot at the same time be material and also perfectly indivisible or endowed with a real unity, I was obliged to have recourse to a formal atom. It was necessary, therefore, to recall and rehabilitate, as it were, the substantial forms which are so much derided to-day, reinstating them in a way which renders them intelligible, and which separates the use we ought to make of them from the abuse which has been made of them. I found then that their nature consists in force, and that from this there ensued something analogous to feeling and desire, and so it was necessary to conceive them in the likeness of the notion we have of souls. But just as the soul cannot be used to give a reason for the detail of the economy of the animal body, so I concluded that these substantial forms also cannot be used to explain the particular problems of nature, necessary as they are to establish its general principles. These substantial forms are named by Aristotle the *first entelechies*. I call them, perhaps more intelligibly, the *primitive forces*. They contain not only the *act*, or the complement of the possibility, but also an original activity."

I have quoted this passage to show how in the course of his straightforward philosophical meditation the notion of material substance disappears from his scheme and is replaced with a new type of reality. It is curious to notice that the dissatisfaction is twofold, theoretical and practical. His logical sense is offended at the contradiction involved in the notion of the material substance, and his common sense is revolted by the degradation of living creatures into mere machines. For theoretical satisfaction he turns from the notion of a material unity to that of a formal unity ; for practical satisfaction he gives priority to the active principle in the living creature over its material structure. He can now indicate in the actual world the real unity ; souls actually conform to the requirements of a real unity ; they are substantial, but their substance is formal, not material. The meaning is quite clear. Leibniz does not hold that our souls are real and our bodies mere appearance. Our bodies are as real as the soul, because the constituents of our bodies are souls. The soul of each of us, what each of us denominates his soul, is a real unity, and it serves as the type or as an analogy of the kind of reality a constituent of the universe is and the kind of composite the universe is. The constituents of the world must be real units ; real units must be indivisible ; material units are divisible to infinity and mathematical points will not compose a continuous extension ; material substance, therefore, has no place whatever in the real universe.

This is not the only direction of the meditation which leads to the disappearance of the notion of material substance. The conclusion is the same when the meditation starts from the nature of the soul. At no point is the self-subsistence of matter called for even as a hypothesis. The notion of extended substance had led, as we have seen, to the opinion that the brutes are machines. This possible yet strangely improbable idea suggests, however, a new line of inquiry. Let us grant that material substance is a *prima facie* interpretation of inanimate nature ; can it equally interpret a living thing ? It can, but only by mechanizing life. Suppose, then, we turn to the living world for our principle. There we have in the soul the principle which will explain the living thing, for the soul is the idea of force or original activity. And more than this, we now know by observation and experiment that a living thing is not an animated mass of inert stuff. Even the microscope shows us this and confirms the view, to which reason leads us, that the real is the active, and that the constituents of the world are not dead matter but active forces. And so from the point of view of the soul material substance has no foothold in the universe.

Leibniz had many other arguments, but so far as his own system of the world is concerned it was not by any argument, but by his failure to rationalize the conception, or fit it into a rational scheme, that the idea of material substance disappeared. He set out to discover what a material thing is, and he could discover nothing which is a material thing.

Let us present this soul-argument in his own words, quoting again from the same article. Starting with the soul as we know it in ourselves he comes to the conclusion that reality is throughout of this nature.

" The soul or the form is a real unity, it is what in ourselves we call *Me*. It finds no place in artificial machines or in masses of matter, however organized they be. A material organism may be likened to an army or a troop, or to a pond full of fish, or to a watch composed of wheels and springs, but were there not real substantial unities composing the collection there would be nothing substantial or real in the collection. A substantial unity is not to be found in the atoms of Democritus. They are material, and *material atoms* are irrational, for besides the contradiction that they are not simple, but composed of parts, even when we consider them, as we are required to, in their attachment to one another, this does not nullify their diversity. Only *substantial atoms*, that is to say, real unities absolutely destitute of parts, can be the source of actions, the absolute first principles of the composition of things, and the ultimate elements in the analysis of things. Being without parts we may call them *metaphysical* points ; they have something *vital* and a kind of *perception*. *Mathematical* points are their points of view from which the universe is expressed in their perceptions, while bodies or corporal substances, in which the organs are closely concentrated into one whole, are in regard to us a single *physical* point.

" Physical points are only in appearance indivisible. Mathematical points are exact, but they are only modalities. Metaphysical points or substantial points (forms or souls) are both exact and real ; without them there would be nothing real, since without real units there would be no multitude."

This distinction between three kinds of points serves admirably to elucidate the mathematical figure which Leibniz had continually in mind, and which served as the scheme of his system—the sphere, at the centre of which infinite radii intersect, forming infinite angles, and whence infinite waves spread outwards—the figure which serves as his illustration at the beginning of his letter to the

Electress (page 60). The centre of the sphere is a point, but if you regard the centre as belonging to the sphere and, so to speak, owning the waves which spread outwards, it is then a physical point, and it represents the unity of the whole sphere. If, however, you confine it to the actual centre it is a mathematical point in the exact mathematical definition, yet it is not nothing, it stands for the point of view, the actual point from which the universe is co-ordinated. If, finally, it is the centre of originating activity, it stands for the force itself which is finding expression in propagated waves, it is then a metaphysical point, exact and real in the absolute meaning.

We shall find that this is the imaginative scheme which supports the conception of substance in the theory of monads.

III

THE MONADS

LEIBNIZ'S philosophy is a constructive metaphysics of reality. This may be surprising in view of the fact that his philosophical writings, all those at least which he published or intended for publication, are without exception controversial. It is easily understood, however, when we see that very early in his life he had worked out a metaphysical theory of his own. His first studies in philosophy led him to two definite conclusions : (1) that the only real unities in nature are formal, not material, and (2) that true individuality is to be found in the living world alone and not in inanimate nature. When these two principles are once clearly apprehended it becomes easy to interpret the metaphysical doctrine.

For a long time Leibniz was content to call the formal unities or substantial forms he was speaking about, souls. This had the advantage that it referred at once to the fact of experience which supplies the very type of a substantial form, the self or ego. We identify the self with the soul, whatever views we may entertain as to the nature of the soul ; and we recognize in the soul the substantial form of which the body is the material organization ; yet obviously to refer to the soul which every one experiences in experiencing, and to add that there are souls everywhere, that nature is full of souls, is to minimize the differences in kind and degree between souls. It is purely by analogy that the simplest substantial form can be described as a soul. Leibniz therefore found the need of a new word, and he chose *Monad*. This word has become for us the distinctive term of Leibniz's philosophy, and the theory of monads is set forth in the *Monadology*. There is besides the *Monadology* another short summary of the theory entitled *Principes de la Nature et de la Grace fondés en Raison*. In sketching the metaphysical theory it is useful to quote from either or both, for sometimes one, sometimes the other, is the more explicit.

The theory of Monads has its origin in a reflective meditation on the nature of mind and body and their union. The guiding thought is that in the mind-body relation we have in miniature the God-world relation. If we can solve the mind-body problem, the solution will yield a metaphysic of reality in its full intension and extension.

The relation of God to the world is remote from us, the relation of the mind to the body is close to us. Before we begin to reflect we have already, in conscious experience itself, direct knowledge of mind and body, so that when we begin to reflect on experience we have not to spread ourselves abroad, as it were, by imagination and reason, we have rather to concentrate our attention on what lies within the actual present experience. Moreover, we have not to go outside our immediate experience in order to pass from the individual to the universal, for in knowing our own mind we know what mind is, and in knowing our own body we know what body is.

Here one may object that we know with the same directness as we know our mind and our body much which is neither our mind nor our body, for we know the objects of the physical world and we recognize other minds or souls in living creatures. These objects and minds are outside us in a way which we do not confuse with what is within the narrower bounds of our mind-body. To this the answer is that, however we interpret experience, and however immediate may seem the reality of the objects we call material, the physical world only exists for us mediately as a modification or affection of the body. In a very real sense, therefore, the physical world is included in our body, and if we endow that world with an independent status, and locate it outside the body, and beyond its sphere of activity, we still must think of it as united to and continuous with our body.

The new metaphysical interest in the seventeenth century had focussed itself on the mind-body problem. Descartes had held that there are two substances, the essential attribute of the one being thought, of the other extension ; that the body is a part of extension ; that the high specialization of structure and multiplicity of function which made it an individual organism were an effect of the movement which God had imparted to extension in the original creative act which produced the world. The soul, on the other hand, he had held to be quite independent of the body, different in its origin and in its destiny. Against this theory of Descartes the materialists had objected that there is no substantial difference between the soul and the body. These were the atomists and known as the new Epicureans. The soul, like the body, they declared, is material, and all reality in its ultimate principle is nothing but atoms and void. Instead of supposing with Descartes an origin of the atoms in the disruption of extension by the introduction of movement, they imagined an eternal rearrangement by aggregation and dispersion of indestructible material units. These were the two opposing principles when Leibniz turned his meditation on philosophy. He was dissatisfied with both. He found each to be plainly self-contradictory when tested by logical analysis. He proposed a third alternative, the theory of monads. He agreed with the atomists that there is only one substance, and that this substance exists in individual units, but he rejected their concept of material units externally related. The individual units are not matter, but force. Extension is not substance, but representation. Movement is not force, but the expression of force, and only force is conserved.

A first reflection on the distinction we make between the mind and the body is that the mind is one and integral, the body is composite, a many. In its first and obvious intention no one will challenge this distinction. Certainly so far as the body is an individual whole it consists of separable parts. It may be likened to a machine, to an army, to a factory, but it is essentially a many, a multitude ; it is one thing, but a composite thing. On the other hand, the mind or the soul, if we mean the subject of experience, the user of the body, the self or the *me*, has no parts. It is complex in its activities, but it is substantially one and indivisible. Even if we accept the modern psycho-analytic doctrine of the self and imagine it as an unruly, turbulent, rebellious crowd of suppressed wishes, held in more or less successful control in an unconscious mind, this does not make the soul composite in the sense in which the body is composite. The very idea of divisibility is destructive of the notion of the soul. Unity is a positive characteristic, for though the soul may have internal diversity and variability, there is no principle on which it can be divided or compounded.

Force is a capacity of action. If force is substance, then while substance is one, substances are of two kinds, simple and composite ; minds which are unities, bodies which are multitudes. But the composite is only an aggregate or assemblage of simple substances, for without simples there could be no compounds. It is these simple substances Leibniz calls monads. *Monas* is a Greek word, meaning unity or what is one. If, then, a monad is essentially what we call a life, a mind, a soul, then the body is composed of souls and all nature is full of souls.

This is a new meaning of the term substance. It is a direct challenge to the old and widely accepted notion of substance. Whether the term had been applied to God, or to the soul, or to the objects of the material world, it had generally suggested the idea of a *substratum*, an underlying support of qualities, attributes and accidents, the static basis of the change and variety which characterizes the actual world. In the new meaning which defines substance as force, the capacity of doing, the conception is no longer of a *static substratum*, but of an *active subject*. It implies experience, whether experience take the subjective form of perceiving, understanding, willing, or the objective form of actions.

Let us first satisfy ourselves of the rationality of this change in the meaning of substance. It is the application of a simple principle. Anything is what it does ; anything which does nothing is nothing. When we substitute the idea of subject for the idea of substratum we still retain the notion of substance, but instead of a *material* identity underlying change we now have a *formal* identity. The difference may be illustrated by an example from the physical world. Ice, snow, vapour, etc., are different forms of an identical matter, the substratum we call water ; rivers, waterfalls, clouds, etc., are permanent forms of a changing matter. The former are accidents of a substantial material ; the latter are the substantial forms of a changing material. So we may speak of the substantial material or of the substantial form of anything. Leibniz's new conception of substance is that the form is prior to the matter. In this he is not proclaiming a new doctrine, but returning to the Platonic conception. He also follows Plato in the doctrine that the forms are intelligible, not sensible. In an important writing entitled " On Nature," which is assigned to the year 1698, he says concerning his theory of substance as force : " This internal force may be conceived, but it cannot be imagined. It is no use to try and represent imaginatively the actual nature of the soul. *Force*, in fact, belongs to that order of things which falls under the understanding, not under the

imagination." In further explanation of this he adds :
" Hobbes and all who agree with him in thinking that
reality is material are right in so far as they are persuaded
that none but corporeal things can be distinctly imagined
and explained. What refutes them is precisely that it is
force, something neither imaginable nor derived from
imaginables, which is at the basis of things. To locate
force simply and directly in God, and to suppose his fiat
to have been pronounced once for all without further
affecting things or leaving after it any effect, is so shallow
an explanation that to offer it is to abandon the rôle of
philosopher and cut the Gordian knot with the sword.
From my *dynamics*, on the other hand, we can draw a
distincter and truer explanation of active force than any
which has heretofore been offered, by considering the real
value we assign it conformably to our experience of the
laws of nature and movement."

The expression " my dynamics " in the last sentence
is a reference to a previous passage in the same article in
which he had proposed to give this name to a special science
of *force* (German *Kraft*, Latin *Virtus*), a science which was
to throw light on the nature of substance. " Active or
acting force is not the same as what the schoolmen named
power, a simple faculty or possibility of acting which to be
carried into act requires an external excitation or independent stimulus. The real active force includes the
action within itself. It is *entelechy*, a power mediating
between the simple faculty of acting and the definite or
effected act. It contains and includes effort. It is self-
determined to action, not requiring to be aided, but only
requiring not to be inhibited. The illustration of a weight
which stretches the cord it is attached to, or of a bent
bow, may elucidate the notion. I hold that this power of
acting is in all substance, and that it is always giving rise
to some action, so that neither spiritual nor corporeal
substance ever ceases to act."

This, then, is the new or reformed idea of substance. It is necessarily individual, and it is necessarily of one kind. The only distinction of substances in nature is between the simple and the composite. There is but one substance, and this substance is individualized. The individuals are the monads.

This reform of the notion of substance is essential to the understanding of the theory of monads, and we may now proceed to inquire into the nature of the monads themselves. They are simple substances. By simple we mean that there are no parts. What has no parts can have neither extension nor shape. There is no possibility of dividing or disintegrating the monads ; they are atoms in the literal meaning of the word. They are indestructible. In this they resemble the atoms of the old philosophy. There is no natural means by which they could come into existence or pass out of existence. We may postulate a supernatural creation to account for their origin out of nothing, and a corresponding supernatural act of annihilation to procure their destruction, but if we do, it must be on independent grounds and for other reasons than any arising in the nature of the monads themselves.

The indestructibility of the monad is the basis of Leibniz's doctrine of the natural immortality of the soul. The ethical and religious import is not in question, but only the logical and metaphysical theory. What appears at once in the conception is that the monads, when they enter into composites, must combine on an entirely different principle from the mechanistic one which applied to the Democritean atoms. Monads without figure and extension cannot by any combination be made to yield figure and extension. Nothing we could possibly mean by the union of souls would produce naturally what we know as the body. If, therefore, monads are the real constituents of nature, nature must be constituted on an entirely different principle from that of materialism and mechanism, for this is based on the primacy of extension and figure. Leibniz has, therefore, two tasks before him in his theory of monads. The first is to explain the inviolable nature of the soul, the simple substance ; and the second is to derive from that inviolable nature the extension, figure and movement which characterize the body, the composite substance.

The monads have neither extension nor figure, for if they had they would have parts. Consequently the only way in which one monad is distinguishable from another is its quality and internal action. Its simplicity is not inconsistent with a multiplicity of its own modifications and with internal change and diversity due to its own nature. " The monads have no windows by which anything can enter or go out." The reference is to the scholastic explanation of sense perception, the notion that substances give off from themselves images or pictorial representations, termed " sensible species," which passing into the mind constitute knowledge. While reintroducing, therefore, the scholastic doctrine of " substantial forms " he wishes to dissociate himself from the scholastic theory of sense knowledge. The whole theory of the monads turns on the nature of perception. For Leibniz, perception is the universal characteristic activity of the monads, even of the bare monad : it is an internal activity, and by means of it the whole universe of the monads is represented in each individual. " The fleeting state which encloses and represents a manifold in the unity, or in the simple substance, is no other than what we call *perception*. We must, however, distinguish perception from apperception or consciousness. It is from neglecting to do so that the Cartesians have gone so wrong. They have supposed that the perceptions we do not apperceive count for nothing, and this is why they hold that only minds (*esprits*) are monads, and that neither animals nor other entelechies have souls (*âmes*) " (*Monadology*, 14).

The problem of perception may be presented in this wise. Our concept of the monad implies that the universe in reality has neither extension, nor shape, nor position, nor movement ; for the monads have none of these characters and they are the real constituents of the universe. In fact, then, there is nothing in reality which corresponds to the perceived qualities of bodies. These qualities, therefore, must be appearances, and so far as they are essential to bodies, the bodies themselves are not realities but appearances, phenomena, such for example as colours and sounds. Perception, then, must be an imperfect or rather an artificial way of knowing reality. It does not enable us to penetrate into the nature of things and know them as they are. There is, indeed, in the rational monads apperception ; this is a higher power than perception, but it is only our own activity in perceiving which we apperceive. Perception is the artifice by which we produce the appearances of things which we distinguish from ourselves and from one another. But in order to represent things outside one another we must first represent extension. This *representation* of extension does not imply or presuppose a real extension, or that things really are outside one another. It is the only way in which we can represent actual multiplicity.

It is important to understand this if we would see the full import of the theory. Extension is not what we perceive ; it is the artifice by which in perceiving a multitude of distinct individuals we represent their togetherness. The doctrine is a peculiarly difficult one, and there is no need to minimize the difficulty ; yet it is a perfectly intelligible doctrine. The difficulty lies in the fact that we are dependent on sense imagery even to represent our dependence. There are many examples, however, within common experience which illustrate the principle exactly.

Thus the musical notes which enter into a melody or compose a symphony or sonata are not extended ; they are a pure succession ; yet we can only represent them by the artifice of a spatial extension in which the successive notes appear to exist simultaneously, a pure fiction of the imagination. A numerical series can only be counted one at a time, yet to represent the series we must use the device of an imaginary extension. Thus a real succession would actually be counted as one, one, one . . . now, now, now . . . for only one " now " exists, and there is no privilege of one over another. If, however, I count the succeeding nows as a series, one, two, three, then for the *three* to have the privilege of being third in the series I must create an imaginary extension in which one and two exist simultaneously with it. It is an artifice or what in the Kantian philosophy is termed a schematism.

This representative or schematic extension itself produces the shapes and movements which characterize our perceptions of the physical world, for the different parts of extension will assume different appearances. Thus the beings, which by this representative extension appear to us as outside one another, appear either constantly in the same order or in a varying order. In the first case we say they are at rest, in the second that they are in movement. Thus arise for us the phenomena of rest and movement. There must, however, be relations between the monads themselves which give rise to these appearances in the representation. Our perceptions, in fact, give rise to reasoning, and the logical principle of sufficient reason governs all our perceptions of matter of fact. The order, therefore, in which we represent things must have its reason in an order which exists between the reals represented. If we knew the reals we should be able to see the generation of every phenomenon in its full particularity. As it is, our ignorance of the reals imposes on us the necessity of following a different route. Instead of explaining phenomena by the reals we have to judge the reality by the phenomena. This we do by imagining in the reality something analogous to the appearances.

Phenomena represent composites, and a composite is a whole whose constituent monads have more immediate relations between themselves than the whole itself has with other composite wholes. Monads, then, must be able to combine in such a way that the immediate relations between them form some analogy to the composites represented in our perceptions. There must be, that is to say, some principle on which the monads form collections or aggregates or composites. These composites, moreover, as we have seen, appear to abide and change and move relatively to one another. This apparent order must correspond to a real order, but the perceived order cannot be that real order.

The monads are active, and this activity is purely internal and self-originated. It is by their internal activity and not by an outward disposition that they are differentiated one from another. What kind of activity do we know which will meet this requirement ? The answer is that understanding and will are such activities. They are also the basis of personal character, giving to each his distinguishing quality. They are entirely internal, originating within, not imposed from without, and yet their whole reference is to the outer world. Understanding and will are highly developed forms of activity which we meet with only in the rational monad, but they are forms of an activity which we must suppose to exist in and form the essential nature of the lowliest monad.

With this introductory consideration of the problem of the monadic activity, let us now turn to Leibniz's own account :

" The monads have no shape, for if they had they would have parts. Consequently, one monad in itself and at any particular moment can only be discerned to

be different from another by its internal qualities and
actions. These can be no other than its *perceptions* (that
is, its representations of the composite, or of what for
the simple monad is without), and its *appetitions* (that is,
its tendencies to pass from one perception to another,
which are the principle of change). For the simplicity of
the substance does not prevent the multiplicity of modifications in the simple substance, and these must consist in
the variety of its relations to things which are without.

" It is like a centre or point which, though itself simple,
is the locus of an infinity of angles formed by the lines
which intersect at it.

" In Nature there is fullness. There are simple substances
effectively separated from one another by their actions,
which actions continually change their relations. Each
simple substance or monad, when it forms the centre of a
composite substance (of an animal, for example) and is
the principle of its *unicity*, is surrounded by a mass composed of an infinity of other monads which constitute the
central monad's body, and according to the affections of
this body the monad represents, in a centre as it were, the
things outside it. This body is organic when it forms a
kind of automatic or natural machine, a machine which is
a machine not only in its ensemble, but even in its smallest
observable component parts. Now since by reason of the
fullness of the world, all is bound up together so that each
body acts on every other body proportionately according
to the distance, and everything is affected reactively, so it
comes about that each monad is a living mirror, a mirror
endowed with internal action, representative of the
universe according to its point of view, the representation
having the same order as the real universe represented.
The perceptions in the monad are produced from one
another by the laws of appetition or of *final causes of good
and evil*, which consist in noticeable perceptions, ordered
or disordered ; the changes of the body and outside

phenomena are produced from one another by the laws of *efficient causes*, that is to say, of movements. Thus there is a perfect harmony between the perceptions of the monad and the movements of bodies, pre-established from the first, between the system of efficient causes and the system of final causes. And in this consists the *accord* and the physical union of the soul and the body without the laws of the one being ever interfered with by the laws of the other.

" Each monad with the body which appertains to it is a living substance. Thus not only is there life everywhere joined to members or organs, but also there is in the monads an infinity of degrees, some more or less dominating the others. When, however, the monad has organs so adjusted that by their means the received impressions, and consequently the perceptions which represent them, stand out in relief and intensified (as, for example, when by means of the humours of the eye the light rays are concentrated and act with more force) it may even lead to feeling, that is, to a perception accompanied by memory, to wit, a perception whose echo, as it were, endures long after and makes itself heard on occasion. Such a living being is an *animal* and its monad is a soul. When this soul is raised to *reason* it becomes something sublimer, and is classed among *minds (esprits)* " (*Principles of Nature and Grace*, 2, 3, 4).

Now although in this passage the theory is expressed in ordinary language and using common-sense imagery, and is consequently open to the charge of inconsistency, the meaning is quite plain. The exigencies of discourse require us to speak of things even in denying that there are things, and to describe these things in spatial terms as outside, extended, massive, changing, even when arguing that space and time, extension and succession, are mere appearance, the ideal representation of realities themselves unextended, simple, self-contained and only internally active. The universe is constituted of the monads, and there is no residue, no remainder. The representation of the universe in each monad is not real, but ideal. The monads differ in degree by the adequacy or inadequacy, the clearness or confusedness and obscurity, by which in each monad the universe is ideally represented.

What we have now to see is how such a universe can be so ordered that organization is possible. Every monad is in some respect dominant over other monads, and in some respect subservient to a dominant monad. Only by being attached to other monads can the dominant monad effectively perform actions. This is the principle which Leibniz rationalized by the idea of a system of pre-established harmony. We may conclude this account of the monads or simple substances by quoting the picturesque passage in the *Monadology* which had been inspired by Leibniz's intense interest in the recently invented microscope and its revelations.

" A world of creatures, living beings, animals, entelechies, souls, exists in the minutest part of matter. Each portion of matter may be conceived as a garden full of plants, as a pond full of fish. But every stem of the plant, every limb of the animal, every drop of sap or blood is also such a garden or pond. And though the ground and air interspersed between the plants of the garden, or the water interspersed between the fish of the pond, may not themselves be plant or fish, yet they contain them, usually of a subtlety which renders them imperceptible. Thus there is nothing arid, sterile, or dead in the universe, no chaos, no confusion, save in appearance ; exactly as a pond would appear to us at a distance were we able to see only the confused movement of the swarming fish and not the fish themselves."

IV

THE PRE-ESTABLISHED HARMONY

THE microscope, if it did not actually suggest to Leibniz the idea of his new system, certainly confirmed it. He refers continually to the researches of the inventors and users of the microscope, Swammerdam, Leeuwenhoek and Malpighi, for the verification of his hypothesis. We may therefore usefully preface our account of the pre-established harmony with a consideration of the philosophical aspect of the nature of reality as revealed by the microscope. We shall see that it indicates how the first purely negative conception of infinity may be turned into a positive conception ; how an agnostic attitude towards the concept of a limit to divisibility may be changed to an affirmation of actual infinity. The self-contradiction involved in the ordinary way of conceiving infinity had led Leibniz to reject the theory of atoms and void. That theory had assumed the actuality of an indivisible material unit, occupying an infinitely divisible extension or space or void, throughout an eternal duration and infinitely divisible succession, despite the obvious self-contradiction the concept involved. It had also assumed that atoms, effectively without parts, could yet combine by partial contacts. On the other hand, the principle of the identity of indiscernibles made it mathematically axiomatic that units literally indivisible if they coincide must coalesce. Again, it is impossible to conceive a limit to the divisibility of space while we affirm its indefinite extensibility. This was the mathematical situation. The infinite for mathematics was a negative conception. There is, however, a metaphysical way of conceiving a positive infinity which in no manner conflicts with geometrical demonstration, and it is this metaphysical infinity which is suggested by the microscope.

When we look through a microscope we see magnified a portion of what we identify as our ordinary extension, and the power of the lenses determines the degree of the magnification. The microscope, therefore, considered simply as a device for magnifying minute objects, may be called in evidence to disprove the atomic theory; for the atom, assuming it to exist, can, theoretically at least, be rendered discernible by magnification. This possibility at once exposes the inconsistency of the conception, for as there is no limit to magnification, so there can be no limit to divisibility. The atom, it is clear, may be magnified till it occupies the field of vision, and then any minutest portion of that field of vision will be magnifiable in its turn. The real atom we are in search of is an atom which cannot be magnified even in appearance, and no such atom is conceivable.

So far, however, we are only considering the microscope as an instrument enabling us to magnify the *appearance* of an object, but what actually the microscope reveals to us is the change which occurs in our view of reality when we take a new standpoint and co-ordinate the world for a new system of reference. Instead of giving us ever new and diminishing dimensions it enables us to carry our ordinary dimensions into new ranges of activity. In a sense there are disclosed to us worlds within worlds, like the boxes within boxes of a Chinese puzzle, but what, in fact, is demonstrated is that every world, however great or small in relation to our normal world of sense experience, is yet of the same size, co-ordinated on the same principle, by axes of co-ordination which are invariable. That is to say, that while, for example, we may be looking at a new world, say the world of a cyclops or of a paramœcium, a world into which we cannot effectively enter, we are co-ordinating that world from the infinitesimal creature's view-point with our own axes of co-ordination. Our universe, accordingly, is seen to be infinite in the positive and absolute meaning that, however the system of reference changes, the dimensions remain constant, and that into whatever system we enter there is actually an infinite extensibility around us and an infinite divisibility below us. If there is no absolute space-time system, no relative space-time system has any privilege. To illustrate this principle in terms of modern physics, it means that were we to shrink to atomic proportions or to expand to proportions which reduced stars to atoms, so long as we co-ordinated our world on the same principle we should find its dimensions had undergone no alteration.

Leibniz had reached this conception on philosophical grounds, and he now found it confirmed by science. " Each portion of matter is not only divisible to infinity, as the ancients recognized, but is also subdivided actually without limit, each part into parts, of which each has some movement of its own ; otherwise it would be impossible that each portion of matter should express the universe " (*Monadology* 65). The science, however, to which Leibniz appealed was the speculation, based on observation, concerning the origin and present state of living forms. Embryology, in the modern meaning, was not even in its infancy; it did not exist. Two theories, both ancient and both rational in their conception, divided the opinion of philosophers. The first was the theory of generation, or epigenesis, which had had the support of Harvey, the discoverer of the circulation of the blood. This was the theory that living forms are generated from a material possessing the potency to produce, but not actually enclosing, the figure or shape of the new creature. The facts of putrefaction, which appeared to be a spontaneous breeding of living forms, and also the structureless character of the egg-yolk before incubation, seemed to confirm this theory. The second and opposing theory was that of preformation. This theory seemed to be scientifically established when Malpighi claimed to have found as the result of extensive observations of incubation that the embryo is fully formed, though infinitesimal, before incubation, and that incubation was not a process of generation, but merely a process of growth, by absorption of the nutritive material of the egg.

The preformation theory was the theory that the actual forms of living beings exist already in the germ, and that in their life as free individuals there is only development and unfolding or expansion, not generation. It carried with it the idea of *emboîtement*; that is, the enclosing of individuals one within another. Thus all the human race to the end of time existed in Adam when the world was brought into existence at the creation. Such a philosophical theory far exceeded any possibility of scientific demonstration, but the microscope and the observations of the first users of it had seemed wonderfully to confirm it. With the history of the theory we are not concerned. It is interesting, however, to know that it held its own throughout the half century which followed the death of Leibniz. It was elaborated by the naturalists, Bonnet, Buffon and Cuvier, but it was definitely disproved and finally discarded in 1759, when C. P. Wolff brought decisive observations of fact to give the victory to the opposite theory of epigenesis.

Let us now see how this preformation theory enters into Leibniz's system of nature and enables him to rationalize his metaphysical conception. The monad or simple substance is formal, not material ; its activity consists in perception and appetition ; and each monad is distinguished from every other monad by its point of view. The conception of a universe requires that these monads shall enter into combinations, and the principle of such composition is open to our inspection in actual experience of the union of soul and body. What, then, is the nature of this union? Leibniz answers that it is the principle of organization by which individual activities of independent units are brought into the harmony of a whole. This is the principle by which man makes a machine. The universe is a living machine which possesses a perfection no artificial machine can attain, inasmuch as it is not only a machine in its entirety, but a machine of which every part is also a machine. We see this principle of organization actually realized in the union of soul and body. The soul impresses its form on the actions of the body, to which it is attached and of which it is the dominant monad, and the body gives figure and shape, that is materiality, to the actions of the soul. At once we see how important is the question of fact. Are we to think of the soul as detachable from the body, able to migrate from one body to another, as some philosophers have held? Is there such a fact as metempsychosis, the passage of the soul from one habitation to another? Does the union take place at some moment of a generative process, and is the union dissolved at the death of the body? Leibniz held on metaphysical grounds that the union is as original and as indestructible as the monad itself, for it is the essence of the monad. He expressed it by saying that the monads could not have been created individually, one at a time, they could only have been created altogether, and they can only perish altogether by an act of annihilation. The preformation theory enabled him to defend his view by an appeal to scientific facts. This is most forcibly set forth in his *Système Nouveau de la Nature*, an article written in 1695. " Now to return to the consideration of the ordinary forms or material souls " (he has been dealing with the peculiar perfections of the rational souls), " the duration, which we must attribute to them, in contrast to that which was attributed to the atoms, might suggest that they must pass from body to body, and that there is what is named metempsychosis, much as some philosophers speak of the transmission of movement and the transmission of species [the scholastic theory]. There is no such passing. It is here that the transformations of MM. Swammerdam, Malpighi and Leeuwenhoek, who are the most excellent experimenters of our time, have come to my support and have made it easier for me to affirm that the animal, and every other organized substance, has not its beginning when we are accustomed to date it and that what appears as generation is only development and a kind of growth. I have been pleased to find, moreover, that the author of *La Recherche de la Vérité* [Malebranche] and also MM. Regis, Hartsoeker and other learned men do not differ very greatly from my opinion.

"There still remains, however, the most important problem as to what becomes of these souls or forms at the death of the animal or at the destruction of the organized individual substance. This is the more embarrassing in as much as it seems eminently irrational to suppose that souls survive uselessly in a chaos of confused matter. The consideration of this problem has brought me finally to the view that the only reasonable conclusion we can come to is that there is not only a conservation of the soul, but also a conservation of the animal itself and its organic machine, although the destruction of its grosser parts may have reduced it to an infinitesimal state far below the range of our senses, such as it was before birth. Moreover, no one can mark exactly the actual moment of death. It may often be simulated for a long time by a simple suspension of noticeable actions, and in simple animals it is, in fact, no more than this, witness the resuscitations of flies drowned in water and buried under powdered chalk. There are also many other like examples which warrant us in believing that there have been many such resuscitations, and that there would be more if mankind knew how to refit the machine. It is probable the great Democritus himself, who was an able anatomical student, had an idea of the same kind, though Pliny, it is true, scoffs at the whole notion. It is natural, then, to suppose that since the animal has always been living and organized (and this fact is beginning to be recognized now by persons of great reputation) it will always continue to be so. For if there is no first birth or entirely new generation of the animal it would seem to follow there can be no final extinction or complete death, taken in the strict metaphysical meaning, and that therefore instead of a transmigration of the soul there is only a transformation of one and the same animal, according as its organs are variously folded and more or less developed."

We are brought, therefore, to what for Leibniz is the fundamental problem : How is this harmony of independent individual activities, each expressing its own nature, each developing according to the law of its own appetition, effected ? If from our twentieth-century outlook the problem appears artificial in its origin and extravagant in its presentation, we must remind ourselves that in the thought of the seventeenth century it was a most vital issue. The problem met the philosopher in some form whatever might be his particular angle of approach. It is not a fantastic cobweb of speculation due to the idiosyncrasy of a man of genius. It is the problem of causality in a form which was inescapable at the stage of philosophical and scientific development which Leibniz represents. He had reformed the notion of substance and found himself confronted with the problem of cause.

The universe, it seems to him, may be likened to a machine, but a machine which is more perfect than any machine of human contrivance, for it is a machine not only in its ensemble, but even in its most infinitesimal part. How, then, and by what agency and power and mode of working, is its efficiency secured? Or, turning from the great universe to the narrower plane within it where the same principle is clearly at work, what is the nature of the union between the soul and the body which secures the harmonious functioning of the living machine, the human being? Two answers were current in the philosophy of the time. One was the direct causation theory and the other the doctrine of occasionalism. The first was the theory of direct action. This was the view that the mind acts directly on the body and that the body directly affects the mind. Descartes had supposed that the mind, or soul, or thinking substance, though unextended, was located in the body at a particular part of the organism which he named the *conarium* and identified anatomically with the structure known to us as the pineal gland. The soul, according to his conception of its nature, had no power to initiate the movements of the body, but it could direct and control them by guiding the animal spirits. Conversely, the animal spirits under the influence of the bodily movements could inform the soul. The body, therefore, could be considered as an automaton under the rule of a rational soul. The unworkability of such a scheme soon became apparent. Bodily actions were conceived as movements mechanically propagated and causally interconnected, mental actions as associated states with no causal efficiency. There were, therefore, two concomitant series of events, each with its own order, having no common factor and consequently no principle on which they could be supposed to interact. This difficulty had led to the theory of occasionalism, the second of the attempts to solve the problem of causality. The affections of the soul, it was said, were not the direct causes of the actions of the body, but the occasion of them. The union of soul and body was not a causal relation at all. Cause could only be attributed to the universal source of power, God, and what we call particular causes are only the occasions on which God exercises power.

These were the two principles by which the activity of the universe was interpreted. Leibniz pointed out a third alternative, one which at once accorded with his new conception of substance, appealed to the logical principle of parsimony, and furnished the basis of a theodicy. It was the principle of the pre-established harmony. There is no action of one substance on another, and there is no occasion for the intervention of God. Every substance originates its own activity and develops its own nature in expressing its activity. To God we must attribute the act of creation. It was the bringing to existence of the monads, simple substances, each with its own individual nature. The work of creation was perfect from the first, being the work of the omniscient, omnipotent God. The harmony is pre-established in the meaning that the work of a perfect artificer cannot be faulty or in need of adjustment. The soul or dominant monad acts in simple accordance with its own nature, and the monads of the body express this nature, not by any direct influence of the soul upon them, nor by an intervention of God, but each acting in accord with its own nature ; the harmony is due to the original act of God in creation. The creative act of a rational being is the determination of a choice among possibilities, for the mode of rational action is the presentation of the possibility in idea before the fiat which makes it actuality. The omniscience of the Creator enabled him to harmonize the activities of the free agents he was creating, in advance of their creation. The created monads are forces, individuals with freedom to develop their own activity, limited only by the activities of one another and the like freedom in all. These individuals are united by ideal relations, and creation therefore must have had regard to this ideal harmony. The very definition of God as the infinitely perfect Being necessarily implies perfection in the creative act itself. Posited in this way, that is to say, granting the premise, which to the intellectual world of Leibniz was a self-evident truth, that the world being finite must have originated in an act of creation by a Being who is infinite, the argument is unassailable. Let us now turn to his own account in his own words.

In a letter to the Abbé Foucher, published in the *Journal des Savants* in 1696, we have what is entitled in the collected editions of his philosophical writings the *Premier Eclaircissement*; it led to a further letter to his correspondent which is entitled *Deuxième Eclaircissement*. The first is as follows :

" Some of my acute and learned friends, having considered my new hypothesis on the great problem of the union of soul and body, and convinced of its importance, have asked me to give them some enlightenment in regard to difficulties they find in it, due, I think, to their not having fully understood it. I may perhaps make it intelligible by the following illustration. Suppose there are two clocks which are in perfect accord with one another. Such an accord could come about in any one of three different ways. The first is that there might be a mutual influence of each on the other ; the second, that both might be under the continual care of an attendant who keeps adjusting them ; the third, that each by itself is keeping time perfectly.

" The first form of explanation, that of influence, was made the subject of an experiment by the late M. Huygens, and it occasioned him no small surprise. He fixed two large pendulums to the same wooden beam ; the continual swinging of these pendulums communicated vibrations to the wooden particles of the beam ; but these vibrations, when both pendulums were swinging, were found to be unable to subsist as separate orders in such wise that one set did not interfere with the other, at least this was so when the two pendulums were not swinging in unison, for it happened in some wonderful way that whenever anyone expressly disturbed their swinging, as soon as they were left alone the regular swing returned, almost like two musical chords which are in unison.

" The second way of making two clocks always accord, however bad the workmanship of the clocks, would be to appoint a clever workman to be constantly attending to them and putting them in accord at every moment they tended to go wrong; and this is what I call the *assistance* hypothesis.

" Finally, the third way would be to construct the two clocks at the beginning with such art and skill that we could be sure of their future accord ; and this is the way which I call that of pre-established agreement.

" Now put soul and body in place of the two clocks. Their accord or sympathy will also come about in one of three ways. The way of *influence* is that of the ordinary philosophy ; but as there is no way of conceiving how material particles, or immaterial qualities, or sensible species, can pass from one of these substances into the other, we must abandon that supposition. The way of *assistance* is that of the system of occasional causes ; but I hold that this is making a *Deus ex machina* for an ordinary and natural event in which, according to rational principles, nothing ought to intervene which is contrary to the general concourse of natural things.

" Thus there remains only my hypothesis, that is to say, the way of the harmony pre-established by a divine prevenient artifice which from the beginning has formed each of these substances in so perfect a manner and regulated each with such precision that, in only following its own laws received with its being, it yet accords perfectly with the other, just as 'though there were a mutual influence, or as if God were always putting forth his hand to bring about the general concourse.

" I do not think this needs further proof, unless someone should want me to prove that God possesses the power required for this prevenient artifice, patterns of which we may even discern among men, proportioned to their skill. Granting that the power is in God, it is clear that this is the most excellent way and the most worthy of him. There are indeed other proofs, but they lie deeper and it is unnecessary to bring them forward here."

The *Deuxième Eclaircissement* is a detailed reply to objections which had been raised by Dr. Pierre Bayle, particularly in his Dictionary article " Rorarius," against the hypothesis of the pre-established harmony and his defence of the Cartesian theory of direct action against the criticisms of Leibniz. Two points in this article are of special interest. Bayle had contended that the continual intervention of God, which the occasional cause theory supposed, was not miraculous. On the other hand he argued that the pre-established harmony was in very truth open to the reproach unjustly urged against occasionalism, for it did introduce the *Deus ex machina*. As this criticism is most generally adopted in the histories of philosophy even to-day, it is important to see how Leibniz himself met the charge by direct reply.

Bayle's objection to the first point was that the system of occasional causes did not suppose the miraculous intervention of God in bringing about the reciprocal dependence of the body and the soul. There was no *Deus ex machina*, for God's intervention was according to general laws and not extraordinary. To this Leibniz replied : " Let us see if the system of occasional causes does not in fact suppose a perpetual miracle. I am told, no : because God would, according to this system, be acting by general laws. I agree, but in my view this is not sufficient to rid the system of miracles. Were God to be continually performing miracles, the miracles would still be miracles, using the term miracle not popularly to denote something rare and marvellous, but philosophically for what surpasses the natural power of the creatures themselves. It is not enough to say that God has made a general law ; for besides the decree there must be a natural means of executing it ; that is to say, what occurs in accordance with a general law must be explicable by the nature which God has given to things. The laws of Nature are not as arbitrary and indifferent as many people imagine. If, for example, God had decreed that all bodies should incline to move in a circle, and that the radii of the circles should be proportional to the magnitudes of the bodies, we should have in that case either to say that there is a way of fulfilling this requirement by the simplest laws, or else to aver that God will execute it miraculously by direct intervention, or perhaps by means of angels charged specially with the task in the way it was formerly supposed the celestial spheres were ruled. It would be much the same as saying that God has endowed bodies with natural and primitive gravities which makes each tend to the centre of its globe without being pushed by other bodies ; for in my opinion this system would require a perpetual miracle or at least the assistance of angels."

This most remarkable argument, simple enough in its first intention, is profound in its insight and sweeping in its application. Any non-natural interpretation of natural phenomena is an appeal to miraculous intervention, and whether the intervention is conceived as uniform and universal or as intermittent and precarious is nothing to the point ; it does not affect its character and cannot save it from condemnation. The bold challenge to Newton's theory of gravitation shows how it can be turned into a touchstone of sound scientific method.

Bayle's counter-charge that the pre-established harmony itself is the *Deus ex machina* is as follows : " Does the internal and active force which, when communicated to the bodily form, produces actions, know the consequences of the actions it will produce ? Not at all, for we know by experience that we are completely ignorant of the perceptions we are going to have, say, an hour hence. Some external principle, therefore, must be guiding the forms in the production of their acts : what is this but the *Deus ex machina* ? How does it differ in this from the system of occasional causes ? "

Leibniz makes this reply : " The force, or rather the soul or form, does not know the coming perceptions distinctly, but it feels them confusedly. There are in every substance some traces of all which has happened to it and some indications of all which will happen to it. But the infinite multitude of these perceptions prevents our distinguishing them ; just as when I hear the confused roar of a mob I am unable to distinguish one voice from another. It does not follow therefore that there must be an external directing principle. On the contrary, the present state of each substance is the natural consequence of its precedent state ; but only an infinite intelligence can see that consequence, for it includes the universe within each soul as well as the universe in each portion of matter."

The system of the pre-established harmony is thus made quite explicit. It does not mean that the Creator of the universe is the cause, efficient or occasional, of the actions of the individual souls or of their perceptions. He has created the monads in the meaning that the whole world of real beings (individual forces) owes its existence to his act. The perfection of God's knowledge made the world a possibility ; the infinite power of God is the source of its existence ; the world itself is a self-regulating automaton.

What is important is to see that the rationale of the system of the pre-established harmony is to be found in the conception of substance as force.   The system is for Leibniz the direct consequence of this conception.   The world which God has created is not the phenomenal world in space and time, not the world which is represented in our perceptions, but the real world of active individual forces.

V

THE SUPREME MONAD

THE pre-established harmony has always seemed to give Leibniz's philosophy a non-natural and even fantastic appearance. We have seen that it followed simply and inevitably from his conception of God as the infinitely perfect Being, *ens realissimum*, the Being in whom all ideas are adequate, all perceptions distinct, all volitions good, all actions the realization of perfect wisdom. If this is our conception of God, then we cannot think a perfect God will be the creator of an imperfect universe. To understand Leibniz, therefore, we must appreciate the logical ground of his conception of God.

Leibniz accepted the ontological argument, as Descartes and Spinoza had accepted it, but he criticized it as containing in its usual presentation a formal defect. The existence of God does not follow directly and necessarily from the idea of perfection, for a most perfect being may not be possible. Before we can conclude from the idea of a most perfect being to the existence of that being, we must demonstrate the possibility of such existence, we must prove that the idea is free from self-contradiction. This means that he agreed that whatever follows from the definition of anything can be predicated of this thing, and that existence follows from the definition of God, but before we can make the inference from the definition we must prove that it is a *real* definition and not nominal, that is, a definition which involves no contradiction. Leibniz proposed accordingly to make the conclusion of the argument : If God is possible God is. In other words, if

God is a possible existence, in the meaning that the predicates in the idea of God are mutually compatible, then God is a necessary existence. Let us inquire therefore how he was led to the conclusion, first, that God is possible, that is, that we can conceive God consistently and without self-contradiction ; and, secondly, that God is necessary, in the sense that without his existence the system of the real is incomplete. The inquiry is particularly interesting and peculiarly instructive. It is interesting because in our own time the theistic implications of spiritual pluralism have appeared sometimes as its chief attraction, sometimes as its chief defect. Among contemporaries some accept the principle because they think it forms the only basis of a theistic doctrine, others accept it because it seems to them easy to discard the theism. To the latter the theism seems a purely gratuitous graft on a self-subsistent system.

The philosophical conception of God has its origin in two necessities of thought, one the necessity of giving unity to nature, that is, to the system of the real, the other the necessity of conceiving the original source of activity. God is, therefore, in philosophy both the idea of self-sufficient being and the idea of the first or self-sufficient cause. In Leibniz's metaphysical system these two necessities of thought take each a special form, corresponding to his definition of substance as force and to his principle of the individuality of the real. God will be both the supreme monad and also the creator of the universe of finite or, as he calls them, created monads.

Leibniz has told us that when he began to reflect on metaphysics, and found himself dissatisfied with the Cartesian philosophy, he first turned to the theory of Democritus, the system of atoms and void. The attraction of that theory to philosophers in all ages has been its naturalism. It does not require the hypostatization of a transcendent cause in order to account for the order of nature. The defect of the theory is internal, and that defect is fatal. The atoms are not real unities. It was this very consideration which led Leibniz to reform the concept of substance and replace the material atoms by spiritual atoms—simple substances, unit forces, immaterial souls, monads. Yet he retained the ideal. His whole philosophical aim was to propound a metaphysic of reality, free from contradiction and with the unity of a system. The conception of God enters quite naturally into his system of the monads. It is not imposed from without. The God does not step out of a machine. For the monads, unlike the atoms, are only differentiated by their qualities, their variety is a diversity of internal activity, their external disposition is not a system of real relations, but an individuality of view-point. There is, indeed, a standard or norm by which they can be compared, otherwise they could not enter into a system. This standard, seeing that their activity consists in perception, is the degree of distinctness in their perceptions, and the consequent adequateness or inadequateness of their ideas. Thus the concept of God enters naturally and necessarily into the system as the ideal of perfection in an activity which is perceptive and appetitive, or as we should say cognitive and conative, and exists in degrees. God in this system is the supreme monad, conceived as perfect, that is, realizing the ideal of perfection, in the meaning that this supreme monad's perceptions are distinct with a discrimination which has no limit to infinity and that all its ideas are adequate. It is this ideal of perfection which Leibniz has before him when he says that if it be possible, then its existence is necessary. He holds that both the hypothetical and the apodeictic propositions, both the possibility and the actuality of God, can be proved by the principles of reason itself. These principles are at the basis of all logical construction.

If our concept of God is in accord with them, then we are entitled to say, what can be and must be, is.

Let us now look at the argument itself in Leibniz's own words. It is the very basis of the monadology, for logical reasoning is the foundation of the metaphysical theory.

" Our reasonings are grounded upon *two great principles*, that of *contradiction*, in virtue of which we judge *false* that which involves a contradiction, and *true* that which is opposed or contradictory to the false ; and that of *sufficient reason*, in virtue of which we hold that there can be no fact real or existing, no statement true, unless there be a sufficient reason why it should be so and not otherwise, although these reasons usually cannot be known by us.

" There are also two kinds of *truths*, those of *reasoning* and those of *fact*. Truths of reasoning are necessary and their opposite is impossible ; truths of fact are contingent and their opposite is possible. When a truth is necessary its reason can be found by analysis, resolving it into more simple ideas and truths, until we come to those which are primary. It is thus that in mathematics speculative theorems and practical canons are reduced by analysis to *definitions*, *axioms* and *postulates*.

" In short, there are *simple ideas*, of which no definition can be given ; there are also axioms and postulates, in a word, *primary principles*, which cannot be proved, and indeed have no need of proof ; and there are *identical propositions*, whose opposite involves an express contradiction.

" But there must also be a *sufficient reason* for contingent truths or truths of fact, that is to say, for the sequence or connection of things which are dispersed throughout the universe of created beings, in which the analyzing into particular reasons might go on into endless detail, because of the immense variety of things in nature

and the infinite division of bodies.   There is an infinity of
present and past forms and motions which go to make the
efficient cause of my present writing ; and there is an
infinity of minute tendencies and dispositions of my soul
which go to make its final cause.   And as all this detail
again involves other prior or more detailed contingent
things, each of which still needs a similar analysis to yield
its reason, we are no further forward ; and the sufficient
or final reason must be outside the sequence or *series*
of particular contingent things, however infinite this
series may be.   Thus the final reason of things must be in
a necessary substance, in which the variety of particular
changes exists only eminently, as in its source ; and this
substance we call *God*.   Now as this substance is a sufficient
reason of all this variety of particulars, which are also
connected together throughout ; *there is only one God,
and this God is sufficient*" (*Monadology*, 31–39).

It is worth remarking parenthetically in this connection
that it is probably the conception of God as a necessary
substance which has led many philosophers to reproach
Leibniz for his denunciation of Spinoza, while himself
affirming a doctrine in all essentials identical.   It is an
entirely unmerited reproach and shows a misunderstanding
of the real point at issue.   The agreement is only in the
terms used.   Leibniz in defining substance as force has
given an entirely new meaning to the conception of God
and an entirely new ground for affirming the necessity of
God's existence.

The two logical principles, that of contradiction and
that of sufficient reason, apply to two different realms of
experience and give rise to two different ideals, the ideal
of consistency and the ideal of originating power. Adopting
the terms which were later made familiar in the philosophy
of Kant, we may say that each principle gives rise to an
Idea of Reason, one the Idea of an all-perfect being, the
other the Idea of a creator.   For Leibniz they are the

Idea of a supreme monad, *monas monadum*, and the Idea of a divine artificer whose power directed by his wisdom is the sufficient reason of a universe of finite monads. These two Ideas are united in the conception of God ; for in the nature of reason there is only one God. We may say, therefore, that two factors enter into the concept of God, and we must now try and make each explicit.

There are two distinctions of prime significance for Leibniz in the construction of his metaphysics of reality. The first is the distinction between distinct and confused perception. The second is the distinction between necessary and contingent truth. It is the latter distinction which is important in our present inquiry. The metaphysical distinction between mind and matter, so fundamentally important in the Cartesian philosophy, has disappeared. Matter, for Leibniz, is ideal representation, only mind is real. There are two orders of things which are the object of our knowledge, a rational order and a factual order ; truths of reason and truths of fact. Corresponding to these two orders of truth is a division in the sciences, between the mathematical sciences and the physical sciences or sciences of nature. The two principles which regulate our procedure in these sciences and direct us in the search for truth are the principle of identity or of non-contradiction and the principle of sufficient reason. Each of these principles transcends the actual subject-matter before us and affirms in its implications, the one an ideal of perfection attracting us as a goal, the other a primary ground of existence, the self-sufficient origin of the causal series.

Thus the two principles lead by a logical necessity to the conception of God, and we may recognize in them the essential forms of two of the classical arguments or proofs of the existence of God—the ontological and the cosmological. It is very significant that the third of these arguments, the teleological, has no place in Leibniz's system. This famous proof of the existence of God based on the evidence of design in nature, which had seemed to St. Thomas Aquinas to exceed in value all the others and to be sufficient in itself, the proof which later in the eighteenth century seemed the sure foundation of natural religion and the practically incontrovertible basis of deism, had no attraction for Leibniz. The reason is clear. The teleological argument would, for Leibniz, be a reversal of the true logical progression, and instead of strengthening the theistic conclusion would weaken and impair it. Instead of arguing that the harmony of nature is evidence of a skilful designer, he reasons that the creator of a world must necessarily have pre-established the harmony. He escapes *ab initio* the discredit which has overtaken the argument. If we reason a priori from the perfection of God to the harmony of nature, then the appearance of physical evil may be ascribed to the finitude of our outlook and to our necessary ignorance of the complete design ; but if we reason a posteriori from the appearances of design to the skill of the designer we are bound to take into account, equally with the instances of adaptation, the absence or deficiency of design, and we must then attribute the presence of evil to the ignorance or powerlessness of the designer.

Leibniz, in fact, while employing the historical philosophical arguments, transforms them almost beyond recognition in accordance with his new system. The ontological argument gives him the conception of the supreme monad ; the cosmological argument gives him the conception of a creator in whom is the sufficient reason of the universe. Is it possible to harmonize these two concepts, to bring the two arguments to converge in the affirmation of the one God, at once the supreme monad and the creator of the universe of finite monads ? This is the crucial test of the system. Are the two Ideas of

Reason mutually consistent and harmonious in the Idea
of God ?   Before we criticize the two concepts, let us
quote Leibniz's own words in the *Principes de la Nature et
de la Grace*.   It is a parallel passage to the one already
quoted from the *Monadology*, but it lays peculiar emphasis
on the creation argument.

" So far we have been dealing with the problem as
simple physicists ; we must now turn to its metaphysical
aspect, making use of the great principle, commonly little
employed, which affirms that *nothing takes place without a
sufficient reason* : that is to say, that nothing happens
without its being possible for one who should know things
sufficiently to give a reason why it is so and not otherwise.
This principle being positive, the first thing we are entitled
to ask is—why is there something rather than nothing ?
Nothing is both simpler and easier to understand than
something.   Further, granting that the existence of
things is necessary, why must they exist thus and not
otherwise ?

" Now the sufficient reason of the existence of the
universe is not to be found in the sequence of contingent
things, that is, in bodies and the representations of them
in souls, because since matter in itself is indifferent to
movement, for the same matter may be moving or at rest,
and since also it is indifferent to the particular movement,
whether it is of one kind or another, we cannot find the
reason of movement in matter and still less the reason of
some particular movement.   And although the actual
movement comes from a precedent movement, and that
again from a precedent movement, yet this carries us no
nearer the goal.   However far back we go the same
question will remain.   The sufficient reason which has no
need of a sufficient reason must be outside the sequence of
contingent things.   It can only be found in a substance
which is cause of itself, a necessary being carrying within
itself the ground of its own existence ; otherwise it would

not be a sufficient reason at which we could finally stop. This ultimate reason of things we call God.

" This simple primitive substance must hold within it in a superlative degree (*éminemment*) the perfection contained in the derivative substances which are its effects. Thus it will have perfect *power*, *knowledge* and *will*, that is, sovereign omnipotence, omniscience and goodness. And since justice, in its usual meaning, is only goodness in conformity with wisdom, there must be sovereign justice in God. The sufficient reason in God of the existence of things, makes things dependent on God in their existing and working. Whatever perfection they have derives from God ; but such imperfection as is found in them comes from the essential and original limitation of the creature."

In all essentials this is the cosmological argument, but with an important change in its form. Instead of stating it in physical terms of causal connection, Leibniz states it in the logical terms of ground and consequence. The principle of sufficient reason is a logical not a dynamical principle, and in using it there is no necessity to introduce the idea of power. Yet there is a plain defect in the argument, and Leibniz is well aware of it. Granting every condition required, we are still without any principle which will supply a passage from the unconditioned self-sufficing reason to the conditioned series of contingent things of which it is the sufficient reason. It is a defect in the cosmological argument itself, an inconsistency in the conception of a first cause. How can the necessity of causal connection be reconciled with the affirmation of a reality not subject to that necessity ? Or more strikingly still, when put in the form of the temporal series—how can the necessity of thinking a before to every moment be consistent with the affirmation of a first moment to which there is no before ? How, then, does Leibniz meet this difficulty ? In effect by appealing to the conception of

God as the supreme monad. The sufficient reason of the universe is the possibility which existed ideally in the supreme being ; a tendency to existence characterizes all ideas ; possibilities naturally seek actualization ; granting therefore the existence of perfect power, wisdom and goodness in God, there must be creation, and the creation will of necessity be the best possible world.

We cannot fail to notice here a serious logical non-sequitur. Why must the supreme monad be the creator of the monadic universe ? Why not, as we should expect, simply one, though the head, of the hierarchy ? Force and ceaseless activity undoubtedly are implied in the concept of a supreme monad, but why should the idea of perfect power, intellect and will imply creation, and creation out of nothing, for so Leibniz defines creation ? If the concept of the supreme monad implies creation, then it would seem to follow that every monad must imply the idea of creation in its degree. This may have been Leibniz's meaning, but if it was it is nowhere explicit. The monads which are entelechies do not create the bodies on which they are dependent and which they dominate. The monadic principle itself would lead to the conception of a world-soul, but this would not satisfy Leibniz's requirement. The world-soul could only be one monad of an ascending series, not the supreme monad. The most perfect being in Leibniz's view has no need of a body or of anything upon which he could be considered dependent. This, however, is a digression. Let us return to Leibniz's own words.

" It follows from the supreme perfection of God that in producing the universe he has chosen the best possible plan, the greatest variety combined with the most perfect order ; ground, place, times as well arranged as possible ; the maximum effect secured by the simplest means ; as much power, knowledge, well-being and goodness in creatures as the universe would admit. For since all

possibles claim existence in God's understanding proportionately to their perfections, the actual world, the
resultant of all these claims, must be the most perfect
which is possible.   Otherwise, it would be impossible to
find a reason why things are thus rather than otherwise "
(*Principes*, 10).

This is the famous theory that the existing universe is
the best of all possible worlds, which is the basis of Leibniz's
optimism.   For the present, however, let us consider it
only in so far as it throws light on the meaning of creation
in Leibniz's philosophy.   The difficulty is to understand
how Leibniz's idea of substance can be reconciled with a
creation theory in any form.

In considering this problem let us accept Leibniz's
conception of God without calling in question the validity
of the a priori argument.   The infinitely perfect being
means a being who is omnipotent, omniscient and benevolent ;   that is, a being who possesses, eminently or in a
superlative degree, power, knowledge and goodness.   The
idea of such perfection, and also of a possible being
possessing such perfection, is given in the idea of the monad·
or simple substance, for imperfection in the monad consists in the confusedness of its perceptions and the inadequacy of its ideas, the degrees of which are determined
by the body to which the monad is attached and on which
it depends for its sense-experience.   The idea of perfection
is necessarily given in the experience of imperfection, and
therefore it is easy to see that the infinitely perfect monad,
if its existence be a possibility, must be a monad whose
perceptions are distinct to infinity and whose ideas are
adequate.   Such a monad would have no need of a body
to mediate its representation, a body would, in fact, be
an imperfection or at least an obstruction.   The only
question it is legitimate to ask in regard to this idea of an
infinitely perfect being is whether it is possible.   If it be
self-contradictory it is impossible and stands condemned.

But how, Leibniz asks, can the existence *in perfection* of power, understanding and will be a contradiction, seeing it is certain they exist *in degree* ? In saying that God is possible we are in effect affirming his necessity, for we are only affirming of the universal what we directly intuit in the particular.

The crucial problem in Leibniz's conception of God, absolute in individuality and rational in personality, is not whether he exists, but how to interpret and rationalize creation. There is no doubt that Leibniz himself considered he had solved this problem, and he regarded his solution as the crowning achievement of his metaphysical enterprise.

Let us look carefully at the difficulty. In the first place we have to ask the question, Why does God, by definition infinitely perfect, create ? This question, however, we may consider already answered in the definition of substance as force or activity. God must as substance be eternally expressing himself. If he ceased to be active he would cease to be God. The question we have really to answer is, Why must God create responsible creatures with a nature which is their own and not his, with an understanding which can err, and a will which can oppose the good ? Can we in effect discern the final cause of the creation as well as recognize the efficient cause ? The answer is that what is admirable in creation is the moral order which has been established in conformity with and in dependence upon the natural order, a realm of grace in a realm of nature.

God has not created the monads individually by individual creative acts : he has created the universe, which is constituted of free individuals and in which they exercise their activity. The universe was possible only by the pre-established harmony of its constituent free activities. What, then, are the monads, and how are they related to God ? How is the freedom, independence and self-origination of their activity consistent with their essential dependence on God ?

We have seen that what Leibniz has in mind when he declares that the monads are not created individually is the fact that no living creature begins to exist at the moment of birth or even at the moment of conception, for birth is but the unfolding and development of a nature which has endured as long as the universe has existed. There is no beginning or end of an individual independent of the beginning and end of the universe. Moreover, the *order* of nature is a precondition of the *existence* of nature. The monads only differ in degree, although the difference in degree between the supreme monad, the infinitely perfect being, and the created monads amounts to a difference in kind, for God exists necessarily, whereas the created monads are contingent. In what meaning, then, are the contingent monads the creation of the necessary monad ? Clearly it is not in the ordinary meaning of creation out of nothing, for the contingent monads, though individually distinct, share the essential nature of the Creator. While therefore Leibniz retained the term creation, he imparts to it a new meaning. " God alone is the primitive unity or simple original substance, of which all the created or derivative monads are productions. They are brought to birth, so to speak, by continual fulgurations of the divinity from moment to moment, they are limited by the receptivity of the created monads, which limitation is an essential part of their nature " (*Monadology*, 47).

This new expression " continual fulgurations " is introduced without explanation, and shows that Leibniz was conscious of the difficulty in using the word creation. The idea of a continual creation of the universe from moment to moment was a Cartesian doctrine which he expressly rejected and which, indeed, would contradict the basic principle of his philosophy. What apparently

he intends to convey by the expression is that the
created monads are essentially derived from the divine
monad, emanations of the essence of God. This is borne
out by the fact that the essential characteristics of the
created monads are perception and appetition, and these
are equally the characteristics of the supreme monad,
the difference being only, as we have seen, in degree.
" In God there is *power*, which is the source of everything,
then *knowledge*, which contains the detail of the ideas, and
finally *will*, which makes changes or productions according
to the principle of the best possible. And what these are
in God responds to the perceptive and appetitive faculties
in the created monads, the faculties which constitute their
basis as subjects. In God the attributes *power*, *knowledge*
and *will* are absolutely infinite or perfect ; and in the
created monads or the entelechies there are only imitations
of the attributes, proportionate to such perfection as the
monads have " (*Monadology*, 48).

The conclusion we are led to is that Leibniz's thought
moves freely within the limits he has laid down for himself
by his intellectualism. He did not, and he could not,
criticize the concepts of power, knowledge and will which
seemed to him to exist eminently in God and derivatively
in God's creatures. In his view reason is absolute and
knowledge is enlightenment. If we accept this position
we shall find it difficult to resist his conclusions or with-
hold our admiration from his conception of the moral
world in the natural world as the divinest of the works of
God.

VI

THE CITY OF GOD

THE conclusion of the *Monadology* is one of the triumphant achievements of the philosophical spirit. The City of God which is there presented is free from every trace of theological and ecclesiastical prejudice. It is the consummation of universal creative activity, the final cause of existence, the supreme manifestation of wisdom, revealed in the emergence of a moral order based upon and continuous with the natural order. In whatever light we regard this conception to-day, with our widened outlook and newer science, in retrospect it stands out as a great emancipation of the human spirit. It finally bursts the bonds of fanatical religious tyranny. The City of God which Leibniz extols, " this truly universal monarchy," as far excels the ideal of St. Augustine, who provided its prototype, as the new dispensation which the Apostle Paul proclaimed excelled the narrow ideal of the Jewish nation from which he derived it. The God of Leibniz is individual and personal, but conceived in no tribal or sectarian spirit. He is not the God of a chosen people or of a select remnant. He has not abandoned his creation, nor even retired for a period before the enemy, preparatory to new strategy after temporary defeat. He has not instituted a moral order independent of the natural order, or in any way opposed to the natural order. Everywhere and in everything, from the lowliest to the highest, nature leads to grace. The moral order is not superposed on the natural order. God is infinitely exalted above us by the perfection in him of intellect and will, but we are in essence one with God. There is no breach between the natural and the spiritual. Each order is complete in itself, yet by way of the natural order we rise to and enter directly into the moral order. God has given existence to the soul, but its possibility, its potentiality, the force and activity it enjoys in its own right, is the divine substance itself, and it has no natural disability by which it is prevented from rising to the highest order, citizenship in the City of God.

Let us now take the steps of the argument in detail. First, however, let us remind ourselves that the distinction between mind and matter, which had been an essential basis of the Christian scheme of a world order, and which had been rationalized and definitely formulated in philosophy in the Cartesian doctrine of dual substance and in the Newtonian physics, has been completely superseded by Leibniz in his reform of the concept of substance. Reality is of one kind; it is activity or force, and it is in its nature individual. The only reals are souls. Matter is phenomenal, an appearance of the real which exists as representation ideally in the mind. In the metaphysical scheme, therefore, we have only souls, ideally related to one another by representative perceptions. It is these representative perceptions which, by their degree of distinctness, give character to the souls and enable us to arrange them in a hierarchical series. We have accordingly to keep constantly in mind that when we speak of material things (bodies, our own and those of others, physical objects such as stones, trees, usable articles of daily life, or scientific objects such as atoms, electrons, radiations which we picture in imagination as existing below the limit of discernibility), these material things have just as much and just as little reality as the sounds, colours, odours, tastes, etc., which we call sensible qualities, or as the rainbows, waterfalls, clouds, sunsets, storms, which we call unsubstantial forms. Material things have no independent reality, they exist only as representations in the mind. This does not mean that representations are the arbitrary creation of the mind in which alone they exist, and it does not mean that there is no causal connection between the substantial reals and their ideal representations ; it means that the real universe can only be known ideally in its representation in the individual mind, and this representation is determined primarily by the activity of the subject of experience.

What, then, do we know of the real world as it is in itself ? Though all knowledge is ideal and though we only know the real as it is ideally represented, yet we can distinguish the reality from its appearance. That is to say, we can conceive the real as it is in itself. Were it otherwise, were we unable to conceive the real, we could not distinguish the ideal as ideal. This concept of the real, the real as it is in itself, is the very basis of our being. It is given in the primary act of self-consciousness itself. I think therefore I am. We affirm existence in the very attempt to doubt it. The real world is the living world, whose unit constituents are individual souls. Every soul has its own inviolable nature and every soul in its perception represents ideally the universe of souls.

The classification of the reals, the monads, which Leibniz adopts, is taken, as in his day so much was taken, uncritically from Aristotle. His division was into three orders, the vegetable, the animal, and the rational soul. Leibniz makes a double use of this division. It serves him to assign a definite place to the individual in a hierarchy, and also it serves to distinguish definite stages in the development or unfolding of the individual. The use of the division is to account for the actual variety in nature. There exist bare monads whose perception is without consciousness of any kind. They are forces, centres of activity, radiating their influences throughout the universe and receiving influences from the whole universe, yet these influences are represented in perceptions which are without any distinctness and completely confused. These are vegetable souls. There are also animal souls, possessing conscious perception in a high degree, able to profit by memory, yet without self-consciousness or apperception. Finally, there are rational souls, souls which are minds, capable of knowing truths of reason, with a high degree of distinctness in their perceptions, not only conscious, but self-conscious, apperceptive monads, minds which in their degree are adumbrations of divinity. Of these three orders of souls we have clear knowledge and direct experience. There may be higher degrees in angelic natures ascending to the ideal of perfection in God.

The other use which Leibniz makes of this division is to rationalize the idea of development or unfolding. The potentialities of the universe are infinite. Every human individual is, for example, in his actuality a choice among infinite possibilities. He exists first in the germ, what Leibniz distinguishes as the " spermatic " individual, awaiting the conditions of free development. Multitudes of spermatic individuals remain indefinitely unactualized. In this state the individual, whatever its potentiality, is indistinguishable from the bare monad and may, indeed, be classed with it. Its force is quiescent, its perception totally confused. This is necessary to the scheme of creation. It is in the actualization of possibilities and in the choice among possibilities of the fittest that the wisdom of God in the pre-established harmony appears.

The universe is a plenum, not in the old meaning that nature abhors a vacuum and that all space is occupied, but in the meaning that the universe consists of forces. Wherever there is the possibility of activity there exists its potentiality. This is the metaphysical basis of the scheme. The natural order is the harmony pre-established by God for the development of these actualized forces.

It involves low forms of activity as well as higher in the meaning that a progression to a higher order must imply the existence of a lower order. The lower is less worthy not in its own nature, but only in relation to the higher.

In the higher range of the natural order, with the rational monads which are *minds* (Leibniz, it should be noted, uses the term *mind* for the rational monad, animals are souls but not minds) we enter another realm, a realm of ends, a moral world in which values are spiritual, incentives are rational, and the goal is the supreme good—the knowledge and love of God. Each mind imitates in its microcosm what God is in the macrocosm. All minds enter by reason and by knowledge of eternal truths into fellowship with God, are members of the City of God, that is, are subjects of a moral government which, without disturbance of the laws of bodies or interference with the course of nature, but by the very order of natural things, passes from a realm of nature to a realm of grace. Nature leads to grace and grace brings nature to perfection.

The natural order is the harmony pre-established by God as the condition of the development of the potencies he has actualized. It involves a hierarchy of forms of activity. There must be lowly forms as well as exalted forms, for this is involved in the idea of progression itself. The lower is not lower in dignity, or less worthy in its own nature, but only lower in relation to the higher order to which it may rise. This natural order, complete in itself, is yet in its turn the condition of a moral order which depends upon it. It is the conception of this moral order arising out of a natural order which enables us to interpret the famous but often misunderstood theory of the best of all possible worlds.

The universe of created monads, the world which God has actualized in the exercise of infinite power, enlightened by omniscience and motivated by good will, is the best of all possible worlds. We may assure ourselves that it must be so by the a priori proof ; that is to say, we can reason that if the world is the creation of God, and if God unites in his essence infinite power, wisdom and goodness, then the world He has produced must reflect the perfection of the Creator. The fact that it does not, that from our human standpoint at any rate it seems otherwise, is the problem of evil. This problem may be met in the usual theological way by contrasting the infinity of God with the insignificance of man, and by recognizing the inadequacy of our view as mortals, with a brief life-span and confined outlook, as a basis for judging a creation which God views in its eternal and infinite aspect. In such case the appeal will be, as in all religious systems, to faith. Such a solution is far from satisfying the philosophical requirements of Leibniz. It is reason which seeks satisfaction. Leibniz's conception is formed from the consideration of the nature of the universe and the necessary conditions which the existence of the universe suppose fulfilled. If the world were a work of art, produced by a divine artist seeking the expression of his intuition in a material which he models to his liking, we should then be justified in judging the world as a successful or unsuccessful expression of the mind of God. But this world in which we find ourselves is not fashioned out of material, it is not a work of art, it is not a machine devised for some ulterior utilitarian purpose. It is a world of free individual natures, each nature acting according to the law of its own being. It is a world of souls, each with its power of self-expression and incentive to express itself, each with its right to development and its natural appetition or urge towards distincter perception. The divine work in creation accordingly was the choice among all possible worlds of that in which the freest and highest expression could be actualized.

In conceiving the world, therefore, and particularly in representing the divine work in creation, there are two

considerations which concern its possibility. The first is
that the material to be created is not some inert substratum, such as atoms and void or extension and movement ; it is free individual active forces, for it is of these
that the actual world consists.

The second consideration is that the real active substances must be compossible. The free active forces must
not only be non-interfering, they must not only not
inhibit one another, but also they must be complementary
to one another. The many must be one. The wisdom of
God is shown in the harmony by which activities subserve
one another without interfering with the individuality of
each.

Keeping in mind these two considerations, let us see
how Leibniz develops his argument. His two principles,
the principle of contradiction and the principle of sufficient
reason, give him the concepts of two realities : first, the
extramundane God as a necessary existence ; second, the
world as a series of contingent facts of which the ultimate
sufficient reason is God. Here is the critical point on which
the whole argument is pivoted. The world itself has no
metaphysical necessity of existence. It could equally
well be conceived as non-existing and as existing. Since
it does exist and the reason of its existence is not in its
essence or idea, it must have a sufficient reason, and that
reason can only be in a being who is not contingent but
necessary. Accordingly he argues that the world must
have been created by God, its creation must have
depended upon God's choice, and God's choice must
have been exercised among infinite possibilities. The
choice must by reason of God's attributes have been the
choice of the best among the possibles. In all this Leibniz
is conceiving God as a perfect mathematician, originating
the world and determining its order by a kind of divine
geometry. Just as the sphere is the form of greatest
capacity, just as the right angle is the fixed determinant

of the angles formed by intersecting lines, so among all possible universes, as among all geometrical figures, there is one which will provide the maximum of reality in its essence, the fullest co-existence of compossibles. It is this universe which God will create, and therefore we can say a priori that the world is the best of all possible worlds. Such is the argument in its abstract mathematical and metaphysical form.

The universe itself, however, is not a metaphysical construction ruled by a mathematical order, for it is essentially and primarily a universe of spiritual values. Its constituent units are free agent forces. The best of all possible worlds cannot be judged therefore by a mathematical standard of perfection, but by its values in the higher spiritual meaning. That world will be the best of all possible worlds which contains the maximum of value. What sort of universe will fulfil this condition? It is clear that such a universe must be one in which moral aspirations are rational and realizable. Could the Christian heaven or the Mohammedan paradise, ideal worlds from which evil in every form, physical or moral, is excluded, possibly fulfil the requirement? Christianity itself has answered the question and recognized the impossibility, for heaven in the Christian theory is the perfected world which is the reward of the good life. If, then, we have regard to virtue and not to virtue's reward, it is only a world such as the existing world with its imperfection and evil which can produce the good life.

We may see, therefore, that Leibniz's theory, that this world with its pain, its sin, its sorrow, its injustice, its misery, is the best of all possible worlds, is neither the hollow mockery nor the patent absurdity it appears at first to be. A world in which beauty, truth and goodness were perfectly realized would be a world in which beauty, truth and goodness could not find expression, and in which ceasing to be ideals they must cease to be values.

If the world is to be judged by a spiritual criterion, that is to say, if it is to offer a real conative activity, not perfection, but infinite perfectibility, then the best possible world is not the world in which imperfection is defect, but a world in which imperfection is a condition of existence. This principle finds abundant illustration in the great works of art. There is no interest in a struggle in which the issue is never in doubt. Satan actually seated on God's throne would be God, and God dethroned would be Satan. There can be no heroes, and therefore no heroism in a world in which there is no conflict, no martyrs in a world in which all motives are understood, no saints and no saintliness in a sinless world, no joy where there can be no repentance, in short no value except in a world which is a world in the making and not ready made.

The a priori argument of Leibniz that the existing world must be the best of all possible worlds because it is the creation of infinite intelligence ; and the a posteriori argument that it is so because we may see everywhere how nature leads to grace, are in no sense whatever irrational. The difficulty which really confronts us is not the difficulty of reconciling our ideal of the best with the shortcoming of that ideal in our actual experience, but a metaphysical difficulty. It lies in the conception of God as a realized perfection. Perfection in the meaning of the ontological argument is inconsistent with the idea of activity. If God is conceived as activity, as really creative and as creating, then he cannot be conceived as already in possession of that for which he is striving. The conception of a really creative God did not and could not present itself to Leibniz. The two logical principles which he formulated so clearly, the principle of contradiction and the principle of sufficient reason, stand confronting one another as the justification of two ultimate facts— a self-sufficient God and a contingent world. The reconciliation which Leibniz attempts is that the moral world

or realm of ends is a City of God. The supreme monad,
the self-sufficient sufficient reason, is not only the creator
of the great machine of nature, he is also the moral ruler
of the universe, the perfect monarch of free subject spirits
constituting a City of God. Let us now read it in his own
words.

" There is a peculiarity in regard to minds or rational
souls. While it is fundamentally true of all animals and
all living things that their beginning is with the beginning of the world and that they last as long as the world,
yet rational animals have this character that the rational
soul is not in them from the first. The infinitesimal
animals which they generate in the sperm, while they are
spermatic animals only, have simple ordinary or sensitive
souls, but when the elect among them, as we say, attain,
by actual conception, their full human nature, then their
sensitive souls are raised in dignity to the prerogative of
minds and become rational souls.

" Among the differences between ordinary souls and
rational minds the chief is this, that while souls in general
are living images of the universe of creatures, rational
minds are images of the divine author of nature himself.
Rational minds are capable of knowing the system of the
universe and to some extent imitating it by architectonic
patterns. Every rational mind is, as it were, a little
divinity in its own department.

" This is what makes rational minds capable of entering
into a kind of society with God, so that to them God is
not as an inventor to his machine (this being his relation
to his other creatures), but as a prince to his subjects, and
as father to his children.

" We are led to conclude that the assemblage of all
rational minds is the City of God. It is the most perfect
state possible under the most perfect monarch.

" This City of God, this really universal monarchy, is a
moral world in the natural world. It is what is noblest

and divinest in the works of God. In it God's glory really consists, since there would be none were his greatness and goodness not known and admired by rational minds. It is also relatively to this divine city that there is goodness in the strict meaning; that is, something other than wisdom and power which manifest themselves everywhere.

"We have already seen that a perfect harmony exists between the two natural realms, the realm of efficient causes and the realm of final causes. We have now to show another harmony between the physical realm of nature and the moral realm of grace; that is to say, between God considered as architect of the machine of the universe and God considered as monarch of the divine city of rational minds.

"This harmony makes things lead to grace by the ways of nature, and shows us that this globe, for example, must be destroyed and renewed by natural ways when the government of minds requires it, for chastisement in the one case and reward in the other.

"We may say, indeed, that in everything God the Architect accords with God the Lawgiver, and thus that sins carry their penalty with them in the order of nature, and even by reason of the mechanical structure of things, and likewise the noblest actions draw forth their reward by ways which are mechanical relatively to bodies, although the result may not, and often does not, follow straightway on the action.

"Finally, under this perfect government, no good action goes unrewarded, no evil action unchastised. Everything works for the success of the good; that is, of those who are not dissatisfied in this great state, who trust in providence after having done their duty, and who love and imitate to the best of their power the author of all good, delighting in the thought of his perfection, following the lead of the " love undefiled " which takes pleasure in the happiness of what it loves. It is what leads the wise and virtuous to work for that which appears to conform to the presumptive or antecedent will of God, and yet to be content with what God brings to pass effectively by his secret, consequent and decisive will. It leads us to recognize that were we able to understand sufficiently the order of the universe we should find it surpass our wisest wishes, and see that a better world than the world which is could not be. Not only is the world the best possible for all in general, it is the best possible for us in particular, if we are attached as we should be to the Author of all, not only as architect and efficient cause of our being, but also as our Lord, the final cause who should be the only goal of our will and who alone can make our happiness " (*Monadology*, 82–90).

VII

ENTELECHIES

IN the preceding chapters the aim has been to present the philosophy of Leibniz from his own standpoint, in its own setting, and in its integrity as a complete world-view. We have now to direct our attention to some of the important concepts which Leibniz was the first to formulate, and which are valuable in themselves and apart from their particular place in a particular system. If Leibniz's philosophy is living to-day it is not because it survives in the systematic form in which he presented it, but because it contains vital principles and fruitful concepts. Judged, not by the dry bones of a dead system, but by the vitality of his interpretative principles, Leibniz stands out in the history of philosophy of the modern period as one of the great intellectual forces which have formed the modern mind and directed the development of Western civilization. We have now to see what were the fruitful ideas which he originated or to which he gave a new direction.

The peculiar genius of Leibniz, like that of Aristotle in the ancient world, directed itself primarily towards the problem of the living world in a profound attempt to bring to clear consciousness the vital principle itself. There was in Leibniz's day an intellectual crisis curiously analogous to that which we are experiencing at the present time in the issue between mechanism and vitalism. The Cartesian philosophy of the seventeenth century had offered a purely mechanistic interpretation of life and of the organization of individual forms of activity. The rational principle in man, his substantial soul, was thought to be quite distinct from the living body, but this living body could, it was held, be completely accounted for by the working of the purely mechanical principles of the propagation of movement in a matter conceived as originally pure extension. In other words, the laws of movement were held sufficient to account for life, though they failed to account for thought. Leibniz met this application of the mechanistic principle with searching criticism and exposed its fundamental weakness. In its place he proposed a new metaphysics based upon a vitalistic principle according to which living activity is the fundamental reality and conditions even mechanistic interpretation. We are going through a similar crisis in science and philosophy to-day. The Darwinian hypothesis of the origin of species by natural selection seemed to the nineteenth century to have definitely established materialistic mechanism as the sufficient interpretation of living activity. Its ideal has not been realized, and we are witnessing to-day a strong reaction. The opposing principle is named the new vitalism to distinguish it from the old vitalism, the analogous principle which Leibniz opposed to the Cartesian mechanism.

Every living creature exhibits in the principle of its organization a unity and a multiplicity which no mathematical formula can express. To indicate it we have to fall back on metaphysics, and metaphysical terms always carry an air of paradox in ordinary discourse. Yet no fact of common experience is more familiar to us than the essential unity of the mind in relation to the diversity, variety and multiplicity of the body, or the unity of the life of an animal or plant in relation to the manifold activities of the structural parts of the organism. It is the life, or soul, or mind, when considered as that which gives integrity to the manifold activities of the individual organism. Leibniz adopted the old Aristotelian term " entelechy." He does not appear to have consulted the text of Aristotle and it is probable that he took the word from the Latin translation of Hermolaus Barbarus, a Venetian writer of the sixteenth century. In the *Théodicée* (87) he says, " Aristotle has given the generic name entelechy or act to the soul. The word entelechy is apparently derived from the Greek word which signifies perfect, and this is why the renowned Hermolaus Barbarus expresses it in Latin *verbatim* as *perfectihabia*, for the act is the accomplishment of the power." The passage is a little obscure as it stands, but Leibniz goes on to elucidate it by reference to the Aristotelian distinction of two kinds of act, the permanent and the successive. The permanent or durable act is identical with the form, and the form may be either substantial or accidental. Leibniz then gives as his own view of this distinction that the substantial form, of which the soul is the instance, is entirely permanent, while the accidental form is only temporary. The act which is transient, that is, the act the nature of which is to be transitory, consists in the action pure and simple. Here, he tells us, comes in the value of the term entelechy, for entelechy carries with it not only the idea of a simple faculty of acting, but also the idea of what we call force, effort, *conatus*, something from which action must follow when there is nothing to stop it.

The term entelechy has been revived in the contemporary discussions of mechanists and vitalists. It is a term which evokes criticism, mainly from those who require of a term that the entity it stands for shall be as isolable and as tractable as the term which stands for it. Since it is clear that entelechy does not exist apart from the organism of which it is entelechy, the term, for these critics, stands self-condemned. So far as there is paradox, however, it is in the fact which the concept expresses, and not in the concept which expresses the fact. Let us, therefore, give attention to the fact.

Every individual living creature appears to be composed of a vast number of special organic structures, each performing its characteristic functions in response to self-solicited stimuli, all the structures being so co-ordinated and interarranged and mutually complement-ary that the assemblage acts integrally as an individual. What is the nature of this unity of the whole, and how is the unity related to the multiplicity ? In a general way we term the unity self, soul, or mind, and the multiplicity, body. Though we distinguish between mind and body, and though the distinction is an ordinary recognized fact of experience, we cannot separate them either actually or ideally, and yet we search in vain for a principle which will provide a satisfactory identity. The ground of the distinction is clear to unscientific reflection, and the more it is made the subject of scientific investigation the more pronounced is the distinction. The ordinary phenomena of waste and repair show us that the material of the body is changing continually, and that indeed the body may not ever be materially identical for two consecutive moments. Its identity therefore cannot be due to any sameness of the elements composing it, for it is changing continually, it must lie in some formal continuity of its successive states. The identity of the body is a formal not a material identity, and this formal identity is in some manner imposed from without and not generated within. The proof of this is that if there is material loss, as when for example an animal loses one of its sense organs, or one of its limbs, or any part of its structural whole not absolutely essential to the continued functioning of the body, the deficiency is not a simple loss mathematically determined, for the body adapts itself by rearrange-ment, and other organs and structures take on novel functions in such way that the body, so long as life is possible, continues working as a whole and not as a

mutilated whole. Moreover, when we study the physiology of the organism in its minute working we find that
the principle which governs the whole, making it always
function as a whole, governs also its constituent parts.
Each organ and each constituent part of each organ
and, so far as we can observe them, each of the constituent cells, functions as an individual, doing its own
work, expressing its own nature in its own characteristic
way, developing its own force from its own individual
standpoint. Only to the outside observer is the expression of the individual activity seen to subserve the
activity of the organism of which it is part.

It is obvious, therefore, that in living creatures and
in the principle of their organization we are confronted
with a phenomenon which will not submit to mechanistic
interpretation in the ordinary meaning of the laws of
motion and the conservation of energy. The body
is not a single interlocking mechanism, the soul is not
the mechanician. Neither the unity nor the multiplicity,
neither the integrity nor the diversity of the organism,
can be interpreted mathematically and mechanistically.
There is some fundamental metaphysical principle
manifesting itself. We require a philosophy of the
organism.

The concept of entelechy is the attempt to give definite
expression to this metaphysics of living activity. The
entelechy is not a dominant cell, or a dominant organ in
an organism, but a dominant monad in a monadic
system. Suppose we could find in the organism itself
an organ or a cell of an organism, by which or from which
the multitudinous activities of the multifarious structures were co-ordinated, the throne of the ruler of a
constitutional monarchy, the seat of the directing
charioteer, a philosophy of the organism in materialistic
and mechanistic concepts might be possible. Not only
has science failed to discover such a dominant organ, but

it has found no slightest indication or reason to believe that it exists unknown. We must seek in philosophy for another principle.

The monadic principle will be found to work in precisely those conditions in which the materialistic principle fails, and the scheme of the monadic activity is self-consistent. The mind is a monad, a simple unit substance, originating its own activity and inviolable in its own nature. It is a dominant monad, for it rules and directs the body to which it is attached and on which it depends for the expression of its activity and the development of its force. The body, which is dominated, itself consists of monads, and these monads each with its own activity, and their composition in the dominated body, are represented ideally in the perceptions of the dominant monad, the mind. The monads of the body have in themselves their own inalienable nature, and in their activity develop their inherent force. The mind has no power to penetrate or interfere with the forces it directs. The activities of the monads of the body subserve the dominant activity of the mind, as the members of the orchestra each playing independently subserve the performance of the symphony (the illustration is one used by Leibniz), and the symphony is the resultant harmony. Each monad is limited in its activity not by any internal interference, penetration, or interaction of any kind, but by the mutual influences which all are exercising at every moment on one another and which are represented in each by its perceptions. The principle of organization, therefore, is the dominating of the individual efforts, not by direct influence or external compulsion, but by securing a harmony of the manifold activities to bring about a single end, which is the end of the dominant monad, and not the common end of the individuals. In Leibniz's view the resultant harmony could not be a natural outcome, it must have been pre-established by God at the creation of the world.

It will be generally admitted that the conception of a pre-established harmony cannot possibly be acceptable to philosophy or to science in any form whatever. It is foreign to our modern way of thinking. To Leibniz it depended on two concepts, one theological the other scientific, both of which appeared to him to be based on facts which were unassailable, but neither of which accords with our present philosophical and scientific knowledge. The first is the concept of an actually existent infinite perfection, the second is the concept of the preformation of every individual living creature. The creation of the world was complete from the first, not in the meaning that its development was pre-determined, but in the meaning that every nature admitting of development was provided for. If, then, we have to reject these two fundamental conceptions in Leibniz's scheme, shall we have any need for his concept of entelechy, and will his monadic system still be applicable to our present science ? Before we attempt to answer, let us look closely at the two offending concepts, the concept of God and the concept of the preformed individual.

It is true that between the rational monad, man, and the supreme monad, God, Leibniz thought the inter-mediate stages might be as infinite as are the stages below us which link us to the bare monad. He called these higher monads, which lie between us and God, genii, and he conceived it possible that it is part of the divine plan that these higher ranks should be open, so that the rational monads may rise higher and higher in the hierarchy. Yet his whole scheme rests ultimately on the affirmation of positive, infinite, perfection in God, who has created the other monads as imperfect adum-brations. The created monads have their own nature, they are free and responsible. God in giving them existence has not determined their actions nor decreed them in any way. He has given existence to a world in which moral value can enjoy its reward. So far, then, as the pre-established harmony depends on Leibniz's conception of God as the infinitely perfect being, the rejection of the concept of God will carry with it the rejection of the pre-established harmony. If, however, in line with the modern recognition of a creative or at least of an emergent power in evolution, we conceive God not as infinite perfection and therefore as a limiting concept, but as the conception of infinite perfectibility, then at every stage of historical evolution there will be harmony as the condition of existence, but it will be a natural not an artificially-imposed harmony.

It is also very important to direct attention to what is really an inconsistency in Leibniz. When he argues that there must be a supreme monad and identifies this with the infinitely perfect God, he is affirming the necessity of a limiting concept, that is, he is affirming an actual last term of an infinite series. God is then presented as the one monad of the series who is not entelechy and has no attachment to a body. God is relieved from this necessity because being perfect He has no obscure perception and no inadequate idea. The same argument, however, ought to lead to the affirmation of a limiting concept at the lower end of the infinite series. The bare monad ought to be a limit, but nowhere does Leibniz even hint at this necessity. He continually declares that the series below the rational monads is actually infinite, every monad, however low in the hierarchy, is an entelechy and has some activity producing distinctness in its perception. It may be infinitely little, but it is not nothing. Moreover, it leads him to a very striking way of expressing the actual infinity of the monadic universe. In a letter to Bernoulli in 1698 he says, " You argue entirely to my mind when you say that changes do not take place *per saltum*. And, further, I do not laugh at your conjecture, but I definitely avow that there are in the world animals as much larger than ourselves, as we are larger than microscopic animalcules. Nor does nature know any limit. And, again, it may be, nay it must be, that in the very smallest grains of dust, and, indeed, in the least atoms, there are worlds not inferior to ours in beauty and variety ; nor is there anything to prevent what may appear a still more wonderful thing, that animals at death are transferred to such worlds ; for I regard death as nothing more than the contraction of an animal." Had Leibniz followed this line of thought in regard to the infinity above us he would have been led to an entirely different concept of God. Instead of the infinitely perfect being, a limit, he would have conceived God as entelechy on the higher level, as a world-soul. It is difficult indeed to read the Fourth Ennead of Plotinus and not be impressed with the remarkable way in which the concept of a world-soul fits in with Leibniz's metaphysical principle. Leibniz was himself aware of it. Whether he had studied Plotinus we do not know, but he was quite familiar with Plato's argument in the *Timæus*, and he turns aside from it with something like dismay. Leibniz had, in fact, started with the conception of God and the pre-established harmony, and as a consequence had to rationalize as best he could a theory of creation.

The second or scientific concept which gave support to Leibniz's system of the pre-established harmony is the preformation theory (already discussed in Chapter IV). Like the theory of special creation, which in the last century appeared to be the only alternative to Darwin's evolution hypothesis, it assumes and even necessitates the assumption of some super-mundane intelligence informing with predispositions the varieties of living species. The preformation theory had in the seventeenth century the peculiar force which the Darwinian theory had in the nineteenth, it was purely and eminently scientific and seemed to be thoroughly confirmed by observation and experiment.

How, then, let us now ask ourselves, does the entelechy principle stand when the support of these two leading concepts of Leibniz is removed ? The reply is that only when these dead encumbrances are removed is the full significance of the principle seen. Leibniz has really discovered the principle of a philosophy of life. He has expounded as no one before him had done the essential nature of living activity, the primacy of life in a metaphysics of reality. Before the rise of biological science, before the principles of embryology and palæontology had been conceived, he had by philosophical reflection and meditation, by his clear logical criticism of the concept of the material atom, proved the impossibility of the origin of life from matter and movement. He sought to discover the true principle of composition in living organized bodies by studying the nature of spiritual units.

His method was primarily a priori, and this in itself in certain scientific circles is a sufficient reproach, yet no one in his age was so markedly under the influence of the scientific spirit. Though his prime interest was metaphysics he followed with the deepest attention every new discovery, keenly intent on its philosophical import. For this reason Leibniz's thought is most modern even when its expression is clothed in the imagery of outworn theological ideas.

We may now summarize the principles of Leibniz's philosophy, for it is by these, and not by any particular application of them, that he stands out in history as a leader of philosophy.

(1) The first is the primacy of activity over inertia. From this it follows that the real constituents of the physical world are not material particles, but unit forces. The universe is not primarily matter and movement, but living force in the form of actual possibilities awaiting the conditions of development.

(2) The second is the principle of the individuality of the real. Individuality characterizes the living world in its full extent. There is no common matrix or substratum. From this it follows that all living activity is development. Every individual when the opportunity comes to it to exert its force expresses its own nature in its activity.

(3) The third is the principle of entelechy. This is the principle by which aggregates of living individual forces form a composite organism which forthwith functions as a whole. Entelechy is the principle by which the actions of the body express the purpose of the soul. It implies that in all living activity there is no interference with the subservient activities in their own sphere.

It is this principle of entelechy which more than any other shows the profound metaphysical insight of Leibniz. The difficulty which confronted him was the need to rationalize a concept which appeared a defiance of the principle of contradiction itself. Entelechy cannot be conceived under the category of substance, for though it exists for itself it is yet wholly dependent on another ; and equally it refuses to come under the category of causality, for taken in itself it is without efficiency or finality. In so far as entelechies are minds or souls it seems easy enough to identify them and distinguish them from the bodies to which they are attached and which they make instrumental to their purposes. This is the easy way of the common philosophy and the only problem which seems to remain is to define the relation between two kinds of reality each obeying an independent order of its own. This, however, is to misunderstand the fact profoundly. There is no entelechy without organization and no organization without entelechy, and the principle of entelechy is universal in the living world.

Leibniz deals with the problem in an entirely original way. He sees that it follows from the nature of monadic activity, which consists in perception and appetition, that the influence of monads on one another, and therefore their relations in the world which they constitute, can only be ideal, and since monadic influences are ideal it is possible for every monad to be dominant in one relation, subservient in another. This is the kind of relation entelechy requires.

A perfect illustration of what entelechy means is seen in the insect communities of the ants and bees. In the organization of the bee-hive or the ant-heap the activities are all individual and the community functions as a whole. It is true there is no evidence of anything distinguishable as entelechy in the meaning of a self, or soul, or mind, but the working of the hive, or of the heap, and the manner in which its activity is schematized, exactly represents the principle. Each individual insect in following its own natural incentive, without external compulsion, direction or interference, works for an end which is not individual, but common to the whole. The individual activities are, in some way and by some principle, so over-ruled that the activities of each are subservient to the whole.

When it is said that the monads exercise a purely ideal influence on one another, what is meant is that throughout the living world there is organization, and wherever there is organization we find the entelechy principle. But why, we may ask, should the influence represented by entelechy be called ideal ? The term ideal has a very wide meaning, but here it is employed in a technical sense. In ordinary practical human life there are two kinds of ways in which man deals with the environment, one when he is manipulating inert matter, another when he is turning to his own purposes the activity of living creatures. Consider, for example, the ordinary agriculturist. In so far as he is dealing with the material environment, building houses, sheds and barns, devising agricultural tools, etc., he is exercising a real influence in the meaning that the matter takes and retains the form he gives it. When, however, he is dealing with living things, crops or live stock, he is exercising an ideal influence on natures which cannot be directly moulded to his purpose. His aim, indeed, is materialistic, the production of human food and clothing, but he can only procure these from the living world by overruling individual natures. Mutton and wool, the end for which he rears his sheep, are no part whatever of the real natures of the sheep considered from their own standpoint as things in themselves. Organic activity throughout the living world is of this type. Only by understanding it is it possible to give a rational account of the relation of mind and body.

VIII

SPACE AND TIME

THE most significant part of Leibniz's philosophy, if we have regard to modern developments in physical science, is the theory of space and time. Space and time in Leibniz's system have their sufficient reason in the real world, but they belong to the representative world, the mirrored universe which exists for each monad in its perceptions. They are therefore ideal, not real in themselves ; they belong to the world of appearance and not to the world of noumenal reality. Yet space and time are not themselves appearances, nor are they objects of perception, they belong to the *order* of perceptions. Space is the order of coexistence, time the order of succession, in the monad's perceptions.

It was Newton's law of gravitation which gave significance to the problem of space and time as determining the nature of physical reality ; and it was Locke's theory of knowledge, and particularly his contention that there was no inconsistency in the idea that matter thinks, which gave the problem philosophical importance. Accordingly in the correspondence with Dr. Clarke, which occupied Leibniz in the last year of his life, the question at issue is whether space and time are absolute or relative. Until this correspondence was started space and time do not appear to have presented to Leibniz a special problem, they were part of the general metaphysical problem. Space and time are formal, not material, realities. If the materialist view of substance and cause is accepted it follows that the formal realities, space and time, are absolute. If materialism is rejected in favour of an idealist theory, and matter is reduced to phenomenon, it will follow that space and time are relative.

In the Cartesian philosophy space and time are practically identical with matter and movement. In the older atomic theory the indestructibility of the atoms and their free mobility were dependent on the distinct and independent existence of space or void and time or lapse. In rejecting both theories, and generally in denying the primacy of quantitative over qualitative distinctions, Leibniz was, in effect, rejecting the absoluteness of space and time and denying the necessity of affirming them as the framework of the universe. The metaphysical problem was simply whether the reality we conceive as substance is material or spiritual, and whether the power we conceive as cause is mechanical transmission of external movement or living force internally controlled and externally expressed. Leibniz's metaphysical theory of substantive units of force, in making matter phenomenal, reduced space and time to forms of order in phenomena.

Newton's discovery of the law of gravitation brought a new situation in regard to the metaphysical problem. The discovery came into direct conflict with the fundamental principle of Descartes's physics, the principle that the essence of matter is extension. Newton's law could only have meaning for a matter which occupies space and for a space which is indifferent whether it is occupied or not. The fundamental quality or property of matter is weight, that is, a certain force of attraction. Matter occupies space in differently constituted individual masses which move with a varying velocity, the universal law of which can be expressed in quantitative terms of mass and distance. Such a universal law assumes the actuality of absolute position and absolute simultaneity, and these assumptions are only intelligible against a metaphysical background. Distrustful of metaphysics, and confining himself to scientific methods of observation and experiment, Newton found himself led to postulate space and time as absolute uniformities. This was in effect to affirm scientific materialism with its consequences in theology and metaphysics. Newton's science, however, received strong support from the philosophy of Locke. All our knowledge, in Locke's view, consists of simple ideas which arise in the mind from sensation and reflection. The direct effect of this empirical principle appeared to be to establish the reality of material or corporeal existence as the basis of all knowledge. Mind could be conceived as an impressible corporeal organ, Nature as a boundless expanse or immobile extension, within which masses of matter, possessing the peculiar force, attraction, move with varying velocities subject to mechanical laws.

Towards this whole conception Leibniz manifested from the first a diametrical opposition. His sharpest antagonism and clearest expression comes out in the correspondence with Clarke. In the letter to the Princess Caroline, which occasioned this correspondence, Leibniz, in satirizing the materialism of Locke and Newton, had indicated the serious consequences of their doctrine in regard to two concepts of peculiar importance to religion, the nature of the soul and the infinity of God. Locke was no longer living, but Newton was very sensitive on these points. Newton had attempted to meet the difficulty of reconciling the infinity of space and time, affirmed in the conception of them as absolute, with the infinity of God. He had taken an analogy from the organism and suggested that space and time were God's *sensorium*. By this he meant that in God's perception there must be something analogous to the soul's perception, and for the soul's perception there must be something in the organism by which the various separate impressions on the sense organs are brought into the unity of the single image which the soul perceives. He suggested that infinite space and time might serve this purpose in God's infinite perception. Leibniz pointed out that this was to conceive God as a world-soul and not as a supra-mundane intelligence. Clarke repudiated indignantly this interpretation of Newton's meaning. Alike for Leibniz and Newton the conception of God as a world-soul was ranked with Spinoza's pantheism as an atheistic doctrine.

Let us give Leibniz's theory of space and time in his own words. " I hold space, and also time, to be something purely relative. Space is an *order of coexistences* as time is an *order of successions*. Space denotes in terms of possibility an order of things which in so far as they exist together exist at the same time, whatever be their several ways of existing. Whenever we see various things together we are conscious of this order between things themselves."

Space and time, then, are neither things in themselves nor properties of things ; they are an order of things. "*Absolute real space*," he says, "is an *Idolon tribus* of English philosophers." How, then, do we come to form notions of space and time, of a real immensity and a real eternity, out of which are cut, as it were, our finite spaces and finite times ? To this question Leibniz has an explicit answer expressed in a carefully developed argument. At every moment of perception a multitude of things are present to our consciousness ; these several things we think of as coexisting, and we represent the order of their coexistence as the simple relation between them which we name situation or distance. But this order of things coexisting at one moment may change or be different at another moment, for our perceptions change as their objects appear to move. When it happens that the same things which coexist in one moment also coexist in a later moment, but with change in their order, we express this change of order by saying that one thing has come into the place of another, or that they have changed places. When there is complete change in the relations of situation to one another of things which continue from moment to moment, we can, by knowing the rules of direction and velocity, not only determine the new relations of situation or distance which each will acquire to the others, but also we can represent what the situations would be if the change had been different. We express this by saying that things have changed their *places*, and then we come to think of all *places* under one comprehensive name *space*. Thus there arises the notion of *space* as something existing absolutely in itself, something within which movements occur. But in order to have this idea of *place*, and with it the comprehensive idea of *space*, there is no necessity to postulate an absolute reality outside and independent of the things which are in this relation of situation to one another. Let us suppose A, B, C, D, E, F to be the objects of perception at one moment ; and then suppose at another moment without any change in the relative position of C, D, E and F, that A and B have changed their positions ; then we say that A is in the *place* of B, B in the *place* of A. We are able therefore to define *place* as that which is the same in two different moments for different existing things whose relation of coexistence with other existing things is unaltered. And we can define *fixed existing things* as those in which there has been no change in the order of coexistence, or which have not moved. And then we can define *space* as the aggregate of places when they are all taken together.

Wherein then lies the difference between " place " and " relation of situation " ? The difference is that the " relation of situation " is in A and B themselves. When

A takes the place of B, its relation of situation to the other bodies is the same as was that of B, but the relation of A is not only the relation of situation and may not be precisely and individually the same as the relation of B. In no single relation can two different subjects, A and B, have precisely the same individual relations to other subjects ; no identical accident can be found in two subjects or pass from one subject to another. But our mind, not satisfied with a convention, wants an identity, something which is actually the same, and as it cannot find the identity in the subjects, it conceives it may lie outside them, and gives it the names of " place " and " space." Place is no more outside the subjects than any other relation is outside.

Space, therefore, can only be ideal, a certain order in which the mind conceives the application of relations. In just the same way our mind can give a kind of reality to the order we find in genealogy. We conceive this order as genealogical lines, the magnitudes of which consist in the number of the generations of a particular person. Yet another instance of the kind is the fiction of metempsychosis. We suppose the same human souls to pass to other bodies, and then we say that the persons change places, and the father or grandfather may become the son or the grandson. These terms, " places," " genealogical lines," " spaces," express real truths, yet are only ideal things. A still more striking instance is the way in which the mind forms out of accidents which belong to subjects something corresponding to accidents outside the subjects. We have an example in the geometrical idea of ratio. The ratio or proportion between two lines, L and M, can be conceived in three ways : (1) as the ratio of the greater L to the lesser M ; (2) as the ratio of the lesser M to the greater L ; and (3) as something abstracted from the two, that is, as the ratio between L and M without regard to anterior or posterior.

In the first case L the greater, in the second case M the lesser, is the subject which owns the accident, as philosophers name the relation. But what is the subject of the accident in the third case ? We should have to reply that the two together, L and M, are the subject of an accident which is itself one and single, and so we should have one accident in two subjects, an accident, as it were, with one foot in one subject, one in another, totally inconsistent with the notion of accident. It would be necessary, therefore, to say that the relation in this third meaning is literally outside, and then it can be neither substance nor accident, but a purely ideal thing, yet not on that account any less useful. Euclid, when he cannot give an absolute meaning to *ratios* in geometry, defines them well enough as the *same ratios*. So when we would explain what *place* is we have to define what the *same place* is. An even more striking illustration of the working of the mind may be seen in the idea of tracks or traces. Things which move in a medium may leave behind in the medium traces of their movement, this gives us the occasion to imagine and form the idea of traces existing even when there is no medium. Such traces are purely ideal and can only mean that, if there had been an immobile medium within which the movement occurred, the trace of the movement might have been left on it. It is in an exactly analogous way that we imagine *places, traces, spaces*, where there are only *relations* and nothing in the nature of absolute reality at all.

The application which Leibniz makes of this argument for the relativity of space and time is from the philosophical standpoint of the first importance. Absolute real space and absolute even-flowing time would conflict with and render nugatory the principle of sufficient reason, the principle upon which all physical science rests, for it governs all our reasoning in regard to matters

of fact. Assume that absolute real space and absolute
even-flowing time are the independent pre-existing conditions of the universe, then in whatever way the
universe has originated, whether by the creative act of
God or by any process of natural generation, it is clear
that not only we cannot give, but there cannot be, a
sufficient reason why it is situated here and not there
in the infinite void, now and not then in the eternal
lapse of time.

Let us quote Leibniz's own words from the third
letter to Clarke :

" There are many ways of refuting the imagination of
those who take space to be a substance, or at least something absolute, but I will confine myself to one proof
only. I say, then, that if space were an absolute being,
it would be impossible to give a sufficient reason for
anything that might happen, yet this principle is with us
an axiom. I prove it in this way. Suppose space is
something absolutely uniform, then without things
occupying it, there is nothing in which one point of space
differs from another. Now from this it follows that,
assuming space to be something in itself other than an
order of bodies among themselves, it is impossible there
should be a reason why God, keeping the same situation
of bodies between themselves, should have placed them
in space thus and not otherwise, why, for instance, the
whole should not be in reverse and that which is now
East be West and what is West, East. If, however,
space is nothing else but the order or relation of things
among themselves, and is nothing at all without bodies
except the possibility of giving order to them, then the
two supposed states, the one which actually is and the
supposititious transposition, would have no difference
at all in themselves. The difference is, then, only to be
found in the chimerical supposition that there is a reality
of space in itself. Apart from this the two supposed

different positions would be exactly the same, two
absolute indiscernibles, consequently there would be no
meaning in asking the reason for preferring one to the
other.

" It is precisely the same in regard to time. Suppose
someone should ask why God did not create the world a
year sooner, and should then go on to infer from the
fact that he did not, that God had done that of which it
is impossible there could be a reason why he had done
it thus and not otherwise. We should have to admit
that his inference would be true if time were something
outside the temporal things. For it would be impossible
that there could be reasons why things should have been
set going at such instants rather than at others, their
succession when set going remaining the same. What
it really proves, however, is that instants apart from
things are nothing, instants consist only in the successive order of things. If the successive order remained
the same, the two states, the imagined anticipation and
the state which now is, would differ in nothing and there
would be no way of discerning the difference."

He goes on to point out that there is no escape from the
conclusion by affirming the sufficient reason to be the
simple will of God ; to do so would be the same thing as
to say that God acts without sufficient reason, and this
would amount to a denial of the principle of sufficient
reason itself.

It is interesting to compare this argument and the
illustration supporting it with the argument for the
modern principle of relativity, the principle that the
laws of nature are the same for observers in different
systems of reference in uniform movement relatively to
one another. Assume an absolute real space and then
suppose that all the magnitudes of our universe should
contract or expand to any extent we like to imagine,
could we by any natural means be made aware that

such contraction or expansion had happened ? There
is no such means. For us it would be completely indifferent. The expanded or contracted world, for every
observer within it, who would, of course, have undergone
the proportionate expansion and contraction in all his
organs of sense perception, would after its change be
identical with the world before its change. There is no
conceivable means by which an observer in the world
could at the same time that he was observing from
within be a disinterested observer without. Consequently an absolute real space is an idle hypothesis. It
is the same with time. Assume that all velocities are
increased or diminished to any imaginable degree, could
we by any means discern the difference by comparing
the velocities of our universe with a supposed absolute
time ? It is clear the different time-flows would be the
same time-flow. Consequently an absolute real time-
flow is as meaningless and useless an hypothesis as an
absolute real space. Leibniz's illustration of the effect of
a shift of the universe in the assumed absolute real space
and time is only different in form. His standpoint is
that of a creation theory.

The metaphysical argument against an absolute real
space and time may be summed up as follows. The
reality of space and time, if they exist absolutely, must be
either substantial or adjectival. In either case the
reality must have a positive character of its own. But
the conceptions of space as the void and of time as the
lapse are simple negations. They are attained by
abstracting from all positive content. They represent
not the presence of anything, but the absence of everything. To affirm the positivity of a pure negation is a
self-contradiction, it is giving the content of the conception the reality which is denied it. Space and time
may, however, be positive conceptions of extension
and duration. But extension and duration are then

adjectival, the attributes of something extended and enduring, and space and time are not this something. It is material things, corporeal things, which are extended and enduring. If we abstract from a material body its extension, it becomes unextended, and ceases to be material ; we have negated its essential character. It is the same with duration. When an extended body moves it does not leave its extension behind in the position it has vacated ; when a living being changes it does not leave its duration in the past. Space and time, therefore, whether we define them negatively as void and lapse, or positively as extension and duration, cannot be independent of things, yet they are neither themselves things nor detachable adjectives of things. What alternative is left ? The alternative that they are not absolute but relative, that they represent the order or arrangement of things between themselves. They are a representation, not of perceptions, which are themselves a representation, but of the order which perceptions take, an order which can have its sufficient reason in the real world.

This, in brief, is Leibniz's theory, and it will be seen at once that it accords with modern relativity theory. It was, in fact, called forth by criticism of the Newtonian postulates of absolute real space and time, which the relativity principle is supplanting. It had, no doubt, a determining influence on Kant in his theory that space and time are the a priori forms of sense perception, but what is particularly to be remarked in Leibniz's doctrine is that while he makes space and time relative he does not make them subjective. They are the product of the co-ordinating activity of the mind, but they characterize nature, the objective world of physics.

In considering Leibniz's criticism of Newton, it is important to keep in mind, that his opposition is not to Newton's physics but to his metaphysics. In so far as

Leibniz can be said to have anticipated the modern mathematical principle of relativity, it is in his idea of individual co-ordinate systems and his practical rejection of the Galilean co-ordinate system which Newton adopted. So far as the formula of the law of gravitation and the idea of a universal influence of all on each are concerned, Leibniz's theory of perception is in effect the subjective counterpart of Newton's universal force of attraction, and there is no suggestion in Leibniz of a return to the Cartesian system or of an interpretation of the laws of movement by the geometry of space. What Leibniz in effect offers is the metaphysical background of the modern principle of relativity, the autonomy of individual standpoints in the observation of nature.

IX

NISI IPSE INTELLECTUS

UNTIL the great work of John Locke came to concentrate his attention upon it, knowledge does not seem to have presented to Leibniz a particular problem. It had its place in the general metaphysical theory. According to Leibniz's " New System " it is by ideal relations alone that the real constituents of the universe are compounded. Knowledge depends on these ideal relations, they are the outcome of the activity of the monad, the expression of its internal force. The activity of the monad consists in perception and appetition, universal and general forms of activity, which in the rational monads become specialized as understanding and will. Perception is representative, that is to say, in perception the external influences of other reals are ideally represented. Knowledge, therefore, is, so to speak, inherent in Leibniz's conception of reality. It is the inalienable nature of the monad to know. The only difference is in degree. Each monad perceives, and the whole universe is represented in its perception, but there are varying degrees of clearness or of confusedness in its perceptions, ranging from complete obscurity to absolute distinctness. Within this activity of perception there is, however, a difference, which amounts to a difference of kind, between sense-knowledge and reason. This is the basis of the hierarchy of the monads. Only the rational monads have knowledge of general principles and eternal truths, and are therefore able to enter into that higher intercourse which characterizes the City of God. Neither the nature of knowledge nor the validity of knowledge stand in Leibniz's path as initial problems obstructing the entrance to the realms of science and philosophy.

It was primarily as an obstacle and obstruction to true philosophy that the problem of knowledge presented itself to Locke. Most of the difficulties on which philosophers were divided would, he thought, be smoothed out or cleared away, if there were a preliminary understanding as to what is the nature and origin of ideas and what are the limitations of knowing. The *Essay on the Understanding* was implicitly, what later Kant's *Critique of Pure Reason* was explicitly, a challenge to every philosophy which aimed to be a metaphysics of reality, to criticise the instrument of knowledge in order to decide in what sense, if any, a metaphysic of reality is possible at all. In Locke it took the form of a preliminary inquiry into the nature and origin of ideas, the immediate objects of the mind when it thinks.

As in the case of Newton so in the case of Locke, the best intention to obey the warning " Beware metaphysics " and the best laid plans to avoid, or at any rate at least to defer, the metaphysical problem are foredoomed to failure. Newton could not, try how he would, interpret his observations of the celestial movements, and frame his laws of motion, without tacitly assuming a metaphysical hypothesis of the nature of space and time, and Locke could not inquire into the origin of ideas without a theory of the nature of the mind and of the ideas which are its objects. Such advantage as Leibniz appears to have in his controversy, alike with Newton and with Locke, arises from the fact that he recognizes the metaphysical problem and accepts it as necessarily first in the order of knowing as well as in the order of being. Unless we already know, we cannot know what it is to know.

It is impossible for the modern student of philosophy

to dissociate Locke's empirical principle as presented in the *Essay on the Understanding* from its subsequent development in the philosophies of Berkeley and Hume, its partial rehabilitation in the philosophy of Condillac, and its reconciliation with the rival principle in the philosophy of Kant. Leibniz's dissertation was before any of this development, yet it did not influence it. His work was unknown to any of those who preceded Kant. Condillac (1715-1780) was deeply influenced by Leibniz's ideas in the *Monadologie* and *Théodicée*, but his own *Traité des Sensations* was written before the *Nouveaux Essais* was published. In considering Leibniz's theory of knowledge, therefore, we have to remember that it finds expression in a contemporary criticism of Locke, but was only given to the world sixty years later, when the empirical principle had produced a real dilemma in philosophical theory.

There was undoubtedly much in Locke's empirical principle with which Leibniz was entirely in sympathy. Notwithstanding his pure intellectualism he had rejected the Cartesian view of sense knowledge. He had no use for the principle of the deceptiveness of the senses nor for the theory of their utilitarian purpose in the protection of the body. Sense knowledge for Leibniz was real knowledge, although confused and obscure. He has no difficulty in subscribing to the maxim, *Nihil est in intellectu quod non prius fuerit in sensu*. He will only object that it is not in the form of ideas that the senses receive external impressions. Before impressions from without can give rise to representative ideas within, an active work of the mind itself must have taken place. Ideas, the objects of the mind when it thinks, are not imposed from without but formed within. Accordingly he qualifies the maxim (usually but erroneously ascribed to Aristotle) by adding *nisi ipse intellectus*, a qualification which in effect completely reverses the whole application of the principle by Locke. The mind is innate to itself.

Locke's philosophy may be summed up in a few definite propositions :

(1) No ideas are innate. All are dependent on and arise from experience.

(2) The mind is a *tabula rasa*. Before experience it is a blank. In experience it is sensitive to and retentive of the impressions it receives.

(3) Activity is, and may be altogether, lodged in corporeal matter. The soul or mind is not necessarily immaterial. It may be the brain which thinks.

(4) There are simple ideas of sensation, that is, of the immediate impressions of external objects on the organs of sense ; there are also simple ideas of reflection, that is, of the fundamental attributes of the mind self-perceived by an inner sense. All knowledge can be resolved into these simple ideas.

Locke's principle, therefore, which in effect places agency in matter and makes mind derivative, is diametrically opposed to Leibniz's principle that minds are internal forces, the real units of nature, and that materiality is a mass effect of confused perception. Leibniz found himself under the necessity of formulating a theory of knowledge. Let us consider what he singles out as the chief differences between himself and Locke.

" The matters on which we disagree are of some importance, to wit, whether the soul in itself is a blank, like a tablet on which nothing yet is written, and whether all that afterwards is traced upon it comes from the senses and experience alone, or whether the soul originally contains the principles of the various notions and interpretations which external objects only call forth on occasion. Locke, following Aristotle, holds the first view, I hold the second, and in this I am in accord with Plato, and also with the scholastics, and, indeed, with all who take literally the passage in which St. Paul declares that the law of God is written in our hearts. (*Romans*, ii. 15.)

" This gives rise to another question, to wit, whether all truths depend on experience, that is, on induction and instances, or whether there are some which have quite another ground. If some events can be foreseen before we have made any actual proof of them, it is clear that something is being contributed by ourselves. The senses, though necessary for all our actual cognitions, are not sufficient to give us the whole of our knowledge, for the senses can never give us anything but instances, that is to say, particular or individual truths. Now it by no means follows that what always has happened always will, and consequently all the instances which confirm a general truth, however great their number, are insufficient to establish its universal necessity. Necessary truths, those of pure mathematics, for example, and especially those of arithmetic and geometry, must have principles whose truth is not dependent on instances and consequently not dependent on the evidence of the senses, although without the senses it might never have occurred to us to think of them. Euclid understood this distinction when he felt it necessary to prove by reason even what is quite evident by experience and sense images. Logic, together with metaphysics and ethics, which give form, the one to theology, the other to jurisprudence, both natural, are full of such truths, and consequently their proof can only come from the internal principles we call innate. We need not imagine that the eternal laws of reason are engraved in the soul as in an open book to be read without difficulty and research; it is enough that they are discoverable within us when we give the attention for which the senses furnish the occasions. Successful experiments serve as confirmation of reason, much as proofs serve in arithmetic. They are the best way of avoiding error in calculations when the reasoning is long. It is in this distinction that the difference lies between human cognitions and those of the brutes. The brutes are purely empirics ; they rule themselves by instances alone, for, as far as we can judge, they never attain to the formation of necessary propositions ; but men are capable of demonstrative sciences. So far as the brutes have the faculty of consequential reasoning it would seem to be in degree and extent far below the capacity of reason which exists in man."

In this passage Leibniz has touched the weak point of Locke's argument for the rejection of innate ideas. It is generally recognized by all his critics that Locke in the first book of the *Essay* combats the theory of innate ideas in a form in which no considerable thinker ever held it. Ideas do not exist before experience in a clear and recognizable form, as Locke seems to think the theory of innate ideas required. " The law of God written in our hearts " is not to be taken to mean that God's commandments are engraved therein in express terms. The question is not to be decided by an appeal to fact whether any ideas are to be found in the mind before experience or not. The mind, in Leibniz's view, is not a *tabula rasa*, waiting to receive its knowledge from the impressions of external objects in the form of ideas ; it is innate " to itself," a nature which will express itself in ideas, in response to the influences it receives. It is dependent on experience for its ideas, but it is not experience which imparts the ideas ; it is experience which gives the occasion for the mind to express itself in ideas. Leibniz is not content, therefore, to insist that there are some ideas which could not have come from experience through the senses, he maintains that no ideas could possibly come to the mind in that way. " I have always held, and still hold, that the idea of God is innate, as Descartes maintained, and also that there are other ideas which could not come from the senses. I now go still further, and in conformity with my new system I hold that all the thoughts and actions of our soul come from its own inner source, and that it is impossible they can be given by the senses." It is along this line that Leibniz develops his opposition to the two first points of Locke's theory.

On the third point, the question of the materiality or immateriality of the mind or soul, his opposition is even more emphatic. Locke, having to meet the challenge that there is no way of conceiving how thought can be a product of material activity, had replied that our conception is no measure of God's power, and he had then cited the analogy of Newton's theory of gravitation, which requires us to attribute an attractive force to matter, though it is not within our power to conceive the nature of such a force. This had been in a published correspondence between Locke and the Bishop of Worcester in 1699. Commenting on it, Leibniz declares that for his own part he is convinced that matter is no more capable of producing feeling mechanically than it is of producing reason. We are not justified in denying what we cannot understand, but we are certainly right in denying what is absolutely unintelligible and inexplicable, at least when the matter in question is in the natural order.

It is clear to us, however, that the fundamental difference between the two philosophers on this question (whether it is conceivable that a corporeal organ, the brain, can be the mind) is really in their metaphysical principles. There can be no question for Leibniz whether matter is capable of thought, because in his view material substance does not exist. Substances, Leibniz insists, be they material or immaterial, cannot be conceived in their bare essence as inactive ; activity is the essence of substance in general. Our power of conceiving is not indeed the measure of God's power, but it is the measure of our natural power, otherwise it would not be possible for any creature to judge what is or is not conformable to the natural order. Locke, on the other hand, conceives material substance as a substratum, with no inherent force of its own, capable of being endowed with just such powers as God chooses to give it. His empirical principle forbids him to go behind the fact, whatever it purports to be, and challenge its rationality, or conceivability, or consistency with any supposed natural order. There is yet another important difference. Materiality for Locke is substantive. For Leibniz, on the other hand, materiality is appearance, simply a mass effect, and for him there is no distinction between material and immaterial substance, for all substance alike is activity or force. The only difference is between the simple and the composite. The mind with its thinking activity in all its modes is a simple substance ; the body, an organization of simple substances, is a composite.

We may now see the peculiar force of Leibniz's argument. The body may indeed be compared to a machine, but it excels all human-made machines in the fact that every minutest part of the machine is also itself a machine. That is to say the body is a living machine, its materiality is an appearance, and thought is the activity not of the machine, but of the immaterial soul attached to it. Thinking (using the term to include all its modes) cannot be a mechanical product, the output of a machine, to which the component parts each contribute in the result. The mind is indivisible on any principle whatever, and it owns all its states. It is quite inconceivable that an extended and therefore divisible body, or organ of a body, could by any imaginable kind of team work among its different parts give rise to that essential unity which thought implies. " It is certain thought cannot be an intelligible modification of matter ; that is to say, a feeling or thinking being is not a mechanical thing like a watch or a mill. We cannot conceive that the mechanical conjunction of magnitudes, shapes, and movements, could produce feeling and thinking in a mass where no such thing existed previously and where no such thing will exist when the machine is out of order." " Should anyone object that God might if he chose endow such a prepared machine with the faculty of thinking, I grant it, but were God really to endow matter with this faculty, without at the same time providing a substance which could be the subject in which such a faculty could naturally inhere, that is to say, if God should make matter think without creating for it an immaterial soul, it would mean that he had miraculously exalted matter to receive a power for which it was not naturally fitted. It would be doing with matter as some scholastics suggest God can do with fire, exalt it in order to give it the power to burn unembodied spirits, a miracle pure and simple."

Locke's distinction of ideas into those which have their origin in sensation and those which have their origin in reflection modified very markedly the sharp contrast between his empirical principle and the intellectualist principle of Leibniz. " Reflection is nothing but attention to what is within us, and the senses do not give us what we already possess. Since then we are, so to speak, innate to ourselves, can it be denied that in the mind itself there is much which is innate, for instance, *being, unity, substance, duration, change, action, perception, pleasure,* and a thousand other things which are objects of our intellectual ideas? It is true these objects are immediate and always present to our understanding, though we may not always be conscious of them owing to our distractions and occupations. Is there, then, anything surprising in saying that the ideas of these objects are innate in us, with all that such a theory implies? Ideas and truths are not external like actions, but innate like inclinations, dispositions, habits, or natural powers. The powers may indeed always be accompanied by the actions, often insensible, which respond to them."

Leibniz illustrates this by comparing two ways in which it might be said that a block of marble contained a statue of Hercules. The block might be of the same texture and character throughout, or it might contain, as veins running through it, the outline of the statue. Of either block we may say that it holds within it a statue of Hercules, but in the one case the material is indifferent to how it is shaped, in the other the shape is already determined by the lines which the veins mark out in it, and the sculptor has only to cut away the stone which conceals them.

The real difference between the two theories is in the distinction, which Leibniz makes and which Locke does not recognize, between perception and apperception. Of far the greater part of our perception we are unconscious, and indeed it is only of a very infinitesimal range that we can ever become conscious. Knowledge, in Locke's view, is an intuition of the relations of ideas ; in Leibniz's view it is ideal representation. Every monad perceives, but the monad's perception is something practically physical in its nature. That is to say, all reality, in Leibniz's view, is activity, and all activity is spiritual, and the influence of this activity spreads throughout the universe from all to each. Thus every monad is a mirror of the universe. How then does this perception become knowledge ? By a selection exercised in the interest of action. "The soul's perceptions always respond naturally to the constitution of the body. When there is a quantity of confused and scarcely distinguishable movement in the brain, as in the case of infants who as yet have had little experience, the thoughts of the soul, corresponding to the order of things, are no distincter than the movements in the brain. Yet the soul is never deprived of the aid of sensation, because sensation is always the body's expression. The body is always being struck by other surrounding bodies in an infinity of ways, though these often make but one confused impression " (*Nouveaux Essais*, II, 17).

Leibniz clearly foresaw the scepticism which must, and as we know inevitably did, overtake the empirical principle. " Our certitude would be small, or rather null, had it no other basis of simple ideas than that which comes from the senses. The ground of our certitude in regard to universal and eternal truths is in the ideas themselves independently of the senses. The ideas of sensible qualities such as colour, taste, etc. (which in fact are only phantoms) come to us from the senses, that is to say, from our confused perceptions."

We may also see in Leibniz's theory of knowledge the first indication of a distinction which in modern times has developed into philosophy of art, the distinction, first explicitly made by Kant, between Æsthetic and Logic. There is for Leibniz no breach of continuity in the ascent from the confused knowledge of the bare monad to the distinct knowledge of the supreme monad, but there is a special quality of confused knowledge which gives it a form of truth different from that of distinct knowledge and which we attribute to imagination and describe as beauty. In the *Principes de la Nature et de Grace* there occurs the significant sentence : " We might know the *beauty* of the universe in each soul if we could unfold all its wrappings which are only sensibly developed in time." And still more strikingly in the Preface to the *Nouveaux Essais* : " These minute perceptions are of greater efficacy than we think. It is they which form that *je ne sais quoi*, those tastes, those images of sense qualities, clear in the mass, but confused in the parts, those impressions which surrounding bodies make on us and which

include the infinite, that bond which binds each being
to the rest of the universe."

Leibniz is, in fact, the first modern philosopher to lay
down the principle in the theory of knowledge, that the
mind in knowing is active and constructive, not passive
and contemplative. Every mind is exposed to all the
influences of all the forces in the universe, but its ideas
are formed within, answering the needs of its own
activity. The distinction between sensible and intelligible ideas is not a difference in kind. The one
arises in confused, the other in distinct perception.
What, then, it will be asked, is the relation between
ideas and things, and in what way do ideas represent
their objects? The answer is that there are no things.
The reality of the universe is not its actuality at any
moment, but its possibility in every moment. Our
ideas represent possibilities. "All intelligible ideas have
their archetypes in the eternal possibilities."

X

THE BEST OF ALL POSSIBLE WORLDS

THE optimism which is the distinguishing character of Leibniz's philosophy, and which made that philosophy a target for the wit and satire of Voltaire, should now appear in its true nature. To affirm that this world, with all its imperfection, suffering and sin, is the best of all possible worlds, however extravagant it may seem, is not a paradox. It is not the *prima facie* absurdity it appears to common sense. It is not enunciated by Leibniz in the spirit of *Credo quia impossibile* ; it is not a chivalrous attempt to justify the ways of God to men ; it is not an appeal to faith or exhortation to indulge the larger hope ; it is the rational corollary which follows naturally from the logical application of a metaphysical principle. We may reject the corollary without in any way detracting from the value of Leibniz's philosophy, but we cannot condemn it as irrational without impugning the metaphysics on which that philosophy is based.

That this is the best of all possible worlds means literally, as the Victorian poet, Tennyson, has beautifully expressed it :—

> That nothing walks with aimless feet ;
>   That not one life shall be destroyed,
>   Or cast as rubbish to the void,
> When God hath made the pile complete ;
>
> That not a worm is cloven in vain ;
>   That not a moth with vain desire
>   Is shrivelled in a fruitless fire,
> Or but subserves another's gain.

The optimism is not based, however, on pious faith in the goodwill of a benevolent power to whom nothing is impossible. We may set aside the argument that the creative work of a Creator, infinite in wisdom, goodness and power, cannot fall short of perfection, and that, therefore, since this world is His creation it is the best possible. Leibniz does, indeed, use this argument and frequently expresses himself in terms of it. But obviously it can be turned in an opposite direction, for if we can argue from the perfection of the Creator to the perfection of the world nothing can prevent us arguing from the imperfection of the world to the imperfection of the Creator. Equally we may set aside the idea that the imperfections of this world may be made good by a system of rewards and punishments in a supernatural sphere. Leibniz accepted the eschatological teachings of the Christian religion, but they do not enter into his metaphysical speculations and logical constructions as essential constituents.

The argument on which Leibniz bases his optimistic conclusion is twofold : it is metaphysical and it is moral. Stated briefly, the metaphysical argument is that the constituents of the universe are indestructible, their existence is one with the existence of the universe. The moral argument is that the ways of nature lead to grace. In the hierarchy of the monads we see that the monads which rise to the self-conscious stage, the rational monads, are able to enter into moral relations with one another, and to become members of the City of God, a moral realm under the most perfect Ruler. The universe is therefore a realm of ends founded on an order of nature. Taking both arguments together the keynote of the whole conception is that the unit substances of which the universe is constituted are not actualities, rigidly circumscribed in space and time, like material atoms, they are eternal possibilities, there is no absolute circumscription of their activities. " Since simple substances always endure, we must not judge of eternity by a few years " (*Nouveaux Essais*, II, 10, 14). The three kinds of monads (the bare monads, the animal monads and the rational monads) are never conceived by Leibniz as constituting exclusive classes. Not only is there a hierarchy, but there is an infinite gradation and there is no limit to the possibility of a monad rising in the hierarchy. The lowest has within it the potentiality of the highest. The Supreme Monad is, indeed, a class apart, but this is by reason of its transcendence. Whether consistent or not, Leibniz conceives God both as beyond and within the hierarchy. One of his commentators (Gottlieb Hanschius, quoted by Condillac in a note to his *Traité des Systèmes*) tells the story that Leibniz remarked to him once, while taking coffee, " There may be in this cup a monad which will one day be a rational soul."

These two concepts—the metaphysical concept of individual substantive units, inviolable in their nature and therefore self-determining or free, and indestructible, because simple and therefore not disruptive ; and the ethical concept of a moral world in the natural world, rendered possible by the ideal relations between the higher monads—are the foundation of his optimism. One gives him the factor of an impelling force below, the other the factor of an attracting purpose above, the activity of the living unit forces.

To see the full significance of his theory, we must set aside any prejudices which are due to scientific theories of modern origin. Leibniz had a very clear conception of the nature of living activity, and also he had the idea of a natural progression from lower to higher forms of life and mind, but we must be careful not to read into his philosophy the modern theory of evolution or the idea of *élan vital*.

It is in the *Théodicée* that the optimistic principle is set forth and defended, and it is there expressed in theological concepts. Can God, such is the problem, countenance imperfection, inflict pain, and permit sin, without himself being responsible for sin and ultimately the author of evil, metaphysical, physical and moral? Leibniz's answer may be given in a sentence. God is concerned with the universe. All value-judgments have regard to the whole. The theological form of the argument has ceased to have any interest for us, largely because for us the part of the physical universe which concerns man has shrunk to such a narrow and insignificant corner of the great whole, if indeed we can think of the physical universe as a whole. There is a curious passage in the *Théodicée* which shews how sensitive Leibniz was to the fact that the progress of physics was rapidly antiquating theodicies by widening the horizon. After referring to various theories associated with Origen's idea of a universal restoration in which even Satan and the fallen angels will be reinstated, he tells how a bold thinker, whom he does not name, " pushing my principles of harmony into arbitrary suppositions which I in no way accept, has constructed a theology almost astronomical." The idea of this theology is that this earth was once a sun, shining by its own effulgence, and under an angelic vice-regent, and that its descent to its present condition was a natural consequence associated with a moral delinquency, perhaps the insubordination of its presiding ruler. By the " pre-established harmony of the realms of nature and grace " the earth when it lost by moral delinquency its natural status became an opaque planet and its inhabitants sinful. The Messianic mission of redemption is then conceived on a world scale, and a full apocalypse of its future history is portrayed, the Son of God coming from his home in the sun to be incarnate and bring about the final reconciliation. Leibniz adds this reflection. " While we have no need of hypotheses or fictions of this kind, in which invention counts for more than revelation and in which even reason is not completely satisfied, yet it does seem that there is no place in the known universe, worthy of being singled out as preferably the seat of the first-born of creatures, who is to restore the universal harmony. We may be sure at least that the sun of our solar system is not such a place."

We can see why this kind of speculation was attractive to Leibniz. The real universe for him was not spatial and therefore the revelation of the vast stellar distances did not affect his scheme, yet it brought home to him a particular difficulty in the application of his optimistic principle. The realm of ethical values on which his optimism was based concerned the human inhabitants of this small planet, and of these by far the larger part, in fact all but an almost insignificant minority, is at present and indefinitely excluded from the City of God. It was some consolation therefore to think that the universe might contain infinite other worlds of monadic natures which, taken in the aggregate with this world of ours, might alter completely the proportions of lost and saved now existing in this world considered in itself alone.

The particular point of interest to us of the scientific era in regard to this conception of the world as the best of possibles, is to see how it resolves itself into an abstract identity of reality and possibility as soon as we divest it of the theistic postulate, an extramundane creator for whom the universe could exist ideally as a possibility before it was realized in act. It is not a little strange that the philosopher who had rejected so definitely an outside theory of knowledge and had enunciated so clearly the principle of the self-centralization of the real, should be remembered chiefly for a judgment on the nature of the universe which assumes the possibility of transcending it. The moment we place ourselves at that truer Leibnizian standpoint, adopt what we call the monadic principle, we see that our view of the universe can only be from within outwards, can only be from our own privileged position within the system we are surveying, and that our outlook is conditioned by our interest as actors. From such a standpoint it is impossible to compare the reality of the universe with its possibility and pass a value-judgment on it as best or worst.

Philosophies are still classed as optimistic or pessimistic but the meaning has changed. It has no longer reference to the conception of Providence, universal or particular. The intellectualist theories, as for example that of Hegel, are for the most part optimisms ; the voluntarist, as for example that of Schopenhauer, are pessimisms. They serve to give tone to the practical or ethical concept. Ought we to face life with confidence or with resignation ? Is there a purpose into which we can enter with joy, or is all incentive and striving a useless revolt against a blind mechanism ?

PART III

INFLUENCE

I

THE SYSTEMATIZATION OF THE LEIBNIZIAN PHILOSOPHY

WE have seen that what Leibniz called his " New System " was really a principle of interpretation. The correspondence of the ideal and the real, the spiritual and the corporeal, the mind and the body, could be explained, he held, rationally and more consistently by the hypothesis of a harmony pre-established by God, than by either of the theories then current, that of causal relation or that of occasional intervention. Apart from this there is nothing systematic, in the accepted meaning of the term " system," in Leibniz's philosophy. On the contrary, the extreme value and the brilliant suggestiveness of that philosophy arise from Leibniz's acute criticisms of systems and his penetrating logical and metaphysical intuitions. We have seen, too, that though a German and attached to the House of Brunswick, he seldom wrote anything, and never anything of philosophical importance, in German. His philosophy was written in Latin or in French, and intended primarily for the literary circles of France and England. The controversies in which he took part were entirely with French and English philosophers. When he claims for a countryman of his own a place in the front rank, it is with submission and almost apologetically, as in his references to " our own " Erhard Weigel. Yet in the century which followed his death he came to be regarded as the typically German philosopher. He had practically no following and little influence in France and England, but he rose to be the apostle of the new philosophical interest in Germany and, still more strange, as setting the standard of philosophical orthodoxy. Before this could happen, however, his philosophy had to change beyond recognition ; it had to be systematized.

This systematization was the work of his follower and younger contemporary, Johann Christian Wolff (1679–1754). In the eighteenth century the two names Leibniz and Wolff are invariably linked together and the philosophy is always referred to as Leibnitio-Wolffian.

Wolff was a brilliant, popular university professor and his life is a straightforward story of continuous literary and academic success. He was one of the first to give university lectures on philosophy in German, discarding the practice which had come down from the scholastic era of lecturing in Latin. He declared one of his ideals to be to make philosophy speak German. His numerous writings were published originally in German and only a few were translated into Latin. He starts the great line of modern German philosophy. He graduated at Leipsic in 1703, and his Latin dissertation, *De philosophia practica universali*, attracted the notice of Leibniz. His first professorship was in mathematics, at the University of Halle, but he lectured also on physics and later added philosophy. He was expelled from Halle by Frederick the Great of Prussia for an expression of opinion supposed to reflect on military discipline, and he then went to Marburg, but later he was recalled by Frederick, and when he died he was Chancellor of the University, Privy Councillor of Prussia, and a Baron of the Holy Roman Empire. His collected writings on philosophy occupy twenty-three large quarto volumes.

It is often charged against Wolff that he was a mere pedagogue and a pure pedant. There seems no reason for such a judgment. It is true we discover in him no spark of originality. On the other hand, he would seem to have realized in an amazing degree the ideal of academic proficiency. His work was to bring the disconnected speculations of philosophy and its medley of principles and maxims and conflicting methods into systematic order, to present philosophy as a concatenation of philosophical sciences, each with its own delimited territory. In fact, he reduced philosophy to a form which fitted it eminently to be a subject of university instruction, and thereby raised it once again to the academic distinction it had enjoyed in the mediæval scholastic period and lost in the renaissance of learning. While receiving his whole inspiration from Leibniz, and faithfully embodying his concepts and principles, he compresses the living thought into rigid frames, modifies the oppositions, tidies up the disorder. We might say, indeed, that we owe to him the staging of the problem which developed so prodigiously in the work of Kant and Kant's successors in the German universities.

The systematization may be said to depend on the definition of philosophy with which he sets out and which in a striking way represents the principle of Leibniz. *Philosophia est scientia possibilium, quatenus esse possunt.* Philosophy is the science of possibles so far as they can be. Philosophical knowledge he then defines as knowledge of the reason of things which are or which become, by which it is understood why they are or become. *Possible* means precisely what Leibniz had defined by the law of identity as that which involves no contradiction. Philosophy does not claim to know all that is possible, but it does claim to extend over the whole field of human knowledge.

Wolff was the first who gave precision to that great division in philosophy, based on the distinction between theoretical and practical, which has become so important in the modern development. The distinction is based on Leibniz's two activities of the soul, perception and appetition. The cognitive faculty gives us metaphysics or theoretical philosophy, the appetitive faculty gives us moral and political philosophy. The one is the philosophy of the understanding, the other of the will.

Theoretical philosophy or metaphysics is therefore, for Wolff, a science of pure reason. There are three principal objects of reason—the World, the Soul, God. These become therefore the subject of three rational sciences. There is, however, a more general science of reason itself which deals with Being or Existence, and it gives the common basis of the three rational objects. Metaphysics therefore is divided into four rational sciences, Ontology, Cosmology, Psychology, Theology.

Practical Philosophy is based on the idea that in questions of right as in questions of fact, and therefore in all matters which concern the direction of the will, reason alone is the principle of knowing. Its subdivisions are, Ethics, Economics and Politics. The object of Ethics is man as man ; of Economics, man as member of the human faculty ; of Politics, man as member of the State.

It is interesting to observe the changes in the concepts which Wolff found necessary in order to bring about this systematization. In every case he seeks to tone down the rigidity and sharp outlines of the original doctrines, with the inevitable effect of making them seem commonplace and insipid. His continual aim is to reconcile opposing principles, to bring all the categories, that is, the rational notions of thought which are applicable to all objects of knowledge, into the scheme of an interconnected chain. He seeks not only to arrange a table of the categories, such as Aristotle had indicated, but to find a principle by which they can be deduced from one another.

His method is rational as opposed to empirical and for this reason his system is known as " dogmatism," not, of course, in the theological meaning, but as a philosophical term of which the opposite is empiricism. Thus he accepts the two logical principles which Leibniz puts at the basis of all our knowledge, the principle of identity and the principle of sufficient reason, but he seeks to unify them by deducing the second from the first or subsuming the one under the other. It is interesting to see how he does this. The Principle of Identity rules in regard to *necessary*, the Principle of Sufficient Reason in regard to *contingent*, truths. The mediation between the two is *possibility*. Possible is what involves no contradiction. The necessary and the contingent can both therefore be defined in terms of possibility. The necessary is that the contradictory of which is impossible ; the contingent that the contradictory of which is possible.

In like manner all the leading concepts of Leibniz are substantially retained in Wolff, but in all cases they are brought into more general accord with common-sense notions. He follows Leibniz in the doctrine that space and time are not things or properties of things, but the order of phenomena. Space and time, and consequently motion, shape and change, do not apply to simple substances, but only to composites. The simples are real units, monads, metaphysical points, and their substance is force. Here, however, Wolff parts from Leibniz. He will not allow a power of perception in the lowest monads, he will not call them souls, they are only *atomi naturæ*. He modifies also the conception of the exclusiveness and self-possession of the monad, which led Leibniz to deny interaction and was the ground of his system of pre-established harmony. Pre-established harmony he admitted as a permissible hypothesis in so far as it did not exclude the possibility of interaction.

The interest and importance of this systematization is that it at once established itself in the universities of Germany, particularly in the kingdom of Prussia, and thereby determined the future direction of philosophical speculation. It was in this system that Immanuel Kant (1724–1804) received his university training. His mind was formed upon it, his early work is under its influence, and the impression of it is stamped on every page of the *Critique of Pure Reason*. The Deduction of the Categories, the Ideas of Reason, the three rational sciences, all appear in the *Critique* in the shape they had assumed in the Wolff systematization. The "dogmatic slumber," to which Kant refers in the *Prolegomena* and from which he tells us he was awakened by reading the *Inquiry* of Hume, was the state of mind induced in him by initiation as a student into Wolff's well-conceived, superbly organized, conceptual system. Moreover, it is not a little significant that the turning-point in Kant's speculative reflection, the new direction which was to produce the three great Critiques, dates from the time when he came into touch with the thought of Leibniz himself, free from the Wolffian veil through which he had hitherto regarded it. This was the first publication (in 1765) of the *Nouveaux Essais*. It was, in effect, for Kant a discovery of the real Leibniz. From that time onward in German philosophy the influence Leibniz had on the development of logical and metaphysical doctrine was direct.

II

THE INFLUENCE OF LEIBNIZ ON THE PHILOSO-
PHICAL DEVELOPMENT IN ENGLAND AND
FRANCE

IT is no chance circumstance that the systematization of Leibniz's philosophy was confined to Germany. Once planted there it bore fruit abundantly. The reason is to be found in certain well-marked and long recognized racial characteristics. The German mentality is distinctly biased towards metaphysics. The German mind finds itself at home in abstract disquisitions. The French and, generally speaking, the Latin mind is as distinctively biased towards science. It is at home in the concrete, it loves the clear precision and definiteness of mathematics, it is predominantly logical. The Anglo-Saxon mind is as distinctively utilitarian and severely practical in its bent. We find accordingly that in Germany the philosophy took root and grew ; in France the direct influence of Leibniz's speculative ideas on the philosophical development was considerable, important and very marked ; in England it was practically null.

In England, the young George Berkeley, almost before he had completed his graduation courses at Trinity College, Dublin, was evolving a theory of spiritual plural-ism, in many respects analogous to, and in its practical outcome closely resembling, the theory of monads. He also criticized and rejected the physics of Newton on the same grounds as those which Leibniz had made the basis of his attack, and by arguments, some of which curiously anticipate the principle of relativity. Yet Berkeley was

not only quite outside the influence of Leibniz, but he
came to his problem from entirely different sources. Apart
from the conclusion at which each arrives, that material
substance does not exist, there is nothing in common
between them. Berkeley accepts and follows the empirical
principle. He is arrested by Locke's derivation of the
idea of material substance, and he criticizes it, from
Locke's standpoint, as a useless and jejune idea, and
finally rejects it as an absurdity. He is left with spiritual
substance existing in finite individual minds and in the
infinite mind of God, and spiritual substance suffices.
This is very different from Leibniz's view that matter,
though not substance, is a real or well-founded phenomenon, arising as a mass effect from confused perception.
Berkeley's spiritual substance, moreover, has no metaphysical support, and when in its turn it has to meet the
sceptical inquiry of Hume, it has nothing to fall back
upon. The Scottish common-sense school sought to meet
the scepticism, but showed no power to surmount it, or to
open a new and original pathway of philosophical inquiry.
The problem was taken up again by the utilitarian philosophers of the nineteenth century (James Mill, John
Stuart Mill, Herbert Spencer and their followers) at the
point where Hume had left it. When the dividing line
appears between the two modern schools of realism and
idealism, the realism is no longer the common-sense
realism of Reid and the Scottish school, but positivism
and scientific naturalism, and the idealism is not the
metaphysical idealism of Leibniz, but the psychological
idealism of Berkeley.

In France, on the other hand, though there was no
development of the Leibnizian philosophy, its direct
influence was very important. Its metaphysical concepts,
logical principles and mathematical and physical ideas
had a very marked effect. This may be illustrated
in the case of three representative philosophers of

eighteenth-century France : Voltaire, Condillac and Maine de Biran.

Voltaire is the representative of the intellectual France of the eighteenth century. He is not a philosopher in the strict academic meaning of the term, but he is one of the acutest critics of philosophical opinion the world has known. He could laugh at metaphysical subtleties, ruthlessly tear the mask from religious superstition, mock with the bitterest sarcasm the extravagant pretensions of philosophers to penetrate the veil which conceals from us the ground of existence. At the same time he could recognize, no one better, genius and real intellectual force, and even when his criticism is malignant, it is scrupulously fair. The Dr. Pangloss of *Candide* is not a caricature of Leibniz, the philosopher whose phrases he is made to repeat, he is merely invented as a satire of Leibniz's optimism. The wittiest of all Voltaire's satirical romances is *Micromegas*. In this a visitor from Sirius is supposed to visit our planet. He amuses himself by listening to the disputes of philosophers. " Et toi, mon ami, dit il à un Leibnitien, qui était là, qu'est ce que ton âme ? C'est, répondit le Leibnitien, une aiguille qui montre les heures pendant que mon corps carillonne ; ou bien, si vous voulez, c'est elle qui carillonne, pendant que mon corps montre l'heure ; ou bien, mon âme est le miroir de l'univers, et mon corps est la bordure du miroir : cela est clair."

Voltaire's most serious philosophical writing was the *Elemens de la Philosophie de Newton*. It contains an interesting defence of Newton against the charge of Leibniz, in the Clarke correspondence, that Newton, together with Locke, had an unworthy conception of God's workmanship in creation. In one chapter (Pt. I Ch. 9) the opposition between the two principles, Newton's and Leibniz's, is stated in so clear a manner that the whole passage is worth quoting :

" If the saying, *Audax Japheti genus*, is ever justified, it is surely in those researches men have dared to make concerning the ultimate elements of the universe, for they seem placed at an infinite distance from the sphere of our knowledge. There is perhaps no more modest opinion than Newton's, who simply believes that the elements of matter are material, that is, that there is an extended and impenetrable being into the inner nature of which the understanding cannot enter. God can divide this matter to infinity or he can annihilate it, but he does not do so; he keeps its parts extended and indivisible to serve as the basis of all the productions of the universe.

" On the other hand, there is perhaps nothing bolder than Leibniz's attempt, starting from his principle of *sufficient reason*, to penetrate if he can into the very causes and inexplicable nature of these elements. Every body, he says, is composed of extended parts : but of what are these extended parts composed ? They are actually, he tells us, divisible and divided to infinity ; all you ever find is extension. Now to say that extension is the sufficient reason of extension is simply a vicious circle, it leads nowhere. We must seek the reason of extended beings, their cause, in beings which are not extended, simple beings, monads. Matter then is only an assemblage of simple beings." He proceeds to set forth Leibniz's view of the nature and activities of the monads, of the nature and origin of ideas, of confused, distinct and adequate perceptions, and of the four kinds of monads. He then passes to criticism.

" The English philosophers have no respect for names and simply reply by laughing, but if I am to refute Leibniz it must be by reasoning. This, then, is what I should like to say to those who hold his views. We all agree with you on your principle of sufficient reason, but are you deducing the right consequence from it ? In the first place, you admit that matter is actually divisible to infinity, that it is impossible to find a smallest part. No point has boundaries, occupies a place, has a shape. Are you then going to form matter of constituents without shape, place or boundaries ? Are you not hurtling against the principle of *contradiction* in your very anxiety to follow that of the *sufficient reason* ? "

(As an argument we can see that Voltaire completely misses the point. According to Leibniz, matter is a phenomenon, a well-founded appearance, not reality. This distinction, however, the distinction between phenomenon and noumenon, had not then become, as it has since Kant, familiar in philosophy.)

The passage concludes : " This is what comes of thinking we can explain things by lemmas, theorems and corollaries. What has anyone proved in this way ? As Cicero said, there is nothing so strange that philosophers will not maintain it. O Metaphysics ! We are as far forward as we were in the times of the Druids."

Just as in religion the great effort of Voltaire was, by satirizing the absurdities of theology and exposing the frauds imposed on human credulity, as he believed by Christianity, to lead men to Natural Religion, so in philosophy he sought to replace the ambitious, soaring attempts of the metaphysicians, their rational systems and inquiries into origins, with the ingenuousness and modesty of Newton and Locke. His influence was immense.

The most notable French philosopher of the eighteenth century is Etienne Bonnot de Condillac (1715–1780). He is chiefly known by his *Traité des Sensations*, a profound and original study, in its main purpose following the principle of Locke that all knowledge comes from experience through impressions on the sense organs, but employing an entirely new device. He supposes a marble statue to be vivified and endowed with conscious sensation by the opening one by one of the special organs of sense. By this artifice he is able to bring a novel analysis to sense know-ledge. Six years before this remarkable treatise appeared, he had published a *Traité des Systèmes*, in which he had described and critically analysed the systems of Descartes, Leibniz, Malebranche and Spinoza. The account of Leibniz's theory of the monads in this treatise is excellent as an exposition, and the refutation which follows the exposition is most important. Before criticizing the theory and proceeding to his refutation Condillac is most careful to present it in its completeness. Most of the critics who had attacked the theory before him had, he tells us, failed to understand the principle and had hastened to charge it with contradictions from which it is free. His own refutation takes an original line ; he does not charge the system with inconsistency ; on the contrary he admits with admiration its coherence. He challenges the principle, and it is therefore an argument with which it is absolutely necessary to come to terms. As a system, he says, it leaves nothing unexplained and some difficulties insoluble in every other system are in this intelligibly explained, and on this account it has the right to claim to be regarded as more than a hypothesis.

His refutation consists in attacking the principles by which Leibniz undertakes to explain phenomena, on the ground that the principles themselves are no more intelli-gible than the phenomena they are required to interpret. He means that the phenomena to be explained, the physical universe, the world of composite extended things, with all the contradictions involved in the concept of extension, cannot be explained by monads which escape these con-tradictions only because they are defined negatively as unextended. He admits indeed that Leibniz also defines the monads positively as force, and conceives them as having perceptions : " but if this force and these per-ceptions are merely words without meaning, his system becomes frivolous ; it amounts to saying there is extension because there is something which is not extended, or there are bodies because there is something which is not body."

That this is a real failure he then proceeds to show in the clear and crisp manner so characteristic of him, and he certainly succeeds in presenting the empirical principle in strong and favourable contrast to the rational principle, without in any way belittling the principle he opposes.

His first argument is that it is impossible to form any notion of the force with which Leibniz endows the monad. " Were our soul to act sometimes without the body, perhaps then we might form an idea of the monad's force : but, simple as the monad is, its dependence on the body is so strong that its action is always in some way confused with the body's action. The force we experience in ourselves is not noticed by us as belonging to a simple being, we feel it spread as it were over our whole composite being. It cannot serve, then, as our model to represent the force which belongs to each monad."

The significance of this argument lies in the principle that the interpretation of our ideas is the reference in them to something actual in our sense experience, that unless there is such a reference the idea is a mere name. Acute as the thrust is, and even admitting the validity of the principle, it fails in as much as it misses the essential point of the theory it is refuting. The force of the monad according to Leibniz is not unexpressed, it expresses itself in perception. Now perception is not a vague term without reference to experience ; on the contrary, it is something we only know by direct experience, and we know it (and this is the real point of the theory) as something which is not and cannot be referred to the body ; it is the unique act of the indivisible, simple substance we know as soul or mind. However multiple or manifold or expanded the object of perception, perception itself is single and unique.

Condillac next proceeds to show that Leibniz has not proved and cannot prove that monads have perceptions, and, further, that he can give no idea of the perceptions which he attributes to the monads. " Our soul has perceptions, that is, it experiences something when objects make an impression on the senses. This we feel, but the nature of the soul and the nature of what it experiences when it has perceptions are so completely unknown that we can never discover what renders us capable of perceiving. How, then, can our imperfect idea of the soul enable us to understand how other beings have perceptions such as it has ? "

This is a very forcible statement of the empirical principle and brings out admirably its complete divergence from the rational principle. According to the empirical principle we know the objects which make impressions on the senses and have their representations in the mind, but our mind itself, since it can make no impression on the senses, is completely unknown. According to the rational principle, on the other hand, our mind in its activity is the one thing we directly know and it gives us the archetype from which we can pass to a metaphysics of reality. Condillac's refutation of Leibniz is, in fact, as probably he would himself have acknowledged, not a refutation but the advocacy of another principle.

Condillac gave a new direction to the philosophical development in France. He started a line of metaphysical speculation which is marked by a close approximation to science, at first more especially to physiology and later to the biological sciences generally and to psychology, a movement which has been continuous from his time to the present day. It was little disturbed and hardly deflected by the great speculative movement of Kant and his successors in Germany. Condillac was acquainted with the Wolffian systematization of Leibniz but unattracted by it.

Maine de Biran (1766-1824) is now regarded as one of the great influences in the French development and one of the most notable in the succession of French philosophers. His very considerable philosophical writings were unknown to his contemporaries and he was himself unrecognized in his life-time.   His works were published posthumously at various periods by different editors, the earliest edition being in 1834, ten years after his death.   He had been a guardsman of Louis XVI, and he lived during the period of the Revolution and the Napoleonic wars in complete retirement.   He devoted himself to the study of philosophy but never directly sought recognition.   His principal works are prize essays, written in response to theses propounded by Academies.   His posthumous works consist of these essays, discovered in manuscript among the archives of the Institute of France, the Berlin and Copenhagen Academies.

Maine de Biran seems to have received his inspiration from the direct study of Leibniz, unsullied by the systematization of Wolff.   He wrote the article on Leibniz for the first edition of the *Biographie Universelle* in 1820.   What he does in his own philosophy is to apply the metaphysical principles of Leibniz, particularly the principle of substance as originating force, to the psychological problem.   He brings the dynamical conception of substance as an interpretative principle to the inquiry initiated by Condillac into the nature of human knowledge.

The central idea which finds expression in all his work is that the first fact of consciousness is a sense of effort.   This sense of effort is a direct and immediate experience of force, and it is this actual experience of force (not a representation) which enables us to form the idea of power, causality, substance, etc. in the world external to us.

" The soul manifests itself as person or self by the actual exercise of its own constitutive force, and can only manifest itself in so far as such exercise is free, or freed from the bonds of necessity or *fatum*, and independent of all the other forces of external nature.   It is thus that without passing out of ourselves, we are able to distinguish and

circumscribe the two opposite realms of freedom and
necessity, to see the part of the self and the part of nature,
of action and passion, of man and the animal.   Leibniz in
his forcible way, opposing the foresight of the mind to the
blind fatality of the body, gives expression to it in the
words :   *Quod in corpore Fatum in animo est Providentia."*
(*Rapports du Physique et du Moral de l'Homme :
Prolégomènes.*)

The same predominant idea of the priority of this
expérience intime finds abundant illustration in all the
writings of Maine de Biran.   The chief value of his work
is that it indicates the line along which the metaphysical
principle of Leibniz is interpretative as a scientific principle.
" There is an immediate internal perception or consciousness of a force which is me myself, and which serves as the
common type for all general and universal notions of the
causes and forces, whose real existence in nature we admit."
By this he means that it would be impossible to form the
notion of cause, or force, or power, or substance, had we
not in ourselves the immediate experience of force.

The curious thing to the student of the history of
philosophy is that at the very time when Kant was
elaborating his answer to Hume's sceptical inquiry, in
his theory that an a priori synthesis is the condition of
the possibility of knowledge, an unknown recluse in
France was meeting Hume's challenge with a direct
response.   Show me, Hume had demanded, the impression
from which is derived the idea of a necessary connection
between matters of fact.   Look for it, now replied Maine de
Biran, not in the external world but in the intimate,
primitive, immediate *fact of experience* within your own
self, in the sense of effort which is the *sine qua non*, the
accompaniment, of every act of consciousness.   It was a
new answer and different from that of Kant, and when it
became known, long after, it led to a fruitful development
of theory which extends to our own time.   Both answers

to Hume were directly inspired by Leibniz, and in effect had been given before Hume's question was asked. Kant's theory of the a priori synthesis is the direct application of Leibniz's *nisi ipse intellectus*. But Kant turns his inquiry into what the factors are which the mind itself contributes to the fact of knowledge. What, he asks, are the a priori conditions which anticipate experience ? He answers Hume by a hypothesis. Unless there be an a priori synthesis, knowledge is impossible, therefore since knowledge is actual there are a priori judgments. Maine de Biran also turns to Leibniz for the answer to Hume but he goes directly to the conception of the monad. His answer is categorical. The immediate primitive act of consciousness is not an impression imposed from without but a stirring felt within, a sense of effort, a *nisus* or *conatus*. This experience does not indeed give us the idea of an existing thing, it gives us rather the archetype of existence in the things which we represent as external to us. This is the essential import of the theory of monads.

The comparison of the application of the Leibnizian principle by Kant and by Maine de Biran leads to another consideration of deep significance in philosophy. The monads of Leibniz are things in themselves. The perceptions of the monads are representative of the real universe, that is, we only know the universe ideally. While therefore the monads are real, their knowledge is ideal. This led Kant to the distinction between phenomena and noumena and to the theory that knowledge is only of phenomena and that we cannot know things in themselves. But we can see now that it is possible to apply the principle in an entirely different way and with a very different result. Our self-knowledge is immediate, direct knowledge of reality as it is in itself. There is in this case no mediating representation. It is this direct, immediate knowledge of the real, or as Leibniz named it, this apperception of the self, which enables us to make our representative knowledge, notwithstanding its ideality, knowledge of the real. If there could be no knowledge of the noumenon there could be no distinction between noumenon and phenomenon. We can *know* things in themselves without being the things we know because we have in our immediate apperception the principle by which to interpret our representative perceptions.

III

THE NEW PHYSICS. PRINCIPLES AND FACTS

IT is only possible to deal with the influence of Leibniz on the science and philosophy of the present time in the manner of an epilogue. The history of science differs from the history of philosophy in this radical respect—that while the one aims at recording the progressive discovery of the nature of the physical universe, the other aims at recording the successive attempts of living minds to penetrate by thought to the principles of things. The history of philosophy is essentially biographical. We cannot dissociate the philosopher from his system in the same way that we are able to dissociate the scientific discoverer's discovery from the scientific discoverer himself. This does not mean that there is no continuity in the development of philosophy, that philosophy is nothing more than a succession of individual lives, each with an outlook on the universe peculiarly its own and passing away with the philosopher's life ; it means that the continuity of philosophy is not objective but spiritual continuity, it is the continuity of a dialogue carried on across the centuries, in which the personality of the interlocutors is the connecting link. Philosophy like science is a process of discovery, but it is a discovery of principles rather than facts, and principles are subjective in the meaning that they refer to the working of the mind in the search for truth.

The distinction between facts and principles arose at the very beginning of the modern scientific era. In a sense modern science begins with a challenge to long accepted principles and an appeal to facts against principles, and

in the scientific development the autonomy of facts and
the subservience of principles became the oriflamme of
the new scientific spirit in its struggle with authority
for emancipation.

Descartes, in a letter to his friend Père Mersenne, in
1638, on the subject of his recently published *Discours de
Méthode*, says : " You ask me if I consider what I have
written on refraction to be a demonstration. My answer is,
yes ; at least so far as it is possible to give a demonstration
without first demonstrating the principles of physics by
metaphysics. This I hope some day to do, but up to now
it has not been done." This demonstration of the principles
of physics exactly describes the task which Leibniz half a
century later kept constantly before him in all his philosophical work. He sought to demonstrate the principles
of physics by metaphysics. To interpret observations and
experiments we must have a metaphysical basis of physics.
His insistence on the necessity brought him into sharp
conflict with Newton. In the twentieth century physics
has come to recognize its dependence on metaphysics, and
Leibniz's original criticism of Newton has been justified.
It is Leibniz's view of space and time, and not Newton's,
which gives modern physics its metaphysical background.

There are two principles which we owe to Leibniz.
One concerns the nature of the real, the other the know-
ability of the real. The first is that reality is activity and
that substance, *ousia*, the *being* of the real, must therefore
be conceived not as an inert substratum but as force. The
second is that knowledge is ideal, we do not know the
universe in its reality, we only know it representatively,
that is ideally. Both principles follow from the recognition
of the fact that our outlook on the universe is from an
unchanging centralized position of individual activity.
This position is fixed for us absolutely by our nature and
we have no power to vary it. The system of the universe
is not surveyed from without or even inwardly contem-

plated, it is an extrapolation of our inner experience. In all its changes the universe must adapt itself continually to our unchanging position at its centre.

To common sense this is a paradox, and as philosophers we have to come to terms with the fact that the two principles run counter to the whole bias of our mentality. They contradict the almost universal interpretation we make of our experience in practical life. To common sense it seems indubitable that we contemplate the universe in which we move freely and exercise as individuals the special functions of our living organism. We seem to be disinterested observers of a world indifferent to us, a world which we may convert to our uses but which is effectively independent and outside. The reality of the universe we regard as essentially revealed to us in our knowledge, however limited may be our power of apprehension. It seems to us absurd to suppose that the universe adapts itself to our standpoint.

Physical science with its strong bent towards practical utility, with its driving force in human economic activity, has always hitherto based itself on the common-sense view, the view that in knowledge an object existing effectively outside the mind is by reason of a real relation between the object and the mind known as it really is. At times, disturbed by the contradictions and paradoxes in the fundamental concepts of space, time, matter and movement, philosophers have recognized that the common-sense view is an assumption, yet in the interest of science the assumption has seemed necessary. And not seldom philosophy has set itself the task of reconciling the inconsistencies of common sense in the interest of objective science. In the latest developments of the mathematico-physical sciences, however, the case is completely altered, and the whole direction of theoretical scientific reasoning has been reversed. Modern science has found it necessary, in its own interest, to reject definitely the " outside theory

of knowledge,'' and to recognize as a condition of all
observation of the phenomena of nature the necessary
position of the observer as himself within the system he is
observing, and by that position himself laying down a
priori the conditions to which the observations must
conform.

This revolutionary conception of the a priori conditions
of scientific observation and experiment, which characterizes twentieth-century science, is not due to the direct
influence of the philosophy of Leibniz or to a rediscovery
of its principles, yet it is not without significance that
precisely the defects which Leibniz indicated in the metaphysical basis of the Newtonian physics have called for a
reconstruction of the whole framework of physical science.

The two metaphysical principles which lie at the basis
of physical science in its new orientation are identical with
the two principles of Leibniz, although we cannot claim
for Leibniz that he had any preconception of the actual
course of scientific development.   It was, indeed, quite
impossible that anyone in the seventeenth and eighteenth
centuries should have foreseen or could have anticipated
the scientific discoveries of the nineteenth century and the
scientific revolution of the twentieth.   In the modern
conception of the universe there are two new theories
which completely reverse the notion of the fundamental
nature of physical reality—the electrical theory of matter
and the relativity theory of space and time.   Each of these
is based on the metaphysical principles of Leibniz.   Before
we consider them let us set side by side the old world-view
and the new.

The old world-view assumed that the physical universe
was an indestructible, inert material, forming masses of
various degrees of condensation, localized in an absolute,
boundless extension or space, and altering the relative
disposition of its parts in an absolute succession or time.

The new world-view considers the universe to be the

assemblage of all events. Events are related by the distance which separates them in space and the interval which separates them in time. Distances and intervals are not absolute but vary for observers in different frames of reference moving relatively to one another. The aspect of the universe, its materiality, is determined for the observer of the events by the frame of reference which supplies the axes of co-ordination (the length, breadth, depth and time axes) by which he measures the distances and intervals. Co-ordination depends on the subjective condition that the system which supplies the observer with the frame of reference is for him at rest, whatever be its relative movement for observers in other systems.

This is a condensed statement but it may serve to make clear in what respect the new world-view is in accord with the metaphysical principle of Leibniz. It will be evident at once that the scientific principle is the objective form of Leibniz's principle of individuality. If we replace Leibniz's theoretical activity of the monad which consists in perception with the practical activity of an observer co-ordinating or measuring, we shall see that the physical principle is identical with the metaphysical principle.

Let us now look at the two concepts of modern physics, the atomic or electronic system and the space-time continuum.

The atom in the present atomic theory is not, as the retention of the term might imply, the physical unit of the older theory. It is not simple, or unitary, or indivisible, but composite and a system. On the other hand, it is not a metaphysical unit ; it is not to be identified with the monad or simple substance. It is conceived as an energetical system of opposing strains or forces in momentary, more or less stable equilibrium. The modern atomic theory is not, like the old atomic theory, an attempt to carry the analysis of the matter of common-sense experience to its ultimate constitution. The new theory is, on the contrary, an intellectual construction, a mathematical schematization of the microcosmic forces which lie behind the macrocosmic appearances. There is in the modern theory no direct or indirect influence of Leibniz, yet it is impossible not to recognize that it is only by the metaphysical principles on which he was continually insisting, and which he was never weary of interpreting, that the method and result of the modern physical construction can be rationalized. A comparison may make the meaning clear. The preformation theory was, as we have seen, the scientific theory which appealed to Leibniz as offering the strongest physical confirmation of his metaphysical principle. There is a curious analogy between it and the modern atomic theory. Both conceive the inferior limits of the analysis of physical reality to be systems. We never pass from the system to elements not systems, out of which the systems are constructed. The principle of individuality will not permit us to construct the individual of elements which are not individual. This is the reason for rejecting mathematical points or indivisible atoms as the basis of physical reality. Suppose, now, that Leibniz had known the modern atomic theory, its electronic systems would certainly not have seemed to claim the place of his monads, but his monads would have been completely at home in the electronic systems. Even the hydrogen atom, which science places at the bottom of the atomic table, would assume the dimensions of the universe to a monad perceiving from within. In fact, Leibniz could have applied his monadic principle to the present theory precisely in the way he applied the principle of entelechy to the preformation theory, when he argued that not only the mind or dominant monad but the body or system of subservient monads could, from the physical standpoint, contract or shrink to infinity. It may be that the modern atomic theory is destined to be outworn and cast aside, as the preformation theory has been discarded, but if so it will be when the metaphysical principles have found a sounder physical conception for their embodiment.

The modern mathematical theory of the four-dimensional continuum in which the three spatial and one temporal dimensions are co-variable is in very remarkable accord with Leibniz's metaphysical principles, although the development of the theory, mathematical and physical, has been quite independent. In expounding Leibniz's doctrine of space and time we have already had occasion to call attention to the remarkable way in which it anticipates the modern relativity principle. What is more remarkable is the way in which the principle of individuality and the principle of the identity of indiscernibles find their complete exemplification in the modern scientific principle. The universe, as we are now taught to think of it, is the assemblage or sum total of events. For all observers of natural phenomena events are separated by a distance in space and an interval in time. An observer can only measure distances and intervals by means of a co-ordinate system, that is, by referring to a space-time framework in which measuring rod and clock have a constant value and record equal spaces in equal times. There is no system of reference to which an observer is attached which is not moving relatively to other systems within the universe. For example, a terrestrial observer is attached to the moving earth. It would seem, then, that to be true measurements universally applicable, every observer's observations require to be corrected or adjusted to allow for the movement of the system from which the observation is being made. Only when the absolute movement of the system is calculated and allowed for can the real distance and interval between the observed events be determined. Such a correction and adjustment was formerly assumed to be not only theoretically possible but practically available. Newton, following Galileo, used the fixed stars as an absolute system of reference for all astronomical moving systems. Modern experiments designed to test the variation of the velocity of light consequent on the movement of the source (experiments which are famous and universally acknowledged) have falsified the assumption that there is an absolute system of reference by which absolute movement can be determined. The absolute space and time of the classical mechanics is found to have no existence ; that is to say, physics cannot utilize such a system if it exists and has not even a theoretical interest in postulating its existence. This has led to the formulation of the principle of relativity. The ground of this principle is the discovery that a subjective condition governs the employment of all co-ordinate systems used by observers of the phenomena of nature. This subjective condition is that the system to which the observer is attached, and for which his space-time co-ordinates are valid, is at rest relatively to all other systems. The objective counterpart of this condition is the fact that the velocity of light *in vacuo* is constant for all observers, independently of the relative movements of the systems of reference to which they are attached. Under this condition it is impossible to determine absolute motion by any experiment whatever, and the hypothesis of relativity is, therefore, that the phenomena of nature will be the same to two observers who move with any uniform velocity whatever relatively to one another. This is now distinguished as the special theory of relativity because it refers only to the conceptions of space and time, and it is with those we are here concerned.

While it is true that this modern development was in no way anticipated or even implied in the ideas of Leibniz regarding the physical universe, it is certainly arguable that the facts on which the modern principle of relativity is founded are rationalized by his metaphysical principles, particularly the principle of individuality and the principle of the identity of indiscernibles, and cannot be rationalized by any other. What corresponds in Leibniz's theory to the systems of reference to which observers are attached is the spheres of activity or ranges of effective action which form zones as it were round the individual activities of the monads. Every monad has, according to Leibniz, its sphere of activity or range of effective action. The whole universe is mirrored in its perception, but the sphere of its efficiency may vary infinitely, expanding or contracting. In all these changes of the monad's range of action the universe adapts itself to the monad's outlook, remaining always identical in its dimensions to the monad, however the system of reference or range of the monad's action may vary, viewed, as the older philosophy might have expressed it, from God's unchanging standpoint. The principle may be illustrated in a way which will apply equally to the Leibnizian monad or to the " observer " of modern physics. Suppose (as we easily may, however extravagant the supposition may appear) that a terrestrial observer should shrink in all his proportions to such a degree that the solar system had become an atomic system. The earth would then, according to the hypothesis, be no more than a rotating electron revolving round a central proton or sun. According to the principle of relativity, and according to Leibniz's principle of indiscernibles, the space-time co-ordinates of the old system would retain the same ratio in the new, the observer would still say that ninety million miles of space and eight minutes of time for the propagation of light separate his new earth from his new sun. To observers in other systems he and his world would be infinitesimal but to himself there would be no change. The difference between the two systems of reference is indiscernible ; to the observer who has passed from the one to the other they are identical.

We have, it is true, when applying Leibniz's metaphysics to the concepts of modern physics, to remember that Leibniz has taken living activity as the basis of reality, whereas the scientific concept of energy is mechanistic, and physics is ever seeking to discover the laws of a non-living world as the condition of living activity. What modern science has come to recognize, however, is that the physical reality it requires can only be attained by an active work of ideal construction, and such work can only be undertaken from individual standpoints under subjective conditions of observation.

IV

RETROSPECT AND PROSPECT

THE extreme variety in the number and kind of ideas with which Leibniz has enriched the intellectual world, combined with the absolute unity of principle and method by which he has interpreted them, above all the conception of the essential unity of the spiritual and the material, of the natural and the moral world, must raise in our minds the highest admiration of his extraordinary genius. Yet more than by any account of his manifold activities, of the fertility of his imagination and the fecundity of his ideas, his philosophical leadership is revealed in the way he conceived the task of philosophy and the nature of its special problem.

The task of philosophy, as it presented itself to Leibniz, was to construct the system of reality from a solipsistic basis. The solipsistic starting-point is not theoretical, it is pure, immediate, fact of experience. The mind is centralized within the system of the real and it comes to self-consciousness, apperceives itself, as an activity of perceiving with a universe ideally represented in its perceptions. I know myself as a spiritual activity expressing my activity in actions through a corporeal reality, my body. This knowing can only proceed from my own experience and can only refer to my own experience. Ideas cannot enter my mind from without by any natural process which can be made intelligible. My knowledge must therefore take account of the basic, immediate, unequivocal fact, that all cognitive activity is solipsistic. Leibniz expressed this in a picturesque image : The

monads have no windows.　It is the essence of his doctrine.
Those who have tried to explain it away or soften the
harshness of the paradox in the interest of common sense,
have either shown their inability to grasp his meaning or
their failure to perceive the real problem of philosophy.
Leibniz was always satirizing the opposite view, the view
that ideas are a mental stuff, a *species intelligibilis*, a kind
of pictorial representation of themselves, given off by
independent things, floating about on their own account,
seeking entrance into minds.

Solipsism is almost invariably regarded as philosophical
lunacy.　It is identified with the megalomaniac theory that
there is no existence other than that of the ideas in the mind
of a knower.　Were anyone to assert as his genuine belief
that other minds had no existence save only as ideas in his
mind, it would clearly be impossible to refute him by
argument, but his belief would carry no conviction.　Such
a solipsism is often supposed to be implicit in the concept
of the windowless monad.　Were it a mere misunderstanding we might pass it by, but it is a common criticism
in philosophical dialectic.　It apparently arises by conversion of the simple and obviously true proposition " The
world is my idea " into the extravagantly absurd proposition " My idea is the world."

The recognition of the solipsistic position as simple
unmistakable fact of experience is indeed the beginning
of philosophical wisdom.　No truth is so little in need of
proof as the proposition " The world is my idea."　Leibniz
was the first to give it prominence and full expression.
However much our knowledge grows, however intimate
becomes our acquaintance with other minds, with those
who live or have lived or will live, our knowledge never
changes from ideality to reality, never ceases to be
privately owned.　We never pass out of our self.　The
great merit of Leibniz is that, while recognizing this fact
in its fullest significance, he yet saw that we can know the

universe without transcending in any way our individual self-centred experience. Indeed only because we cannot transcend the self can we know what is other than ourself without passing into that other and ceasing to be self. Knowing is an ideal relation not a real relation, that is, it is not a relation of interacting objects but of individual subjects.

How, then, can pure subjective experience become objective knowledge ? If the mind cannot issue from itself, and if there is no intelligible way by which what is without can enter in, how can knowledge acquire validity ? More especially, if with Leibniz we hold that the only reality effectively confronting the mind as outside it is constituted of other minds, how do these minds communicate, and what is the nature of their intercourse ? Before recalling Leibniz's own solution in his theory of perception, let us look at the problem from the general standpoint of philosophy and state briefly the idealist answer.

There is one realm of human experience in which we have a case in point of the mind externalizing itself, expressing outwardly its inward intuition, giving objective form to what is essentially spiritual meaning ; this is the realm of artistic production, or of what in philosophy we name æsthetic activity. The artist in producing a work of art gives expression to his intuition. The artistic work is a process from within outwards. Art is essentially spiritual activity even when its embodiment is material. Nothing in a work of art which belongs to its artistic character comes from without into the mind. It is true that to give complete externalization to his expression the artist needs material and this material he does not create. But it is equally true that this material does not enter the mind from without or impose itself on the mind. So far as the pure artistic work is concerned the material is chosen *ad hoc* and utilized for a special purpose. If then we concentrate attention on what is essential in artistic production we may find the clue to the solution of the whole problem of knowledge, for we may see how a purely internal, self-contained, autonomous, subjective power or force, in the process of active self-development, in passing from potentiality to actuality, exteriorizes itself and becomes objective. Artists are not a special class of rational minds, great artists are only those who exemplify in a high or superlative degree what is common to human nature. Every one can verify, by reflection on his own experience, the æsthetic activity by which his intuitions find expression in objective imagery without ever passing out of his possession. If this be true with regard to imagination and the artistic faculty, is it different with regard to understanding and the logical faculty? The idealist principle in philosophy is that it is not. It is our concepts and judgments which invest the physical world with an independent outside reality or thinghood, and in this conceptual activity we are no more issuing out of ourselves than in artistic production. Concepts no more than images besiege the mind from without. They are inwardly formed and express what we regard as laws of nature. Not alone on its formal side but also on its material side, knowledge is the constructive work of the mind in interpreting experience. This, briefly stated, and in its extreme generality, is the idealist position in philosophy.

It follows from this principle that systems of philosophy are really of the nature of works of art. Leibniz's system of the pre-established harmony, his conception of the City of God, his idea of creation and preformation, are, like the great works of art, the constructive work of the philosopher's mind in expressing his rationalizing activity of interpreting his own experience. We must say the same of the theories and hypotheses of modern physics. The objective reference in knowledge is no less real for an idealism, which takes account of the essential fact that the mind can only express what exists already intuitively in its nature, just as a tree can only bear the fruit which by nature it is fitted to produce, than it is for a realism with its outside theory of knowledge as revelation.

The recognition of the solipsistic basis of the idealist construction of the system of the real by no means precludes the possibility of rationalizing a scheme of inter-subjective intercourse; on the contrary, it affords the only ground of the possibility of intercourse. Intercourse is not a real but an ideal relation between minds. It supposes no invasion of one mind by another, no interchange of content real or ideal. What intercourse implies is the possibility of the internal responsive expression of one mind to the outward expression of its own intuition by another. Such expressive response depends on the natural accord of similar subjective natures, and only where there is such accord is there the possibility of intercourse.

With these principles the philosophy of Leibniz is in complete agreement, expressed in the imagery and concepts which were the intellectual patrimony of his historical period. Let us recall his theory of perception. In perception the mind represents to itself the influences which are pouring in upon it from every point in the universe. The universe, Leibniz says, is mirrored in every monad's perception. Our knowledge of the universe is not received by contemplating the reflection in the mirror. The mind does not look on the mirror as one regards the reflection of his face in a glass, it experiences the universe as opposition felt within to an activity developing outwards. The mind represents the opposition it is meeting by sense imagery formed by itself from within. The degree in which this perception grows in clearness and distinctness marks the rise of the monad in the rational hierarchy. The mind can never transcend its limitations. However high it rises in the scale of existence its perception of the universe is its own self-limitation viewed from within and internal   The universe is revealed to the mind in the fullness of its reality and is known as it is in itself, but the knowledge of it is ideal; for in its immediacy it is opposition, which the mind must interpret, and this interpretation is a mathematical and metaphysical work of ideal construction.

We may say, then, that Leibniz was the first philosopher of the modern period to indicate the true way of idealism, and we may claim without exaggeration that the modern world has adopted his view. It is nothing to the point that his own system of the pre-established harmony, his views of creation, preformation and development, have all been thrown aside as outworn creeds and discredited hypotheses. We to-day conceive the task of philosophy and science as he conceived it, and if our theories and hypotheses are destined in their turn to become old-fashioned and discarded it will be when they are replaced by more adequate ones. What lives of Leibniz in the thought of to-day is the principle and method to which more than any philosopher in the modern period he has given forcible expression.

BIBLIOGRAPHY

A complete edition of the Works of Leibniz, including all the papers in the Library of Hanover, is in course of publication under the direction of the Akademie der Wissenschaften of Berlin (see page 5).

The Collected Editions are:

1. L. DUTENS. *Leibnitii Opera Omnia.* 6 vols. Geneva, 1768.
2. G. H. PERTZ. *Leibnizens gesammalte Werke.* 12 vols. Berlin, 1843-63.
3. FOUCHER DE CAREIL. Paris, 1859-75. Seven volumes published.
4. ONNO KLOPP. *Die Werke von Leibniz.* 10 vols. 1864-77.

The Editions of the Philosophical Works are:

1. RASPE. *Œuvres philosophiques latines et françoises.* Amsterdam and Leipsic, 1765.
2. J. E. ERDMANN. *Leibnitii Opera Philosophica.* 1 vol. 1840.
3. A. JACQUES. *Œuvres de Leibniz.* 2 vols. Paris, 1846.
4. PAUL JANET. *Œuvres philosophiques.* 2 vols. Paris, 1866.
5. C. J. GERHARDT. *Die philosophischen Schriften von G. W. Leibniz.* 7 vols. 1875-90.

The English Translations are:

1. R. LATTA. *The Monadology and other Writings.* Oxford, 1898.
2. G. M. DUNCAN. *The Philosophical Works of Leibniz.* New Haven, 1890.
3. A. G. LANGLEY. *The New Essays.* London, 1894.
4. G. R. MONTGOMERY. *Discourse on Metaphysics, Correspondence with Arnauld, and Monadology.* Open Court Publishing Co.

INDEX

ÆSTHETIC, 175
Aquinas, St. Thomas, 119
Aristotle, 78, 129, 139, 168, 188
Arnauld, 16, 22
Augustine, St., 127

BÁLE, Council of, 20
Barbarus, Hermolaus, 141
Bayle, 4, 34, 35, 108
Berkeley, 43, 74, 167, 191
Bossuet, 17, 18, 21
Boyneburg, 10, 13
Brinon, Madame de, 18
Bruno, 54
Brunswick-Lüneburg, Duke of, 13

CALCULUS, 17, 48
Calixtins, 20
Caroline, Princess of Wales, 47
Catholic Reunion, 17
Charles II, 5
Christina, Queen of Sweden, 17, 36
Clarke, Dr. Samuel, 47, 153
Condillac, 167, 195
Constance, Council of, 20
Cosmological Argument, 118

DARWINIAN THEORY, 140, 147
Democritus, 53, 103, 114

Descartes, 26, 31, 37, 76, 85, 204
Dodard, 63

EPIGENESIS, 99

FONTENELLE, 9, 14
Force, 86

GALILEO, 209
Gassendi, 26
George I, 14

HANSCHIUS, GOTTLIEB, 179
Harvey, 99
Hegel, 182
Hesse-Rheinfels, Ernest of, 21
Hobbes, 26, 88
Hume, 43, 167, 192, 200
Huygens, 31, 106

JAMES II, 7
Jansenists, 16
Joseph I, 12

KANT, 45, 117, 163, 167, 175, 187, 189
Ker of Kersland, 55

LEEUWENHOEK, 63, 68, 97, 102
Locke, 4, 43, 44, 153, 165
Louis XIV, 4, 6, 12
Luxembourg, Duke of, 35

EPIC AND ROMANCE
by W. P. Ker

This classic work by a great Medieval scholar is a fascinating description of the principal forms of narrative literature that emerged from the Middle Ages. Focusing upon Epic and Romance as products, respectively, of the "heroic age" and the "age of chivalry", the author examines these forms in general and then proceeds to a specific discussion of the contributions of three major schools — the Teutonic Epic, the French Epic, and the Icelandic Histories.

The Teutonic Epic is considered in the light of its tragic conception, scale of treatment, and style. A list of extant poems and fragments in the older Teutonic languages is included. **Beowulf** is discussed and analyzed separately. Then, moving on to the Icelandic Sagas, the author examines Iceland's place in the heroic tradition, matter and form in the sagas, tragic imagination, comedy, the art of narrative, northern prose romances, and other like topics. He follows this with a discussion of the Old French Epic (chansons de geste) and Romance and the Old French Romantic Schools. Competition of epic and romance in the 12th century, comedy, "humors", romantic additions to heroic styles, blending of classical and Celtic influences are among the subjects covered.

Besides the Homeric epics and **Beowulf**, this volume considers such works as **Maldon, Roland, Alboin,** the **Helgi** poems, **Volospa, Laxdaela, Roman de Troie, Tristram, Flamenca, Troilus and Criseyde,** and many others.

Index. xxiv + 398pp. 5⅜ x 8.

T355 Paperbound $1.95

GUIDE TO PHILOSOPHY
by C. E. M. Joad

Joad's GUIDE TO PHILOSOPHY examines systematically the central questions of all philosophical thought since classical times: Is there a plan to the universe? Is mind unique and independent, or a mere secretion of the brain? Is there such a thing as free will?

These and similar questions in theory of knowledge, critical and constructive metaphysics are examined, for the most part, in terms of opposed solutions: subjective idealism vs. realism, teleology vs. chance, causation vs. temporalism, logical positivism vs. vitalism and modern idealism.

Under each problem are considered the solutions and contributions of the great philosophers: Plato, Aristotle, the Scholastics, Kant, Hegel, Leibniz, William James, Whitehead, and many others.

This clear and impartial book by the most gifted expositor in modern philosophy is written for the intelligent reader without specialized training in philosophy. It is not simply a catalogue of varied opinions about varied questions, but a brilliant integration of the greatest problems in human life, done with full awareness of modern needs and special problems.

"The finest introduction to philosophy," BOSTON TRANSCRIPT. "Especially successful in relating classical difficulties to . . . modern physics," JOURNAL OF PHILOSOPHY.

Classified bibliography. Index. 592pp.

T138 Paperbound. **$1.95**

LANGUAGE, TRUTH AND LOGIC by A. J. Ayer

First published in 1936, this first full-length presentation in English of the Logical Positivism of Carnap, Neurath, and others has gone through 10 printings to become a classic of thought and communication. It not only surveys one of the most important areas of modern thought; it also shows you how to apply analytical methods to your own field of work and dispel the confusion that arises from imperfect understanding of the uses of language. A first-rate antidote for fuzzy thought and muddled writing, this remarkable book has helped philosophers, writers, speakers, teachers, students, and general readers alike.

Mr. Ayer sets up specific tests by which you can easily evaluate statements of ideas. You will also learn how to distinguish ideas that cannot be verified by experience — those expressing religious, moral, or aesthetic experience, those expounding theological or metaphysical doctrine, and those dealing with a priori truth. The basic thesis of this work is that philosophy should not squander its energies upon the unknowable, but should perform its proper function in criticism and analysis.

PARTIAL CONTENTS: Elimination of metaphysics, Function of philosophy. Nature of philosophic analysis. The a priori. Truth and probability. Critique of ethics and theology. The self and the common world. Solutions of outstanding philosophical disputes.

"A delightful book...I should like to have written it myself," Bertrand Russell.

Index. 160 pp. 5⅜ x 8.   T10 Paperbound **$1.25**

THE MYSTERIES OF MITHRA
by Franz Cumont

This is the definitive coverage of a great ideological struggle between the west and the orient in the first centuries of the Christian era. At this time, Mithraism, a mystery religion originating in Persia, spread rapidly through the Roman Empire, and achieved such strength that Europe almost became Mithraic. Dr. Cumont, the world's greatest authority on aspects of classical religions, here discusses the origins of this colorful oriental religion, and its association with the Roman army. Then utilizing fragmentary monuments and texts, in one of the greatest feats of scholarly detection, he reconstructs the mystery teachings and secret doctrines, the hidden organization and cult of Mithra. Mithraic art is discussed, analyzed, and shown in 70 illustrations. 239pp. 5⅜ x 8.

Paperbound **$1.50**

Catalog
of
DOVER BOOKS

BOOKS EXPLAINING SCIENCE

(Note: The books listed under this category are general introductions, surveys, reviews, and non-technical expositions of science for the interested layman or scientist who wishes to brush up. Dover also publishes the largest list of inexpensive reprints of books on intermediate and higher mathematics, mathematical physics, engineering, chemistry, astronomy, etc., for the professional mathematician or scientist. For our complete Science Catalog, write Dept. catrr., Dover Publications, Inc., 180 Varick Street, New York 14, N. Y.)

CONCERNING THE NATURE OF THINGS, Sir William Bragg. Royal Institute Christmas Lectures by Nobel Laureate. Excellent plain-language introduction to gases, molecules, crystal structure, etc. explains "building blocks" of universe, basic properties of matter, with simplest, clearest examples, demonstrations. 32pp. of photos; 57 figures. 244pp. 5⅜ x 8.

T31 Paperbound **$1.35**

MATTER AND LIGHT, THE NEW PHYSICS, Louis de Broglie. Non-technical explanations by a Nobel Laureate of electro-magnetic theory, relativity, wave mechanics, quantum physics, philosophies of science, etc. Simple, yet accurate introduction to work of Planck, Bohr, Einstein, other modern physicists. Only 2 of 12 chapters require mathematics. 300pp. 5⅜ x 8.

T35 Paperbound **$1.60**

THE COMMON SENSE OF THE EXACT SCIENCES, W. K. Clifford. For 70 years, Clifford's work has been acclaimed as one of the clearest, yet most precise introductions to mathematical symbolism, measurement, surface boundaries, position, space, motion, mass and force, etc. Prefaces by Bertrand Russell and Karl Pearson. Introduction by James Newman. 130 figures. 249pp. 5⅜ x 8.

T61 Paperbound **$1.60**

THE NATURE OF LIGHT AND COLOUR IN THE OPEN AIR, M. Minnaert. What causes mirages? haloes? "multiple" suns and moons? Professor Minnaert explains these and hundreds of other fascinating natural optical phenomena in simple terms, tells how to observe them, suggests hundreds of experiments. 200 illus; 42 photos. xvi + 362pp.

T196 Paperbound **$1.95**

SPINNING TOPS AND GYROSCOPIC MOTION, John Perry. Classic elementary text on dynamics of rotation treats gyroscopes, tops, how quasi-rigidity is induced in paper disks, smoke rings, chains, etc, by rapid motion, precession, earth's motion, etc. Contains many easy-to-perform experiments. Appendix on practical uses of gyroscopes. 62 figures. 128pp.

T416 Paperbound **$1.00**

A CONCISE HISTORY OF MATHEMATICS, D. Struik. This lucid, easily followed history of mathematics from the Ancient Near East to modern times requires no mathematical background itself, yet introduces both mathematicians and laymen to basic concepts and discoveries and the men who made them. Contains a collection of 31 portraits of eminent mathematicians. Bibliography. xix + 299pp. 5⅜ x 8.

T255 Paperbound **$1.75**

THE RESTLESS UNIVERSE, Max Born. A remarkably clear, thorough exposition of gases, electrons, ions, waves and particles, electronic structure of the atom, nuclear physics, written for the layman by a Nobel Laureate. "Much more thorough and deep than most attempts . . . easy and delightful," CHEMICAL AND ENGINEERING NEWS. Includes 7 animated sequences showing motion of molecules, alpha particles, etc. 11 full-page plates of photographs. Total of nearly 600 illus. 315pp. 6⅛ x 9¼.

T412 Paperbound **$2.00**

WHAT IS SCIENCE?, N. Campbell. The role of experiment, the function of mathematics, the nature of scientific laws, the limitations of science, and many other provocative topics are explored without technicalities by an eminent scientist. "Still an excellent introduction to scientific philosophy," H. Margenau in PHYSICS TODAY. 192pp. 5⅜ x 8.

S43 Paperbound **$1.25**

FADS AND FALLACIES IN THE NAME OF SCIENCE, Martin Gardner. The standard account of the various cults, quack systems and delusions which have recently masqueraded as science: hollow earth theory, Atlantis, dianetics, Reich's orgone theory, flying saucers, Bridey Murphy, psionics, irridiagnosis, many other fascinating fallacies that deluded tens of thousands. "Should be read by everyone, scientist and non-scientist alike," R. T. Birge, Prof. Emeritus, Univ. of California; Former President, American Physical Society. Formerly titled, "In the Name of Science." Revised and enlarged edition. x + 365pp. 5⅜ x 8.
T394 Paperbound **$1.50**

THE STUDY OF THE HISTORY OF MATHEMATICS, THE STUDY OF THE HISTORY OF SCIENCE, G. Sarton. Two books bound as one. Both volumes are standard introductions to their fields by an eminent science historian. They discuss problems of historical research, teaching, pitfalls, other matters of interest to the historically oriented writer, teacher, or student. Both have extensive bibliographies. 10 illustrations. 188pp. 5⅜ x 8. T240 Paperbound **$1.25**

THE PRINCIPLES OF SCIENCE, W. S. Jevons. Unabridged reprinting of a milestone in the development of symbolic logic and other subjects concerning scientific methodology, probability, inferential validity, etc. Also describes Jevons' "logic machine," an early precursor of modern electronic calculators. Preface by E. Nagel. 839pp. 5⅜ x 8. S446 Paperbound **$2.98**

SCIENCE THEORY AND MAN, Erwin Schroedinger. Complete, unabridged reprinting of "Science and the Human Temperament" plus an additional essay "What is an Elementary Particle?" Nobel Laureate Schroedinger discusses many aspects of modern physics from novel points of view which provide unusual insights for both laymen and physicists. 192 pp. 5⅜ x 8.
T428 Paperbound **$1.35**

BRIDGES AND THEIR BUILDERS, D. B. Steinman & S. R. Watson. Information about ancient, medieval, modern bridges; how they were built; who built them; the structural principles employed; the materials they are built of; etc. Written by one of the world's leading authorities on bridge design and construction. New, revised, expanded edition. 23 photos; 26 line drawings, xvii + 401pp. 5⅜ x 8. T431 Paperbound **$1.95**

HISTORY OF MATHEMATICS, D. E. Smith. Most comprehensive non-technical history of math in English. In two volumes. Vol. I: A chronological examination of the growth of mathematics from primitive concepts up to 1900. Vol. II: The development of ideas in specific fields and areas, up through elementary calculus. The lives and works of over a thousand mathematicians are covered; thousands of specific historical problems and their solutions are clearly explained. Total of 510 illustrations, 1355pp. 5⅜ x 8. Set boxed in attractive container. T429, T430 Paperbound, the set **$5.00**

PHILOSOPHY AND THE PHYSICISTS, L. S. Stebbing. A philosopher examines the philosophical implications of modern science by posing a lively critical attack on the popular science expositions of Sir James Jeans and Arthur Eddington. xvi + 295pp. 5⅜ x 8.
T480 Paperbound **$1.65**

ON MATHEMATICS AND MATHEMATICIANS, R. E. Moritz. The first collection of quotations by and about mathematicians in English. 1140 anecdotes, aphorisms, definitions, speculations, etc. give both mathematicians and layman stimulating new insights into what mathematics is, and into the personalities of the great mathematicians from Archimedes to Euler, Gauss, Klein, Weierstrass. Invaluable to teachers, writers. Extensive cross index. 410pp. 5⅜ x 8.
T489 Paperbound **$1.95**

NATURAL SCIENCE, BIOLOGY, GEOLOGY, TRAVEL

A SHORT HISTORY OF ANATOMY AND PHYSIOLOGY FROM THE GREEKS TO HARVEY, C. Singer. A great medical historian's fascinating intermediate account of the slow advance of anatomical and physiological knowledge from pre-scientific times to Vesalius, Harvey. 139 unusually interesting illustrations. 221pp. 5⅜ x 8. T389 Paperbound **$1.75**

THE BEHAVIOUR AND SOCIAL LIFE OF HONEYBEES, Ronald Ribbands. The most comprehensive, lucid and authoritative book on bee habits, communication, duties, cell life, motivations, etc. "A MUST for every scientist, experimenter, and educator, and a happy and valuable selection for all interested in the honeybee," AMERICAN BEE JOURNAL. 690-item bibliography. 127 illus.; 11 photographic plates. 352pp. 5⅜ x 8⅜. S410 Clothbound **$4.50**

TRAVELS OF WILLIAM BARTRAM, edited by Mark Van Doren. One of the 18th century's most delightful books, and one of the few first-hand sources of information about American geography, natural history, and anthropology of American Indian tribes of the time. "The mind of a scientist with the soul of a poet," John Livingston Lowes. 13 original illustrations, maps. Introduction by Mark Van Doren. 448pp. 5⅜ x 8. T326 Paperbound **$2.00**

STUDIES ON THE STRUCTURE AND DEVELOPMENT OF VERTEBRATES, Edwin Goodrich. The definitive study of the skeleton, fins and limbs, head region, divisions of the body cavity, vascular, respiratory, excretory systems, etc., of vertebrates from fish to higher mammals, by the greatest comparative anatomist of recent times. "The standard textbook," JOURNAL OF ANATOMY. 754 illus. 69-page biographical study. 1186-item bibliography. 2 vols. Total of 906pp. 5⅜ x 8.
Vol. I: S449 Paperbound **$2.50**
Vol. II: S450 Paperbound **$2.50**

DOVER BOOKS

THE BIRTH AND DEVELOPMENT OF THE GEOLOGICAL SCIENCES, F. D. Adams. The most complete and thorough history of the earth sciences in print. Covers over 300 geological thinkers and systems; treats fossils, theories of stone growth, paleontology, earthquakes, vulcanists vs. neptunists, odd theories, etc. 91 illustrations, including medieval, Renaissance wood cuts, etc. 632 footnotes and bibliographic notes. 511pp. 308pp. 5⅜ x 8.   T5 Paperbound **$2.00**

FROM MAGIC TO SCIENCE, Charles Singer. A close study of aspects of medical science from the Roman Empire through the Renaissance. The sections on early herbals, and "The Visions of Hildegarde of Bingen," are probably the best studies of these subjects available. 158 unusual classic and medieval illustrations. xxvii + 365pp. 5⅜ x 8.   T390 Paperbound **$2.00**

SAILING ALONE AROUND THE WORLD, Captain Joshua Slocum. Captain Slocum's personal account of his single-handed voyage around the world in a 34-foot boat he rebuilt himself. A classic of both seamanship and descriptive writing. "A nautical equivalent of Thoreau's account," Van Wyck Brooks. 67 illus. 308pp. 5⅜ x 8.   T326 Paperbound **$1.00**

TREES OF THE EASTERN AND CENTRAL UNITED STATES AND CANADA, W. M. Harlow. Standard middle-level guide designed to help you know the characteristics of Eastern trees and identify them at sight by means of an 8-page synoptic key. More than 600 drawings and photographs of twigs, leaves, fruit, other features. xiii + 288pp. 4⅝ x 6½.
T395 Paperbound **$1.35**

FRUIT KEY AND TWIG KEY ("Fruit Key to Northeastern Trees," "Twig Key to Deciduous Woody Plants of Eastern North America"), **W. M. Harlow.** Identify trees in fall, winter, spring. Easy-to-use, synoptic keys, with photographs of every twig and fruit identified. Covers 120 different fruits, 160 different twigs. Over 350 photos. Bibliographies. Glossaries. Total of 143pp. 5⅝ x 8⅜.   T511 Paperbound **$1.25**

INTRODUCTION TO THE STUDY OF EXPERIMENTAL MEDICINE, Claude Bernard. This classic records Bernard's far-reaching efforts to transform physiology into an exact science. It covers problems of vivisection, the limits of physiological experiment, hypotheses in medical experimentation, hundreds of others. Many of his own famous experiments on the liver, the pancreas, etc., are used as examples. Foreword by I. B. Cohen. xxv + 266pp. 5⅜ x 8.
T400 Paperbound **$1.50**

THE ORIGIN OF LIFE, A. I. Oparin. The first modern statement that life evolved from complex nitro-carbon compounds, carefully presented according to modern biochemical knowledge of primary colloids, organic molecules, etc. Begins with historical introduction to the problem of the origin of life. Bibliography. xxv + 270pp. 5⅜ x 8.   S213 Paperbound **$1.75**

A HISTORY OF ASTRONOMY FROM THALES TO KEPLER, J. L. E. Dreyer. The only work in English which provides a detailed picture of man's cosmological views from Egypt, Babylonia, Greece, and Alexandria to Copernicus, Tycho Brahe and Kepler. "Standard reference on Greek astronomy and the Copernican revolution," SKY AND TELESCOPE. Formerly called "A History of Planetary Systems From Thales to Kepler." Bibliography. 21 diagrams. xvii + 430pp. 5⅜ x 8.
S79 Paperbound **$1.98**

URANIUM PROSPECTING, H. L. Barnes. A professional geologist tells you what you need to know. Hundreds of facts about minerals, tests, detectors, sampling, assays, claiming, developing, government regulations, etc. Glossary of technical terms. Annotated bibliography. x + 117pp. 5⅜ x 8.   T309 Paperbound **$1.00**

DE RE METALLICA, Georgius Agricola. All 12 books of this 400 year old classic on metals and metal production, fully annotated, and containing all 289 of the 16th century woodcuts which made the original an artistic masterpiece. A superb gift for geologists, engineers, libraries, artists, historians. Translated by Herbert Hoover & L. H. Hoover. Bibliography, survey of ancient authors. 289 illustrations of the excavating, assaying, smelting, refining, and countless other metal production operations described in the text. 672pp. 6¾ x 10¾. Deluxe library edition.   S6 Clothbound **$10.00**

DE MAGNETE, William Gilbert. A landmark of science by the man who first used the word "electricity," distinguished between static electricity and magnetism, and founded a new science. P. F. Mottelay translation. 90 figures. lix + 368pp. 5⅜ x 8.   S470 Paperbound **$2.00**

THE AUTOBIOGRAPHY OF CHARLES DARWIN AND SELECTED LETTERS, Francis Darwin, ed. Fascinating documents on Darwin's early life, the voyage of the "Beagle," the discovery of evolution, Darwin's thought on mimicry, plant development, vivisection, evolution, many other subjects Letters to Henslow, Lyell, Hooker, Wallace, Kingsley, etc. Appendix. 365pp. 5⅜ x 8.   T479 Paperbound **$1.65**

A WAY OF LIFE AND OTHER SELECTED WRITINGS OF SIR WILLIAM OSLER. 16 of the great physician, teacher and humanist's most inspiring writings on a practical philosophy of life, science and the humanities, and the history of medicine. 5 photographs. Introduction by G. L. Keynes, M.D., F.R.C.S. xx + 278pp. 5⅜ x 8.   T488 Paperbound **$1.50**

LITERATURE

WORLD DRAMA, B. H. Clark. 46 plays from Ancient Greece, Rome, to India, China, Japan. Plays by Aeschylus, Sophocles, Euripides, Aristophanes, Plautus, Marlowe, Jonson, Farquhar, Goldsmith, Cervantes, Molière, Dumas, Goethe, Schiller, Ibsen, many others. One of the most comprehensive collections of important plays from all literature available in English. Over ⅓ of this material is unavailable in any other current edition. Reading lists. 2 volumes. Total of 1364pp. 5⅜ x 8.
Vol. I, T57 Paperbound **$2.00**
Vol. II, T59 Paperbound **$2.00**

MASTERS OF THE DRAMA, John Gassner. The most comprehensive history of the drama in print. Covers more than 800 dramatists and over 2000 plays from the Greeks to modern Western, Near Eastern, Oriental drama. Plot summaries, theatre history, etc. "Best of its kind in English," NEW REPUBLIC. 35 pages of bibliography. 77 photos and drawings. Deluxe edition. xxii + 890pp. 5⅜ x 8.
T100 Clothbound **$5.95**

THE DRAMA OF LUIGI PIRANDELLO, D. Vittorini. All 38 of Pirandello's plays (to 1935) summarized and analyzed in terms of symbolic techniques, plot structure, etc. The only authorized work. Foreword by Pirandello. Biography. Bibliography. xiii + 350pp. 5⅜ x 8.
T435 Paperbound **$1.98**

ARISTOTLE'S THEORY OF POETRY AND THE FINE ARTS, S. H. Butcher, ed. The celebrated "Butcher translation" faced page by page with the Greek text; Butcher's 300-page introduction to Greek poetic, dramatic thought. Modern Aristotelian criticism discussed by John Gassner. lxxvi + 421pp. 5⅜ x 8.
T42 Paperbound **$2.00**

EUGENE O'NEILL: THE MAN AND HIS PLAYS, B. H. Clark. The first published source-book on O'Neill's life and work. Analyzes each play from the early THE WEB up to THE ICEMAN COMETH. Supplies much information about environmental and dramatic influences. ix + 182pp. 5⅜ x 8.
T379 Paperbound **$1.25**

INTRODUCTION TO ENGLISH LITERATURE, B. Dobrée, ed. Most compendious literary aid in its price range. Extensive, categorized bibliography (with entries up to 1949) of more than 5,000 poets, dramatists, novelists, as well as historians, philosophers, economists, religious writers, travellers, and scientists of literary stature. Information about manuscripts, important biographical data. Critical, historical, background works not simply listed, but evaluated. Each volume also contains a long introduction to the period it covers.

Vol. I: **THE BEGINNINGS OF ENGLISH LITERATURE TO SKELTON, 1509, W. L. Renwick. H. Orton.** 450pp. 5⅛ x 7⅛.
T75 Clothbound **$3.50**
Vol. II: **THE ENGLISH RENAISSANCE, 1510-1688, V. de Sola Pinto.** 381pp. 5⅛ x 7⅛.
T76 Clothbound **$3.50**
Vol. III: **THE AUGUSTANS AND ROMANTICS, 1689-1830, H. Dyson, J. Butt.** 320pp. 5⅛ x 7⅛.
T77 Clothbound **$3.50**
Vol. IV: **THE VICTORIANS AND AFTER, 1830-1914, E. Batho, B. Dobrée.** 360pp. 5⅛ x 7⅛.
T78 Clothbound **$3.50**

EPIC AND ROMANCE, W. P. Ker. The standard survey of Medieval epic and romance by a foremost authority on Medieval literature. Covers historical background, plot, literary analysis, significance of Teutonic epics, Icelandic sagas, Beowulf, French chansons de geste, the Niebelungenlied, Arthurian romances, much more. 422pp. 5⅜ x 8.
T355 Paperbound **$1.95**

THE HEART OF EMERSON'S JOURNALS, Bliss Perry, ed. Emerson's most intimate thoughts, impressions, records of conversations with Channing, Hawthorne, Thoreau, etc., carefully chosen from the 10 volumes of The Journals. "The essays do not reveal the power of Emerson's mind . . .as do these hasty and informal writings," N. Y. TIMES. Preface by B. Perry. 370pp. 5⅜ x 8.
T447 Paperbound **$1.85**

A SOURCE BOOK IN THEATRICAL HISTORY, A. M. Nagler. (Formerly, "Sources of Theatrical History.") Over 300 selected passages by contemporary observers tell about styles of acting, direction, make-up, scene designing, etc., in the theatre's great periods from ancient Greece to the Théâtre Libre. "Indispensable complement to the study of drama," EDUCATIONAL THEATRE JOURNAL. Prof. Nagler, Yale Univ. School of Drama, also supplies notes, references. 85 illustrations. 611pp. 5⅜ x 8.
T515 Paperbound **$2.75**

THE ART OF THE STORY-TELLER, M. L. Shedlock. Regarded as the finest, most helpful book on telling stories to children, by a great story-teller. How to catch, hold, recapture attention; how to choose material; many other aspects. Also includes: a 99-page selection of Miss Shedlock's most successful stories; extensive bibliography of other stories. xxi + 320pp. 5⅜ x 8.
T245 Clothbound **$3.50**

THE DEVIL'S DICTIONARY, Ambrose Bierce. Over 1000 short, ironic definitions in alphabetical order, by America's greatest satirist in the classical tradition. "Some of the most gorgeous witticisms in the English language," H. L. Mencken. 144pp. 5⅜ x 8.
T487 Paperbound **$1.00**

MUSIC

A DICTIONARY OF HYMNOLOGY, John Julian. More than 30,000 entries on individual hymns, their authorship, textual variations, location of texts, dates and circumstances of composition, denominational and ritual usages, the biographies of more than 9,000 hymn writers, essays on important topics such as children's hymns and Christmas carols, and hundreds of thousands of other important facts about hymns which are virtually impossible to find anywhere else. Convenient alphabetical listing, and a 200-page double-columned index of first lines enable you to track down virtually any hymn ever written. Total of 1786pp. 6¼ x 9¼. 2 volumes.   T133. The Set, Clothbound **$15.00**

STRUCTURAL HEARING, TONAL COHERENCE IN MUSIC, Felix Salzer. Extends the well-known Schenker approach to include modern music, music of the middle ages, and Renaissance music. Explores the phenomenon of tonal organization by discussing more than 500 compositions, and offers unusual new insights into the theory of composition and musical relationships. "The foundation on which all teaching in music theory has been based at this college," Leopold Mannes, President, The Mannes College of Music. Total of 658pp. 6½ x 9¼. 2 volumes.   S418 The set, Clothbound **$8.00**

A GENERAL HISTORY OF MUSIC, Charles Burney. The complete history of music from the Greeks up to 1789 by the 18th century musical historian who personally knew the great Baroque composers. Covers sacred and secular, vocal and instrumental, operatic and symphonic music; treats theory, notation, forms, instruments; discusses composers, performers, important works. Invaluable as a source of information on the period for students, historians, musicians. "Surprisingly few of Burney's statements have been invalidated by modern research . . . still of great value," NEW YORK TIMES. Edited and corrected by Frank Mercer. 35 figures. 1915pp. 5½ x 8½. 2 volumes.   T36 The set, Clothbound **$12.50**

JOHANN SEBASTIAN BACH, Phillip Spitta. Recognized as one of the greatest accomplishments of musical scholarship and far and away the definitive coverage of Bach's works. Hundreds of individual pieces are analyzed. Major works, such as the B Minor Mass and the St. Matthew Passion are examined in minute detail. Spitta also deals with the works of Buxtehude, Pachelbel, and others of the period. Can be read with profit even by those without a knowledge of the technicalities of musical composition. "Unchallenged as the last word on one of the supreme geniuses of music," John Barkham, SATURDAY REVIEW SYNDICATE. Total of 1819pp. 5⅜ x 8. 2 volumes.   T252 The set, Clothbound **$10.00**

HISTORY

THE IDEA OF PROGRESS, J. B. Bury. Prof. Bury traces the evolution of a central concept of Western civilization in Greek, Roman, Medieval, and Renaissance thought to its flowering in the 17th and 18th centuries. Introduction by Charles Beard. xl + 357pp. 5⅜ x 8.
T39 Clothbound **$3.95**
T40 Paperbound **$1.95**

THE ANCIENT GREEK HISTORIANS, J. B. Bury. Greek historians such as Herodotus, Thucydides, Xenophon; Roman historians such as Tacitus, Caesar, Livy; scores of others fully analyzed in terms of sources, concepts, influences, etc., by a great scholar and historian. 291pp. 5⅜ x 8.   T397 Paperbound **$1.50**

HISTORY OF THE LATER ROMAN EMPIRE, J. B. Bury. The standard work on the Byzantine Empire from 395 A.D. to the death of Justinian in 565 A.D., by the leading Byzantine scholar of our time. Covers political, social, cultural, theological, military history. Quotes contemporary documents extensively. "Most unlikely that it will ever be superseded," Glanville Downey, Dumbarton Oaks Research Library. Genealogical tables. 5 maps. Bibliography. 2 vols. Total of 965pp. 5⅜ x 8.   T398, T399 Paperbound, the set **$4.00**

GARDNER'S PHOTOGRAPHIC SKETCH BOOK OF THE CIVIL WAR, Alexander Gardner. One of the rarest and most valuable Civil War photographic collections exactly reproduced for the first time since 1866. Scenes of Manassas, Bull Run, Harper's Ferry, Appomattox, Mechanicsville, Fredericksburg, Gettysburg, etc.; battle ruins, prisons, arsenals, a slave pen, fortifications; Lincoln on the field, officers, men, corpses. By one of the most famous pioneers in documentary photography. Original copies of the "Sketch Book" sold for $425 in 1952. Introduction by E. Bleiler. 100 full-page 7 x 10 photographs (original size). 244pp. 10¾ x 8½.
T476 Clothbound **$6.00**

THE WORLD'S GREAT SPEECHES, L. Copeland and L. Lamm, eds. 255 speeches from Pericles to Churchill, Dylan Thomas. Invaluable as a guide to speakers; fascinating as history past and present; a source of much difficult-to-find material. Includes an extensive section of informal and humorous speeches. 3 indices: Topic, Author, Nation. xx + 745pp. 5⅜ x 8.
T468 Paperbound **$2.49**

FOUNDERS OF THE MIDDLE AGES, E. K. Rand. The best non-technical discussion of the transformation of Latin paganism into medieval civilization. Tertullian, Gregory, Jerome, Boethius, Augustine, the Neoplatonists, other crucial figures, philosophies examined. Excellent for the intelligent non-specialist. "Extraordinarily accurate," Richard McKeon, THE NATION. ix + 365pp. 5⅜ x 8.   T369 Paperbound **$1.85**

THE POLITICAL THOUGHT OF PLATO AND ARISTOTLE, Ernest Barker. The standard, comprehensive exposition of Greek political thought. Covers every aspect of the "Republic" and the "Politics" as well as minor writings, other philosophers, theorists of the period, and the later history of Greek political thought. Unabridged edition. 584pp. 5⅜ x 8.
T521 Paperbound **$1.85**

PHILOSOPHY

THE GIFT OF LANGUAGE, M. Schlauch. (Formerly, "The Gift of Tongues.") A sound, middle-level treatment of linguistic families, word histories, grammatical processes, semantics, language taboos, word-coining of Joyce, Cummings, Stein, etc. 232 bibliographical notes. 350pp. 5⅜ x 8.
T243 Paperbound **$1.85**

THE PHILOSOPHY OF HEGEL, W. T. Stace. The first work in English to give a complete and connected view of Hegel's entire system. Especially valuable to those who do not have time to study the highly complicated original texts, yet want an accurate presentation by a most reputable scholar of one of the most influential 19th century thinkers. Includes a 14 x 20 fold-out chart of Hegelian system. 536pp. 5⅜ x 8.
T254 Paperbound **$2.00**

ARISTOTLE, A. E. Taylor. A lucid, non-technical account of Aristotle written by a foremost Platonist. Covers life and works; thought on matter, form, causes, logic, God, physics, metaphysics, etc. Bibliography. New index compiled for this edition. 128pp. 5⅜ x 8.
T280 Paperbound **$1.00**

GUIDE TO PHILOSOPHY, C. E. M. Joad. This basic work describes the major philosophic problems and evaluates the answers propounded by great philosophers from the Greeks to Whitehead, Russell. "The finest introduction," BOSTON TRANSCRIPT. Bibliography, 592pp. 5⅜ x 8.
T297 Paperbound **$2.00**

LANGUAGE AND MYTH, E. Cassirer. Cassirer's brilliant demonstration that beneath both language and myth lies an unconscious "grammar" of experience whose categories and canons are not those of logical thought. Introduction and translation by Susanne Langer. Index. x + 103pp. 5⅜ x 8.
T51 Paperbound **$1.25**

SUBSTANCE AND FUNCTION, EINSTEIN'S THEORY OF RELATIVITY, E. Cassirer. This double volume contains the German philosopher's profound philosophical formulation of the differences between traditional logic and the new logic of science. Number, space, energy, relativity, many other topics are treated in detail. Authorized translation by W. C. and M. C. Swabey. xii + 465pp. 5⅜ x 8.
T50 Paperbound **$2.00**

THE PHILOSOPHICAL WORKS OF DESCARTES. The definitive English edition, in two volumes, of all major philosophical works and letters of René Descartes, father of modern philosophy of knowledge and science. Translated by E. S. Haldane and G. Ross. Introductory notes. Total of 842pp. 5⅜ x 8.
T71 Vol. 1, Paperbound **$2.00**
T72 Vol. 2, Paperbound **$2.00**

ESSAYS IN EXPERIMENTAL LOGIC, J. Dewey. Based upon Dewey's theory that knowledge implies a judgment which in turn implies an inquiry, these papers consider such topics as the thought of Bertrand Russell, pragmatism, the logic of values, antecedents of thought, data and meanings. 452pp. 5⅜ x 8.
T73 Paperbound **$1.95**

THE PHILOSOPHY OF HISTORY, G. W. F. Hegel. This classic of Western thought is Hegel's detailed formulation of the thesis that history is not chance but a rational process, the realization of the Spirit of Freedom. Translated and introduced by J. Sibree. Introduction by C. Hegel. Special introduction for this edition by Prof. Carl Friedrich, Harvard University. xxxix + 447pp. 5⅜ x 8.
T112 Paperbound **$1.85**

THE WILL TO BELIEVE and HUMAN IMMORTALITY, W. James. Two of James's most profound investigations of human belief in God and immortality, bound as one volume. Both are powerful expressions of James's views on chance vs. determinism, pluralism vs. monism, will and intellect, arguments for survival after death, etc. Two prefaces. 429pp. 5⅜ x 8.
T294 Clothbound **$3.75**
T291 Paperbound **$1.65**

INTRODUCTION TO SYMBOLIC LOGIC, S. Langer. A lucid, general introduction to modern logic, covering forms, classes, the use of symbols, the calculus of propositions, the Boole-Schroeder and the Russell-Whitehead systems, etc. "One of the clearest and simplest introductions," MATHEMATICS GAZETTE. Second, enlarged, revised edition. 368pp. 5⅜ x 8.
S164 Paperbound **$1.75**

MIND AND THE WORLD-ORDER, C. I. Lewis. Building upon the work of Peirce, James, and Dewey, Professor Lewis outlines a theory of knowledge in terms of "conceptual pragmatism," and demonstrates why the traditional understanding of the a priori must be abandoned. Appendices. xiv + 446pp. 5⅜ x 8.
T359 Paperbound **$1.95**

THE GUIDE FOR THE PERPLEXED, M. Maimonides One of the great philosophical works of all time, Maimonides' formulation of the meeting-ground between Old Testament and Aristotelian thought is essential to anyone interested in Jewish, Christian, and Moslem thought in the Middle Ages. 2nd revised edition of the Friedländer translation. Extensive introduction. lix + 414pp. 5⅜ x 8.
T351 Paperbound **$1.85**

THE PHILOSOPHICAL WRITINGS OF PEIRCE, J. Buchler, ed. (Formerly, "The Philosophy of Peirce.") This carefully integrated selection of Peirce's papers is considered the best coverage of the complete thought of one of the greatest philosophers of modern times. Covers Peirce's work on the theory of signs, pragmatism, epistemology, symbolic logic, the scientific method, chance, etc. xvi + 386pp. 5 3⁄8 x 8.
T216 Clothbound **$5.00**
T217 Paperbound **$1.95**

HISTORY OF ANCIENT PHILOSOPHY, W. Windelband. Considered the clearest survey of Greek and Roman philosophy. Examines Thales, Anaximander, Anaximenes, Heraclitus, the Eleatics, Empedocles, the Pythagoreans, the Sophists, Socrates, Democritus, Stoics, Epicureans, Sceptics, Neo-platonists, etc. 50 pages on Plato; 70 on Aristotle. 2nd German edition tr. by H. E. Cushman. xv + 393pp. 5⅜ x 8.
T357 Paperbound **$1.75**

INTRODUCTION TO SYMBOLIC LOGIC AND ITS APPLICATIONS, R. Carnap. A comprehensive, rigorous introduction to modern logic by perhaps its greatest living master. Includes demonstrations of applications in mathematics, physics, biology. "Of the rank of a masterpiece," Z. für Mathematik und ihre Grenzgebiete. Over 300 exercises. xvi + 241pp. 5⅜ x 8.
Clothbound **$4.00**
S453 Paperbound **$1.85**

SCEPTICISM AND ANIMAL FAITH, G. Santayana. Santayana's unusually lucid exposition of the difference between the independent existence of objects and the essence our mind attributes to them, and of the necessity of scepticism as a form of belief and animal faith as a necessary condition of knowledge. Discusses belief, memory, intuition, symbols, etc. xii + 314pp. 5⅜ x 8.
T235 Clothbound **$3.50**
T236 Paperbound **$1.50**

THE ANALYSIS OF MATTER, B. Russell. With his usual brilliance, Russell analyzes physics, causality, scientific inference, Weyl's theory, tensors, invariants, periodicity, etc. in order to discover the basic concepts of scientific thought about matter. "Most thorough treatment of the subject," THE NATION. Introduction. 8 figures. viii + 408pp. 5⅜ x 8.
T231 Paperbound **$1.95**

THE SENSE OF BEAUTY, G. Santayana. This important philosophical study of why, when, and how beauty appears, and what conditions must be fulfilled, is in itself a revelation of the beauty of language. "It is doubtful if a better treatment of the subject has since appeared," PEABODY JOURNAL. ix + 275pp. 5⅜ x 8.
T238 Paperbound **$1.00**

THE CHIEF WORKS OF SPINOZA. In two volumes. Vol. I: The Theologico-Political Treatise and the Political Treatise. Vol. II: On the Improvement of Understanding, The Ethics, and Selected Letters. The permanent and enduring ideas in these works on God, the universe, religion, society, etc., have had tremendous impact on later philosophical works. Introduction. Total of 862pp. 5⅜ x 8.
T249 Vol. I, Paperbound **$1.50**
T250 Vol. II, Paperbound **$1.50**

TRAGIC SENSE OF LIFE, M. de Unamuno. The acknowledged masterpiece of one of Spain's most influential thinkers. Between the despair at the inevitable death of man and all his works, and the desire for immortality, Unamuno finds a "saving incertitude." Called "a masterpiece," by the ENCYCLOPAEDIA BRITANNICA. xxx + 332pp. 5⅜ x 8.
T257 Paperbound **$1.95**

EXPERIENCE AND NATURE, John Dewey. The enlarged, revised edition of the Paul Carus lectures (1925). One of Dewey's clearest presentations of the philosophy of empirical naturalism which reestablishes the continuity between "inner" experience and "outer" nature. These lectures are among the most significant ever delivered by an American philosopher. 457pp. 5⅜ x 8.
T471 Paperbound **$1.85**

PHILOSOPHY AND CIVILIZATION IN THE MIDDLE AGES, M. de Wulf. A semi-popular survey of medieval intellectual life, religion, philosophy, science, the arts, etc. that covers feudalism vs. Catholicism, rise of the universities, mendicant orders, and similar topics. Bibliography. viii + 320pp. 5⅜ x 8.
T284 Paperbound **$1.75**

AN INTRODUCTION TO SCHOLASTIC PHILOSOPHY, M. de Wulf. (Formerly, "Scholasticism Old and New.") Prof. de Wulf covers the central scholastic tradition from St. Anselm, Albertus Magnus, Thomas Aquinas, up to Suarez in the 17th century; and then treats the modern revival of scholasticism, the Louvain position, relations with Kantianism and positivism, etc. xvi + 271pp. 5⅜ x 8.
T296 Clothbound **$3.50**
T283 Paperbound **$1.75**

A HISTORY OF MODERN PHILOSOPHY, H. Höffding. An exceptionally clear and detailed coverage of Western philosophy from the Renaissance to the end of the 19th century. Both major and minor figures are examined in terms of theory of knowledge, logic, cosmology, psychology. Covers Pomponazzi, Bodin, Boehme, Telesius, Bruno, Copernicus, Descartes, Spinoza, Hobbes, Locke, Hume, Kant, Fichte, Schopenhauer, Mill, Spencer, Langer, scores of others. A standard reference work. 2 volumes. Total of 1159pp. 5⅜ x 8.
T117 Vol. 1, Paperbound **$2.00**
T118 Vol. 2, Paperbound **$2.00**

LANGUAGE, TRUTH AND LOGIC, A. J. Ayer. The first full-length development of Logical Positivism in English. Building on the work of Schlick, Russell, Carnap and the Vienna school, Ayer presents the tenets of one of the most important systems of modern philosophical thought. 160pp. 5⅜ x 8.
T10 Paperbound **$1.25**

ORIENTALIA AND RELIGION

THE MYSTERIES OF MITHRA, F. Cumont. The great Belgian scholar's definitive study of the Persian mystery religion that almost vanquished Christianity in the ideological struggle for the Roman Empire. A masterpiece of scholarly detection that reconstructs secret doctrines, organization, rites. Mithraic art is discussed and analyzed. 70 illus. 239pp. 5⅜ x 8.
T323 Paperbound **$1.85**

CHRISTIAN AND ORIENTAL PHILOSOPHY OF ART. A. K. Coomaraswamy. The late art historian and orientalist discusses artistic symbolism, the role of traditional culture in enriching art, medieval art, folklore, philosophy of art, other similar topics. Bibliography. 148pp. 5⅜ x 8.
T378 Paperbound **$1.25**

TRANSFORMATION OF NATURE IN ART, A. K. Coomaraswamy. A basic work on Asiatic religious art. Includes discussions of religious art in Asia and Medieval Europe (exemplified by Meister Eckhart), the origin and use of images in Indian art, Indian Medieval aesthetic manuals, and other fascinating, little known topics. Glossaries of Sanskrit and Chinese terms. Bibliography. 41pp. of notes. 245pp. 5⅜ x 8.
T368 Paperbound **$1.75**

ORIENTAL RELIGIONS IN ROMAN PAGANISM, F. Cumont. This well-known study treats the ecstatic cults of Syria and Phrygia (Cybele, Attis, Adonis, their orgies and mutilatory rites); the mysteries of Egypt (Serapis, Isis, Osiris); Persian dualism; Mithraic cults; Hermes Trismegistus, Ishtar, Astarte, etc. and their influence on the religious thought of the Roman Empire. Introduction. 55pp. of notes; extensive bibliography. xxiv + 298pp. 5⅜ x 8.
T321 Paperbound **$1.75**

ANTHROPOLOGY, SOCIOLOGY, AND PSYCHOLOGY

PRIMITIVE MAN AS PHILOSOPHER, P. Radin. A standard anthropological work based on Radin's investigations of the Winnebago, Maori, Batak, Zuni, other primitive tribes. Describes primitive thought on the purpose of life, marital relations, death, personality, gods, etc. Extensive selections of õriginal primitive documents. Bibliography. xviii + 420pp. 5⅜ x 8.
T392 Paperbound **$2.00**

PRIMITIVE RELIGION, P. Radin. Radin's thoroughgoing treatment of supernatural beliefs, shamanism, initiations, religious expression, etc. in primitive societies. Arunta, Ashanti, Aztec, Bushman, Crow, Fijian, many other tribes examined. "Excellent," NATURE. New preface by the author. Bibliographic notes. x + 322pp. 5⅜ x 8.   T393 Paperbound **$1.85**

SEX IN PSYCHO-ANALYSIS, S. Ferenczi. (Formerly, "Contributions to Psycho-analysis.") 14 selected papers on impotence, transference, analysis and children, dreams, obscene words, homosexuality, paranoia, etc. by an associate of Freud. Also included: THE DEVELOPMENT OF PSYCHO-ANALYSIS, by Ferenczi and Otto Rank. Two books bound as one. Total of 406pp. 5⅜ x 8.
T324 Paperbound **$1.85**

THE PRINCIPLES OF PSYCHOLOGY, William James. The complete text of the famous "long course," one of the great books of Western thought. An almost incredible amount of information about psychological processes, the stream of consciousness, habit, time perception, memory, emotions, reason, consciousness of self, abnormal phenomena, and similar topics. Based on James's own discoveries integrated with the work of Descartes, Locke, Hume, Royce, Wundt, Berkeley, Lotse, Herbart, scores of others. "A classic of interpretation," PSYCHIATRIC QUARTERLY. 94 illus. 1408pp. 2 volumes. 5⅜ x 8.
T381 Vol. 1, Paperbound **$2.50**
T382 Vol. 2, Paperbound **$2.50**

THE POLISH PEASANT IN EUROPE AND AMERICA, W. I. Thomas, F. Znaniecki. Monumental sociological study of peasant primary groups (family and community) and the disruptions produced by·a new industrial system and emigration to America, by two of the foremost sociologists of recent times. One of the most important works in sociological thought. Includes hundreds of pages of primary documentation; point by point analysis of causes of social decay, breakdown of morality, crime, drunkenness, prostitution, etc. 2nd revised edition. 2 volumes. Total of 2250pp. 6 x 9.   T478 2 volume set, Clothbound **$12.50**

FOLKWAYS, W. G. Sumner. The great Yale sociologist's detailed exposition of thousands of social, sexual, and religious customs in hundreds of cultures from ancient Greece to Modern Western societies. Preface by A. G. Keller. Introduction by William Lyon Phelps. 705pp. 5⅜ x 8.
S508 Paperbound **$2.49**

BEYOND PSYCHOLOGY, Otto Rank. The author, an early associate of Freud, uses psychoanalytic techniques of myth-analysis to explore ultimates of human existence. Treats love, immortality, the soul, sexual identity, kingship, sources of state power, many other topics which illuminate the irrational basis of human existence. 291pp. 5⅜ x 8.   T485 Paperbound **$1.75**

ILLUSIONS AND DELUSIONS OF THE SUPERNATURAL AND THE OCCULT, D. H. Rawcliffe. A rational, scientific examination of crystal gazing, automatic writing, table turning, stigmata, the Indian rope trick, dowsing, telepathy, clairvoyance, ghosts, ESP, PK, thousands of other supposedly occult phenomena. Originally titled "The Psychology of the Occult." 14 illustrations. 551pp. 5⅜ x 8.
T503 Paperbound **$2.00**

DOVER BOOKS

YOGA: A SCIENTIFIC EVALUATION, Kovoor T. Behanan. A scientific study of the physiological and psychological effects of Yoga discipline, written under the auspices of the Yale University Institute of Human Relations. Foreword by W. A. Miles, Yale Univ. 17 photographs. 290pp. 5⅜ x 8.
T505 Paperbound **$1.65**

HOAXES, C. D. MacDougall. Delightful, entertaining, yet scholarly exposition of how hoaxes start, why they succeed, documented with stories of hundreds of the most famous hoaxes. "A stupendous collection . . . and shrewd analysis, "NEW YORKER. New, revised edition. 54 photographs. 320pp. 5⅜ x 8.
T465 Paperbound **$1.75**

CREATIVE POWER: THE EDUCATION OF YOUTH IN THE CREATIVE ARTS, Hughes Mearns. Named by the National Education Association as one of the 20 foremost books on education in recent times. Tells how to help children express themselves in drama, poetry, music, art, develop latent creative power. Should be read by every parent, teacher. New, enlarged, revised edition. Introduction. 272pp. 5⅜ x 8.
T490 Paperbound **$1.50**

LANGUAGES

NEW RUSSIAN-ENGLISH, ENGLISH-RUSSIAN DICTIONARY, M. A. O'Brien. Over 70,000 entries in new orthography! Idiomatic usages, colloquialisms. One of the few dictionaries that indicate accent changes in conjugation and declension. "One of the best," Prof. E. J. Simmons, Cornell. First names, geographical terms, bibliography, many other features. 738pp. 4½ x 6¼.
T208 Paperbound **$2.00**

MONEY CONVERTER AND TIPPING GUIDE FOR EUROPEAN TRAVEL, C. Vomacka. Invaluable, handy source of currency regulations, conversion tables, tipping rules, postal rates, much other travel information for every European country plus Israel, Egypt and Turkey. 128pp. 3½ x 5¼.
T260 Paperbound **60¢**

MONEY CONVERTER AND TIPPING GUIDE FOR TRAVEL IN THE AMERICAS (including the United States and Canada), **C. Vomacka.** The information you need for informed and confident travel in the Americas: money conversion tables, tipping guide, postal, telephone rates, etc. 128pp. 3½ x 5¼.
T261 Paperbound **65¢**

DUTCH-ENGLISH, ENGLISH-DUTCH DICTIONARY, F. G. Renier. The most convenient, practical Dutch-English dictionary on the market. New orthography. More than 60,000 entries: idioms, compounds, technical terms, etc. Gender of nouns indicated. xviii + 571pp. 5½ x 6¼.
T224 Clothbound **$2.50**

LEARN DUTCH!, F. G. Renier. The most satisfactory and easily-used grammar of modern Dutch. Used and recommended by the Fulbright Committee in the Netherlands. Over 1200 simple exercises lead to mastery of spoken and written Dutch. Dutch-English, English-Dutch vocabularies. 181pp. 4¼ x 7¼.
T441 Clothbound **$1.75**

PHRASE AND SENTENCE DICTIONARY OF SPOKEN RUSSIAN, English-Russian, Russian-English. Based on phrases and complete sentences, rather than isolated words; recognized as one of the best methods of learning the idiomatic speech of a country. Over 11,500 entries, indexed by single words, with more than 32,000 English and Russian sentences and phrases, in immediately usable form. Probably the largest list ever published. Shows accent changes in conjugation and declension; irregular forms listed in both alphabetical place and under main form of word. 15,000 word introduction covering Russian sounds, writing, grammar, syntax. 15-page appendix of geographical names, money, important signs, given names, foods, special Soviet terms, etc. Travellers, businessmen, students, government employees have found this their best source for Russian expressions. Originally published as U.S. Government Technical Manual TM 30-944. iv + 573pp. 5⅝ x 8⅜.
T496 Paperbound **$2.75**

PHRASE AND SENTENCE DICTIONARY OF SPOKEN SPANISH, Spanish-English, English-Spanish. Compiled from spoken Spanish, emphasizing idiom and colloquial usage in both Castilian and Latin-American. More than 16,000 entries containing over 25,000 idioms—the largest list of idiomatic constructions ever published. Complete sentences given, indexed under single words —language in immediately usable form, for travellers, businessmen, students, etc. 25-page introduction provides rapid survey of sounds, grammar, syntax, with full consideration of irregular verbs. Especially apt in modern treatment of phrases and structure. 17-page glossary gives translations of geographical names, money values, numbers, national holidays, important street signs, useful expressions of high frequency, plus unique 7-page glossary of Spanish and Spanish-American foods and dishes. Originally published as U.S. Government Technical Manual TM 30-900. iv + 513pp. 5⅝ x 8⅜.
T495 Paperbound **$1.75**

SAY IT language phrase books

"SAY IT" in the foreign language of your choice! We have sold over ½ million copies of these popular, useful language books. They will not make you an expert linguist overnight, but they do cover most practical matters of everyday life abroad.

Over 1000 useful phrases, expressions, with additional variants, substitutions.

Modern! Useful! Hundreds of phrases not available in other texts: "Nylon," "air-conditioned," etc.

The ONLY inexpensive phrase book **completely indexed.** Everything is available at a flip of your finger, ready for use.

Prepared by native linguists, travel experts.

Based on years of travel experience abroad.

This handy phrase book may be used by itself, or it may supplement any other text or course; it provides a living element. Used by many colleges and institutions: Hunter College; Barnard College; Army Ordnance School, Aberdeen; and many others.

Available, 1 book per language:

Danish (T818) 75¢
Dutch T(817) 75¢
English (for German-speaking people) (T801) 60¢
English (for Italian-speaking people) (T816) 60¢
English (for Spanish-speaking people) (T802) 60¢
Esperanto (T820) 75¢
French (T803) 60¢
German (T804) 60¢
Modern Greek (T813) 75¢
Hebrew (T805) 60¢

Italian (T806) 60¢
Japanese (T807) 60¢
Norwegian (T814) 75¢
Russian (T810) 75¢
Spanish (T811) 60¢
Turkish (T821) 75¢
Yiddish (T815) 75¢
Swedish (T812) 75¢
Polish (T808) 75¢
Portuguese (T809) 75¢

LISTEN & LEARN language record sets

LISTEN & LEARN is the only language record course designed especially to meet your travel needs, or help you learn essential foreign language quickly by yourself, or in conjunction with any school course, by means of the automatic association method. Each set contains three 33⅓ rpm long- playing records — 1½ hours of recorded speech by eminent native speakers who are professors at Columbia, N.Y.U., Queens College and other leading universities. The sets are priced far below other sets of similar quality, yet they contain many special features not found in other record sets:

* Over 800 selected phrases and sentences, a basic vocabulary of over 3200 words.
* Both English and foreign language recorded; with a pause for your repetition.
* Designed for persons with limited time; no time wasted on material you cannot use immediately.
* Living, modern expressions that answer modern needs: drugstore items, "air-conditioned," etc.
* 128-196 page manuals contain everything on the records, plus simple pronunciation guides.
* Manual is fully indexed; find the phrase you want instantly.
* High fidelity recording—equal to any records costing up to $6 each.

The phrases on these records cover 41 different categories useful to the traveller or student interested in learning the living, spoken language: greetings, introductions, making yourself understood, passing customs, planes, trains, boats, buses, taxis, nightclubs, restaurants, menu items, sports, concerts, cameras, automobile travel, repairs, drugstores, doctors, dentists, medicines, barber shops, beauty parlors, laundries, many, many more.

"Excellent . . . among the very best on the market," Prof. Mario Pei, Dept. of Romance Languages, Columbia University. "Inexpensive and well-done . . . an ideal present," CHICAGO SUNDAY TRIBUNE. "More genuinely helpful than anything of its kind which I have previously encountered," Sidney Clark, well-known author of "ALL THE BEST" travel books. Each set contains 3   33⅓ rpm   pure vinyl records, 128- 196 page   with full record text, and album. One language per set. LISTEN & LEARN record sets are now available in—

FRENCH	the set $4.95	GERMAN	the set $4.95
ITALIAN	the set $4.95	SPANISH	the set $4.95
RUSSIAN	the set $5.95	JAPANESE *	the set $5.95

* Available Sept. 1, 1959

UNCONDITIONAL GUARANTEE: Dover Publications stands behind every Listen and Learn record set. If you are dissatisfied with these sets for any reason whatever, return them within 10 days and your money will be refunded in full.

DOVER BOOKS

ART HISTORY

STICKS AND STONES, Lewis Mumford. An examination of forces influencing American architecture: the medieval tradition in early New England, the classical influence in Jefferson's time, the Brown Decades, the imperial facade, the machine age, etc. "A truly remarkable book," SAT. REV. OF LITERATURE. 2nd revised edition. 21 illus. xvii + 228pp. 5⅜ x 8.
T202 Paperbound **$1.60**

THE AUTOBIOGRAPHY OF AN IDEA, Louis Sullivan. The architect whom Frank Lloyd Wright called "the master," records the development of the theories that revolutionized America's skyline. 34 full-page plates of Sullivan's finest work. New introduction by R. M. Line. xiv + 335pp. 5⅜ x 8.
T281 Paperbound **$1.85**

THE MATERIALS AND TECHNIQUES OF MEDIEVAL PAINTING, D. V. Thompson. An invaluable study of carriers and grounds, binding media, pigments, metals used in painting, al fresco and al secco techniques, burnishing, etc. used by the medieval masters. Preface by Bernard Berenson. 239pp. 5⅜ x 8.
T327 Paperbound **$1.85**

PRINCIPLES OF ART HISTORY, H. Wölfflin. This remarkably instructive work demonstrates the tremendous change in artistic conception from the 14th to the 18th centuries, by analyzing 164 works by Botticelli, Dürer, Hobbema, Holbein, Hals, Titian, Rembrandt, Vermeer, etc., and pointing out exactly what is meant by "baroque," "classic," "primitive," "picturesque," and other basic terms of art history and criticism. "A remarkable lesson in the art of seeing," SAT. REV. OF LITERATURE. Translated from the 7th German edition. 150 illus. 254pp. 6⅛ x 9¼.
T276 Paperbound **$2.00**

FOUNDATIONS OF MODERN ART, A. Ozenfant. Stimulating discussion of human creativity from paleolithic cave painting to modern painting, architecture, decorative arts. Fully illustrated with works of Gris, Lipchitz, Leger, Picasso, primitive, modern artifacts, architecture, industrial art, much more. 226 illustrations. 368pp. 6⅛ x 9¼.
T215 Paperbound **$1.95**

HANDICRAFTS, APPLIED ART, ART SOURCES, ETC.

WILD FOWL DECOYS, J. Barber. The standard work on this fascinating branch of folk art, ranging from Indian mud and grass devices to realistic wooden decoys. Discusses styles, types, periods; gives full information on how to make decoys. 140 illustrations (including 14 new plates) show decoys and provide full sets of plans for handicrafters, artists, hunters, and students of folk art. 281pp. 7⅞ x 10¾. Deluxe edition.
T11 Clothbound **$8.50**

METALWORK AND ENAMELLING, H. Maryon. Probably the best book ever written on the subject. Tells everything necessary for the home manufacture of jewelry, rings, ear pendants, bowls, etc. Covers materials, tools, soldering, filigree, setting stones, raising patterns, repoussé work, damascening, niello, cloisonné, polishing, assaying, casting, and dozens of other techniques. The best substitute for apprenticeship to a master metalworker. 363 photos and figures. 374pp. 5½ x 8½.
T183 Clothbound **$7.50**

SHAKER FURNITURE, E. D. and F. Andrews. The most illuminating study of Shaker furniture ever written. Covers chronology, craftsmanship, houses, shops, etc. Includes over 200 photographs of chairs, tables, clocks, beds, benches, etc. "Mr. & Mrs. Andrews know all there is to know about Shaker furniture," Mark Van Doren, NATION. 48 full-page plates. 192pp. Deluxe cloth binding. 7⅞ x 10¾.
T7 Clothbound **$6.00**

PRIMITIVE ART, Franz Boas. A great American anthropologist covers theory, technical virtuosity, styles, symbolism, patterns, etc. of primitive art. The more than 900 illustrations will interest artists, designers, craftworkers. Over 900 illustrations. 376pp. 5⅜ x 8.
T25 Paperbound **$1.95**

ON THE LAWS OF JAPANESE PAINTING, H. Bowie. The best possible substitute for lessons from an oriental master. Treats both spirit and technique; exercises for control of the brush; inks, brushes, colors; use of dots, lines to express whole moods, etc. 220 illus. 132pp. 6⅛ x 9¼.
T30 Paperbound **$1.95**

HANDBOOK OF ORNAMENT, F. S. Meyer. One of the largest collections of copyright-free traditional art: over 3300 line cuts of Greek, Roman, Medieval, Renaissance, Baroque, 18th and 19th century art motifs (tracery, geometric elements, flower and animal motifs, etc.) and decorated objects (chairs, thrones, weapons, vases, jewelry, armor, etc.). Full text. 3300 illustrations. 562pp. 5⅜ x 8.
T302 Paperbound **$2.00**

THREE CLASSICS OF ITALIAN CALLIGRAPHY. Oscar Ogg, ed. Exact reproductions of three famous Renaissance calligraphic works: Arrighi's OPERINA and IL MODO, Tagliente's LO PRESENTE LIBRO, and Palatino's LIBRO NUOVO. More than 200 complete alphabets, thousands of lettered specimens, in Papal Chancery and other beautiful, ornate handwriting. Introduction. 245 plates. 282pp. 6⅛ x 9¼.
T212 Paperbound **$1.95**

THE HISTORY AND TECHNIQUES OF LETTERING, A. Nesbitt. A thorough history of lettering from the ancient Egyptians to the present, and a 65-page course in lettering for artists. Every major development in lettering history is illustrated by a complete alphabet. Fully analyzes such masters as Caslon, Koch, Garamont, Jenson, and many more. 89 alphabets, 165 other specimens. 317pp. 5⅜ x 8.
T427 Paperbound **$2.00**

LETTERING AND ALPHABETS, J. A. Cavanagh. An unabridged reissue of "Lettering," containing the full discussion, analysis, illustration of 89 basic hand lettering tyles based on Caslon, Bodoni, Gothic, many other types. Hundreds of technical hints on construction, strokes, pens, brushes, etc. 89 alphabets, 72 lettered specimens, which may be reproduced permission-free. 121pp. 9¾ x 8. T53 Paperbound **$1.25**

THE HUMAN FIGURÉ IN MOTION, Eadweard Muybridge. The largest collection in print of Muybridge's famous high-speed action photos. 4789 photographs in more than 500 action-strip-sequences (at shutter speeds up to 1/6000th of a second) illustrate men, women, children—mostly undraped—performing such actions as walking, running, getting up, lying down, carrying objects, throwing, etc. "An unparalleled dictionary of action for all artists," AMERICAN ARTIST. 390 full-page plates, with 4789 photographs. Heavy glossy stock, reinforced binding with headbands. 7⅞ x 10¾. T204 Clothbound **$10.00**

ANIMALS IN MOTION, Eadweard Muybridge. The largest collection of animal action photos in print. 34 different animals (horses, mules, oxen, goats, camels, pigs, cats, lions, gnus, deer, monkeys, eagles—and 22 others) in 132 characteristic actions. All 3919 photographs are taken in series at speeds up to 1/1600th of a second, offering artists, biologists, cartoonists a remarkable opportunity to see exactly how an ostrich's head bobs when running, how a lion puts his foot down, how an elephant's knee bends, how a bird flaps his wings, thousands of other hard-to-catch details. "A really marvelous series of plates," NATURE. 380 full-pages of plates. Heavy glossy stock, reinforced binding with headbands. 7⅞ x 10¾. T203 Clothbound **$10.00**

THE BOOK OF SIGNS, R. Koch. 493 symbols—crosses, monograms, astrological, biological symbols, runes, etc.—from ancient manuscripts, cathedrals, coins, catacombs, pottery. May be reproduced permission-free. 493 illustrations by Fritz Kredel. 104pp. 6⅛ x 9¼. T162 Paperbound **$1.00**

A HANDBOOK OF EARLY ADVERTISING ART, C. P. Hornung. The largest collection of copyright-free early advertising art ever compiled. Vol. I: 2,000 illustrations of animals, old automobiles, buildings, allegorical figures, fire engines, Indians, ships, trains, more than 33 other categories! Vol II: Over 4,000 typographical specimens; 600 Roman, Gothic, Barnum, Old English faces; 630 ornamental type faces; hundreds of scrolls, initials, flourishes, etc. "A remarkable collection," PRINTERS' INK.

Vol. I: Pictorial Volume. Over 2000 illustrations. 256pp. 9 x 12. T122 Clothbound **$10.00**
Vol. II: Typographical Volume. Over 4000 speciments. 319pp. 9 x 12. T123 Clothbound **$10.00**
Two volume set, Clothbound, only **$18.50**

DESIGN FOR ARTISTS AND CRAFTSMEN, L. Wolchonok. The most thorough course on the creation of art motifs and designs. Shows you step-by-step, with hundreds of examples and 113 detailed exercises, how to create original designs from geometric patterns, plants, birds, animals, humans, and man-made objects. "A great contribution to the field of design and crafts," N. Y. SOCIETY OF CRAFTSMEN. More than 1300 entirely new illustrations. xv + 207pp. 7⅞ x 10¾. T274 Clothbound **$4.95**

HANDBOOK OF DESIGNS AND DEVICES, C. P. Hornung. A remarkable working collection of 1836 basic designs and variations, all copyright-free. Variations of circle, line, cross, diamond, swastika, star, scroll, shield, many more. Notes on symbolism. "A necessity to every designer who would be original without having to labor heavily," ARTIST and ADVERTISER. 204 plates. 240pp. 5⅜ x 8. T125 Paperbound **$1.90**

THE UNIVERSAL PENMAN, George Bickham. Exact reproduction of beautiful 18th century book of handwriting. 22 complete alphabets in finest English roundhand, other scripts, over 2000 elaborate flourishes, 122 calligraphic illustrations, etc. Material is copyright-free. "An essential part of any art library, and a book of permanent value," AMERICAN ARTIST. 212 plates. 224pp. 9 x 13¾. T20 Clothbound **$10.00**

AN ATLAS OF ANATOMY FOR ARTISTS, F. Schider. This standard work contains 189 full-page plates, more than 647 illustrations of all aspects of the human skeleton, musculature, cutaway portions of the body, each part of the anatomy, hand forms, eyelids, breasts, location of muscles under the flesh, etc. 59 plates illustrate how Michelangelo, da Vinci, Goya, 15 others, drew human anatomy. New 3rd edition enlarged by 52 new illustrations by Cloquet, Barcsay. "The standard reference tool," AMERICAN LIBRARY ASSOCIATION. "Excellent," AMERICAN ARTIST. 189 plates, 647 illustrations. xxvi + 192pp. 7⅞ x 10⅝. T241 Clothbound **$6.00**

AN ATLAS OF ANIMAL ANATOMY FOR ARTISTS, W. Ellenberger, H. Baum, H. Dittrich. The largest, richest animal anatomy for artists in English. Form, musculature, tendons, bone structure, expression, detailed cross sections of head, other features, of the horse, lion, dog, cat, deer, seal, kangaroo, cow, bull, goat, monkey, hare, many other animals. "Highly recommended," DESIGN. Second, revised, enlarged edition with new plates from Cuvier, Stubbs, etc. 288 illustrations. 153pp. 11⅜ x 9. T82 Clothbound **$6.00**

ANIMAL DRAWING: ANATOMY AND ACTION FOR ARTISTS, C. R. Knight. 158 studies, with full accompanying text, of such animals as the gorilla, bear, bison, dromedary, camel, vulture, pelican, iguana, shark, etc., by one of the greatest modern masters of animal drawing. Innumerable tips on how to get life expression into your work. "An excellent reference work,' SAN FRANCISCO CHRONICLE. 158 illustrations. 156pp. 10½ x 8½. T426 Paperbound **$2.00**

THE CRAFTSMAN'S HANDBOOK, Cennino Cennini. The finest English translation of IL LIBRO DELL' ARTE, the 15th century introduction to art technique that is both a mirror of Quatrocento life and a source of many useful but ‑nearly forgotten facets of the painter's art. 4 illustrations. xxvii + 142pp. D. V. Thompson, translator. 6⅛ x 9¼. T54 Paperbound **$1.50**

THE BROWN DECADES, Lewis Mumford. A picture of the "buried renaissance" of the post-Civil War period, and the founding of modern architecture (Sullivan, Richardson, Root, Roebling), landscape development (Marsh, Olmstead, Eliot), and the graphic arts (Homer, Eakins, Ryder). 2nd revised, enlarged edition. Bibliography. 12 illustrations. xiv + 266 pp. 5⅜ x 8. T200 Paperbound **$1.65**

STIEGEL GLASS, F. W. Hunter. The story of the most highly esteemed early American glassware, fully illustrated. How a German adventurer, "Baron" Stiegel, founded a glass empire; detailed accounts of individual glasswork. "This pioneer work is reprinted in an edition even more beautiful than the original," ANTIQUES DEALER. New introduction by Helen McKearin. 171 illustrations, 12 in full color. xxii + 338pp. 7⅞ x 10¾. T128 Clothbound **$10.00**

THE HUMAN FIGURE, J. H. Vanderpoel. Not just a picture book, but a complete course by a famous figure artist. Extensive text, illustrated by 430 pencil and charcoal drawings of both male and female anatomy. 2nd enlarged edition. Foreword. 430 illus. 143pp. 6⅛ x 9¼. T432 Paperbound **$1.45**

PINE FURNITURE OF EARLY NEW ENGLAND, R. H. Kettell. Over 400 illustrations, over 50 working drawings of early New England chairs, benches, beds cupboards, mirrors, shelves, tables, other furniture esteemed for simple beauty and character. "Rich store of illustrations . . . emphasizes the individuality and varied design," ANTIQUES. 413 illustrations, 55 working drawings. 475pp. 8 x 10¾. T145 Clothbound **$10.00**

BASIC BOOKBINDING, A. W. Lewis. Enables both beginners and experts to rebind old books or bind paperbacks in hard covers. Treats materials, tools; gives step-by-step instruction in how to collate a book, sew it, back it, make boards, etc. 261 illus. Appendices. 155pp. 5⅜ x 8. T169 Paperbound **$1.35**

DESIGN MOTIFS OF ANCIENT MEXICO, J. Enciso. Nearly 90% of these 766 superb designs from Aztec, Olmec, Totonac, Maya, and Toltec origins are unobtainable elsewhere! Contains plumed serpents, wind gods, animals, demons, dancers, monsters, etc. Excellent applied design source. Originally $17.50. 766 illustrations, thousands of motifs. 192pp. 6⅛ x 9¼. T84 Paperbound **$1.85**

AFRICAN SCULPTURE, Ladislas Segy. 163 full-page plates illustrating masks, fertility figures, ceremonial objects, etc., of 50 West and Central African tribes—95% never before illustrated. 34-page introduction to African sculpture. "Mr. Segy is one of its top authorities," NEW YORKER. 164 full-page photographic plates. Introduction. Bibliography. 244pp. 6⅛ x 9¼. T396 Paperbound **$2.00**

THE PROCESSES OF GRAPHIC REPRODUCTION IN PRINTING, H. Curwen. A thorough and practical survey of wood, linoleum, and rubber engraving; copper engraving; drypoint, mezzotint, etching, aquatint, steel engraving, die sinking, stencilling, lithography (extensively); photographic reproduction utilizing line, continuous tone, photoengravure, collotype; every other process in general use. Note on color reproduction. Section on bookbinding. Over 200 illustrations, 25 in color. 143pp. 5½ x 8½. T512 Clothbound **$4.00**

CALLIGRAPHY, J. G. Schwandner. First reprinting in 200 years of this legendary book of beautiful handwriting. Over 300 ornamental initials, 12 complete calligraphic alphabets, over 150 ornate frames and panels, 75 calligraphic pictures of cherubs, stags, lions, etc., thousands of flourishes, scrolls, etc., by the greatest 18th century masters. All material can be copied or adapted without permission. Historical introduction. 158 full-page plates. 368pp. 9 x 13. T475 Clothbound **$10.00**

* * *

A DIDEROT PICTORIAL ENCYCLOPEDIA OF TRADES AND INDUSTRY, Manufacturing and the Technical Arts in Plates Selected from "L'Encyclopédie ou Dictionnaire Raisonné des Sciences, des Arts, et des Métiers," of Denis Diderot, edited with text by C. Gillispie. Over 2000 illustrations on 485 full-page plates. Magnificent 18th century engravings of men, women, and children working at such trades as milling flour, cheesemaking, charcoal burning, mining, silverplating, shoeing horses, making fine glass, printing, hundreds more, showing details of machinery, different steps in sequence, etc. A remarkable art work, but also the largest collection of working figures in print, copyright‑free, for art directors, designers, etc. Two vols. 920pp. 9 x 12. Heavy library cloth. T421 Two volume set **$18.50**

* * *

SILK SCREEN TECHNIQUES, J. Biegeleisen, M. Cohn. A practical step-by-step home course in one of the most versatile, least expensive graphic arts processes. How to build an inexpensive silk screen, prepare stencils, print, achieve special textures, use color, etc. Every step explained, diagrammed. 149 illustrations, 8 in color. 201pp. 6⅛ x 9¼. T433 Paperbound **$1.45**

PUZZLES, GAMES, AND ENTERTAINMENTS

MATHEMATICS, MAGIC AND MYSTERY, Martin Gardner. Astonishing feats of mind reading, mystifying "magic" tricks, are often based on mathematical principles anyone can learn. This book shows you how to perform scores of tricks with cards, dice, coins, knots, numbers, etc., by using simple principles from set theory, theory of numbers, topology, other areas of mathematics, fascinating in themselves. No special knowledge required. 135 illus. 186pp. 5⅜ x 8.   T335 Paperbound **$1.00**

MATHEMATICAL PUZZLES FOR BEGINNERS AND ENTHUSIASTS, G. Mott-Smoth. Test your problem-solving techniques and powers of inference on 188 challenging, amusing puzzles based on algebra, dissection of plane figures, permutations, probabilities, etc. Appendix of primes, square roots, etc. 135 illus. 2nd revised edition. 248pp. 5⅜ x 8.
T198 Paperbound **$1.00**

LEARN CHESS FROM THE MASTERS, F. Reinfeld. Play 10 games against Marshall, Bronstein, Najdorf, other masters, and grade yourself on each move. Detailed annotations reveal principles of play, strategy, etc. as you proceed. An excellent way to get a real insight into the game. Formerly titled, "Chess by Yourself." 91 diagrams. vii + 144pp. 5⅜ x 8.
T362 Paperbound **$1.00**

REINFELD ON THE END GAME IN CHESS, F. Reinfeld. 62 end games of Alekhine, Tarrasch, Morphy, other masters, are carefully analyzed with emphasis on transition from middle game to end play. Tempo moves, queen endings, weak squares, other basic principles clearly illustrated. Excellent for understanding why some moves are weak or incorrect, how to avoid errors. Formerly titled, "Practical End-game Play." 62 diagrams. vi + 177pp. 5⅜ x 8.
T417 Paperbound **$1.25**

101 PUZZLES IN THOUGHT AND LOGIC, C. R. Wylie, Jr. Brand new puzzles you need no special knowledge to solve! Each one is a gem of ingenuity that will really challenge your problem-solving technique. Introduction with simplified explanation of scientic puzzle solving. 128pp. 5⅜ x 8.   T167 Paperbound **$1.00**

THE COMPLETE NONSENSE OF EDWARD LEAR. The only complete edition of this master of gentle madness at a popular price. The Dong with the Luminous Nose, The Jumblies, The Owl and the Pussycat, hundreds of other bits of wonderful nonsense. 214 limericks, 3 sets of Nonsense Botany, 5 Nonsense Alphabets, 546 fantastic drawings, much more. 320pp. 5⅜ x 8.   T167 Paperbound **$1.00**

28 SCIENCE FICTION STORIES OF H. G. WELLS. Two complete novels, "Men Like Gods" and "Star Begotten," plus 26 short stories by the master science-fiction writer of all time. Stories of space, time, future adventure that are among the all-time classics of science fiction. 928pp. 5⅜ x 8.   T265 Clothbound **$3.95**

SEVEN SCIENCE FICTION NOVELS, H. G. Wells. Unabridged texts of "The Time Machine," "The Island of Dr. Moreau," "First Men in the Moon," "The Invisible Man," "The War of the Worlds," "The Food of the Gods," "In the Days of the Comet." "One will have to go far to match this for entertainment, excitement, and sheer pleasure," N. Y. TIMES. 1015pp. 5⅜ x 8.   T264 Clothbound **$3.95**

MATHEMAGIC, MAGIC PUZZLES, AND GAMES WITH NUMBERS, R. V. Heath. More than 60 new puzzles and stunts based on number properties: multiplying large numbers mentally, finding the date of any day in the year, etc. Edited by J. S. Meyer. 76 illus. 129pp. 5⅜ x 8.
T110 Paperbound **$1.00**

FIVE ADVENTURE NOVELS OF H. RIDER HAGGARD. The master story-teller's five best tales of mystery and adventure set against authentic African backgrounds: "She," "King Solomon's Mines," "Allan Quatermain," "Allan's Wife," "Maiwa's Revenge." 821pp. 5⅜ x 8.
T108 Clothbound **$3.95**

WIN AT CHECKERS, M. Hopper. (Formerly "Checkers.") The former World's Unrestricted Checker Champion gives you valuable lessons in openings, traps, end games, ways to draw when you are behind, etc. More than 100 questions and answers anticipate your problems. Appendix. 75 problems diagrammed, solved. 79 figures. xi + 107pp. 5⅜ x 8.
T363 Paperbound **$1.00**

CRYPTOGRAPHY, L. D. Smith. Excellent introductory work on ciphers and their solution, history of secret writing, techniques, etc. Appendices on Japanese methods, the Baconian cipher, frequency tables. Bibliography. Over 150 problems, solutions. 160pp. 5⅜ x 8.
T247 Paperbound **$1.00**

CRYPTANALYSIS, H. F. Gaines. (Formerly, "Elementary Cryptanalysis.") The best book available on cryptograms and how to solve them. Contains all major techniques: substitution, transposition, mixed alphabets, multafid, Kasiski and Vignere methods, etc. Word frequency appendix. 167 problems, solutions. 173 figures. 236pp. 5⅜ x 8.   T97 Paperbound **$1.95**

FLATLAND, E. A. Abbot. The science-fiction classic of life in a 2-dimensional world that is considered a first-rate introduction to relativity and hyperspace, as well as a scathing satire on society, politics and religion. 7th edition. 16 illus. 128pp. 5⅜ x 8.
T1 Paperbound **$1.00**

DOVER BOOKS

HOW TO FORCE CHECKMATE, F. Reinfeld. (Formerly "Challenge to Chessplayers.") No board needed to sharpen your checkmate skill on 300 checkmate situations. Learn to plan up to 3 moves ahead and play a superior end game. 300 situations diagrammed; notes and full solutions. 111pp. 5⅜ x 8. **T439 Paperbound $1.25**

MORPHY'S GAMES OF CHESS, P. W. Sergeant, ed. Play forcefully by following the techniques used by one of the greatest chess champions. 300 of Morphy's games carefully annotated to reveal principles. Bibliography. New introduction by F. Reinfeld. 235 diagrams. x + 352pp. 5⅜ x 8. **T386 Paperbound $1.75**

MATHEMATICAL RECREATIONS, M. Kraitchik. Hundreds of unusual mathematical puzzlers and odd bypaths of math, elementary and advanced. Greek, Medieval, Arabic, Hindu problems; figurate numbers, Fermat numbers, primes; magic, Euler, Latin squares; fairy chess, latruncles, reversi, jinx, ruma, tetrachrome other positional and permutational games. Rigorous solutions. Revised second edition. 181 illus. 330pp. 5⅜ x 8. **T163 Paperbound $1.75**

MATHEMATICAL EXCURSIONS, H. A. Merrill. Revealing stimulating insights into elementary math, not usually taught in school. 90 problems demonstrate Russian peasant multiplication, memory systems for pi, magic squares, dyadic systems, division by inspection, many more. Solutions to difficult problems. 50 illus. 5⅜ x 8. **T350 Paperbound $1.00**

MAGIC TRICKS & CARD TRICKS, W. Jonson. Best introduction to tricks with coins, bills, eggs, ribbons, slates, cards, easily performed without elaborate equipment. Professional routines, tips on presentation, misdirection, etc. Two books bound as one: 52 tricks with cards, 37 tricks with common objects. 106 figures. 224pp. 5⅜ x 8. **T909 Paperbound $1.00**

MATHEMATICAL PUZZLES OF SAM LOYD, selected and edited by **M. Gardner.** 177 most ingenious mathematical puzzles of America's greatest puzzle originator, based on arithmetic, algebra, game theory, dissection, route tracing, operations research, probability, etc. 120 drawings, diagrams. Solutions. 187pp. 5⅜ x 8. **T498 Paperbound $1.00**

THE ART OF CHESS, J. Mason. The most famous general study of chess ever written. More than 90 openings, middle game, end game, how to attack, sacrifice, defend, exchange, form general strategy. Supplement on "How Do You Play Chess?" by F. Reinfeld. 448 diagrams. 356pp. 5⅜ x 8. **T463 Paperbound $1.85**

HYPERMODERN CHESS as Developed in the Games of its Greatest Exponent, ARON NIMZOVICH, F. Reinfeld, ed. Learn how the game's greatest innovator defeated Alekhine, Lasker, and many others; and use these methods in your own game. 180 diagrams. 228pp. 5⅜ x 8. **T448 Paperbound $1.35**

A TREASURY OF CHESS LORE, F. Reinfeld, ed. Hundreds of fascinating stories by and about the masters, accounts of tournaments and famous games, aphorisms, word portraits, little known incidents, photographs, etc., that will delight the chess enthusiast, captivate the beginner. 49 photographs (14 full-page plates), 12 diagrams. 315pp. 5⅜ x 8. **T458 Paperbound $1.75**

A NONSENSE ANTHOLOGY, collected by **Carolyn Wells.** 245 of the best nonsense verses ever written: nonsense puns, absurd arguments, mock epics, nonsense ballads, "sick" verses, dog-Latin verses, French nonsense verses, limericks. Lear, Carroll, Belloc, Burgess, nearly 100 other writers. Introduction by Carolyn Wells. 3 indices: Title, Author, First Lines. xxxiii + 279pp. 5⅜ x 8. **T499 Paperbound $1.25**

SYMBOLIC LOGIC and THE GAME OF LOGIC, Lewis Carroll. Two delightful puzzle books by the author of "Alice," bound as one. Both works concern the symbolic representation of traditional logic and together contain more than 500 ingenious, amusing and instructive syllogistic puzzlers. Total of 326pp. 5⅜ x 8. **T492 Paperbound $1.50**

PILLOW PROBLEMS and A TANGLED TALE, Lewis Carroll. Two of Carroll's rare puzzle works bound as one. "Pillow Problems" contain 72 original math puzzles. The puzzles in "A Tangled Tale" are given in delightful story form. Total of 291pp. 5⅜ x 8. **T493 Paperbound $1.50**

PECK'S BAD BOY AND HIS PA, G. W. Peck. Both volumes of one of the most widely read of all American humor books. A classic of American folk humor, also invaluable as a portrait of an age. 100 original illustrations. Introduction by E. Bleiler. 347pp. 5⅜ x 8. **T497 Paperbound $1.35**

Dover publishes books on art, music, philosophy, literature, languages, history, social sciences, psychology, handcrafts, orientalia, puzzles and entertainments, chess, pets and gardens, books explaining science, intermediate and higher mathematics mathematical physics, engineering, biological sciences, earth sciences, classics of science, etc. Write to:

Dept. catrr.
Dover Publications, Inc.
180 Varick Street, N. Y. 14, N. Y.